JUDGMENT
IN MANAGERIAL
DECISION MAKING

JUDGMENT IN MANAGERIAL DECISION MAKING

SECOND EDITION

MAX H. BAZERMAN
J.L. KELLOGG GRADUATE SCHOOL OF MANAGEMENT
NORTHWESTERN UNIVERSITY

JOHN WILEY & SONS
New York   Chichester   Brisbane   Toronto   Singapore

To My Parents

Library of Congress Cataloging-in-Publication Data:

Bazerman, Max H.
   Judgment in managerial decision making /Max H. Bazerman. — 2nd ed.
     p.   cm.
   Includes bibliographical references.
   ISBN 0-471-50763-6
   1. Decision-making. 2. Management. I. Title.
HD30.23.B38   1990
658.4′03—dc20
                                                90-30997
                                                  CIP

Printed in the United States of America

10 9 8 7 6 5 4 3

PREFACE

Between 1981 and 1983, I was on the faculty of the Organizational Behavior Department at Boston University. At the time, I was working with Maggie Neale on several laboratory studies on decision biases in negotiation. The faculty at Boston University provided me with a number of excellent colleagues. Yet these colleagues knew very little about the emerging research on judgment. This lack of awareness, in colleagues that I respected, motivated me to write this book. I wanted to help make the area of judgment a more central part of the management literature. I wanted to present this information to managers, students, and researchers in an interesting manner that would improve their judgment capabilities.

The field of organizational behavior has a history of interest in the process of decision making—dating back to March and Simon's classic book in 1958. However, organizational behavior lost interest in the area of decision making just when behavioral decision research was emerging as a field of its own during the 1970s. Behavioral decision research has developed considerably over the last 20 years and can provide many insights concerning managerial decision making. This book attempts to embed behavioral decision research into the organizational context. This is done by providing managerial examples and examining judgment in a variety of organizational contexts. The first five chapters of the book provide the reader with an opportunity to examine their individual judgment. Starting with Chapter 6, the book moves to a variety of interpersonal contexts that affect judgment.

The audience for this book is anyone who is interested in improving their judgment. The first edition was used in economics, psychology, and organizational behavior courses, and in a variety of executive programs. The book does not assume advanced knowledge of statistics, psychology, economics, or decision making. Rather, the book attempts to provide new research insights in a very accessible form. To the psychology audience, the book offers a systematic framework for using psychological findings to improve judgment. To the economics audience, the book offers a critical review of the many ways in which the classic economic model of decision making has been called into question in recent years. And to the management community, this book offers an opportunity to examine the barriers to and opportunities for making better managerial decisions.

In the first edition, I noted that many fine colleagues influenced by understanding of judgment: Bob Atkin, Joel Brockner, John Carroll, Ed Conlon, Pete Fader, Toni Giuliano, Paul Goodman, Tim Hall, Tom Kochan, Roy Lewicki, Leigh

McAlister, Jeff Rubin, and David Schoorman. In addition, my research was influenced substantially through interdisciplinary research with Bill Samuelson and Hank Farber (both economists). From 1983 to 1985, I was a member of the faculty at MIT, where Harry Katz, Tom Kochan, and Bob McKersie were constant sources of intellectual inspiration. Most importantly, many of the ideas in this book were developed in joint research and discussions with Maggie Neale.

In creating the first edition, four people read the entire manuscript and provided extremely helpful feedback and support during the three years of its creation. These people are John Carroll, Marla Felcher, Tim Hall, and Roy Lewicki. Each helped in important ways as I was putting together my understanding of judgment.

In July 1985, just as I was finishing the first edition, I moved to the Organization Behavior Department of the J.L. Kellogg Graduate School of Management at Northwestern University. While my prior collaboration with Hank Farber, John Carroll, and Maggie Neale has continued, the last four years have provided me with a number of new opportunities. First, the quality of the doctoral students in our department creates an excellent environment to develop my ideas on judgment. Second, my exposure to managers through the school's executive development programs has provided me with a greater appreciation of judgmental issues that are most important in managerial life. Third, the support of Dean Don Jacobs has been critical to making this a wonderful place to work. This is simply a fun and intellectually exciting place to be. Fourth, the development of the Dispute Resolution Research Center, under the direction of Jeanne Brett, has provided an interdisciplinary forum for developing ideas about negotiations and multi-party decision making. Much of my recent research has been supported by the Center, and the opportunity to discuss my research with Bob Bies, Jeanne Brett, Reid Hastie, Roger Myerson, Tom Tyler, and Bob Weber has provided an ongoing source of ideas. And finally, my new coauthors and colleagues (George Loewenstein, Beta Mannix, Harris Sondak, Leigh Thompson, Tom Tripp, Kathleen Valley, and Sally White) have been central to the many improvements that have occurred in my understanding of judgment. I often think that my most important ability is to get excellent people to work with me.

This book has changed in a number of ways since the first edition. The research on individual decision making has been updated, and the examples used to illustrate the research have been improved. The coverage of judgment in negotiation has been expanded to two chapters. Chapter 8, which examines multi-party decision making, has undergone a complete overhaul as a result of a great deal of new research in this area. This edition closes with a detailed discussion of decision making improvement strategies (using some of the material that was in Chapter 6 of the first edition). Most importantly, this edition has benefited from useful feedback that I obtained on the first edition.

This edition also benefited from the excellent critical review and editing of Sally White. I hired Sally to do a final reading of the book. Instead, she provided a detailed and critical critique of each chapter, offered specific reorganizing suggestions, and drafted numerous changes that have improved this edition.

This book has been significantly improved as a result of Sally's work. Finally, there have been 20 or 30 times where I needed to make judgments concerning the contents of the book. In these cases, I walked down the hall to Maggie Neale's office. I told her the problem of the day, and she provided the obvious answer. If you can't make a good decision on your own, it is important to know who can. Maggie has been a consistent source of good advice over the last decade or so.

Max H. Bazerman

CONTENTS

ONE
INTRODUCTION TO MANAGERIAL DECISION MAKING

Robert Davis, head of the legal staff of a Fortune 500 company, has delayed making one of the most critical recommendations in the organization's history. The company is faced with a class action suit from a hostile group of consumers. While the organization believes that it is innocent, it realizes that a court may not have the same perspective. The organization is expected to lose $50 million if the suit is lost in court. Davis predicts a 50% chance of losing the case. The organization has the option of settling out of court by paying $25 million to the "injured" parties. Davis's senior staff has been collecting information and organizing the case for over six months. It is time for action. What should Davis recommend?

Decisions of this level of importance are made every day, yet we understand very little about how managers and professionals make them. We know a great deal about using computers to integrate data and make routine decisions, but computers cannot make decisions involving values and risk preferences. Here, human judgment is required. What advice can we offer Robert Davis? We cannot tell him the degree to which he should take risk. This is a value judgment. It does not have a right or a wrong answer. We can, however, demonstrate a number of cognitive biases that are likely to affect his judgment. The knowledge of these biases can be used to make more objective decisions, in accordance with the values of Robert Davis and his organization. This book addresses the need to improve managerial judgment by identifying cognitive biases and suggesting strategies for overcoming them.

Research evidence suggests that *at least* two types of biases are likely to affect Davis's recommendation. First, it is very possible that Robert Davis's senior staff is biased in believing in the innocence of their firm. They may fall victim to "groupthink," believing their side is invulnerable to attacks from the "opposition." This bias is common among cohesive groups (see Chapter 8). If this is the case, Mr. Davis may underestimate the likelihood of actually losing the case in court.

The way in which the information about the problem is presented, or "framed," represents a second potential bias. Robert Davis may identify his situation as follows:

Option A settle out of court and accept a sure *loss* of $25,000,000, or

Option B go to court expecting a 50 percent probability of a $50,000,000 *loss.*

Alternatively, Mr. Davis could define his situation this way:

Option C settle out of court and *save* $25,000,000 that could be lost in court, or

Option D go to court expecting a 50 percent probability of *saving* $50,000,000.

Options A and B are framed negatively—that is, in terms of possible losses. Options C and D are framed positively—that is, in terms of possible gains. A is equivalent to C, and B is equivalent to D. A consistent decision maker would choose A and C, or B and D. Choosing A and D, or B and C, would be inconsistent. Surprisingly, most MBA students (over 80 percent) select option B in the first situation and option C in the second situation. Research has shown that individuals tend to take risks concerning choices framed in terms of possible losses and tend to avoid risks concerning choices framed in terms of possible gains—even though both sets of choice are objectively the same! We will cover the psychological explanation for this counterintuitive effect in detail in Chapter 3. For now, it is sufficient to say that decision makers are systematically affected by the way in which information is presented.

How can this brief analysis help Robert Davis? It does not tell him what to do. It does not guarantee him that his recommendation will turn out to be optimal, but it can help him to make a good decision. Robert Davis's problem is complicated, yet many of the decision processes that he must employ are quite simple. If he understands the cognitive biases influencing his judgment, he can begin to change his decision processes to reduce these biases. This book can help Robert Davis (and you) by examining biases that typically affect judgment. In addition, this book can help Davis think through the decision processes of other parties in his organization and the decision processes of the opponent consumer group so that he can better anticipate their behaviors.

Although most managerial decisions do not involve sums as large as $50 million, situations that require careful judgment arise continually in our daily lives. Such judgment is a major component of managerial work at all levels of the corporate world and constitutes a critical human resource in any organization. Many managers accept judgment as innate; "some people have it and others don't." This attitude can waste a lot of potential human resources in organizations. Judgment may be partially innate, but training can have a significant effect on the quality of managerial judgment.

THE ANATOMY OF A DECISION

Judgment refers to the cognitive aspects of the decision-making process. To understand judgment, we first need to identify the components of the decision-making process that require judgment. To get started, consider the following decision situations:

- You are finishing your MBA with a major in finance at a well-known school. Your credentials are quite good, and you expect to obtain numerous job offers. How are you going to select your job?
- You are the director of the marketing division of a rapidly expanding high-technology company. You need to hire a new product manager for a new "secret" product that the company plans to introduce to the market in 15 months. How are you going to hire the appropriate individual?
- You are the owner of a venture capital firm, and you have a number of proposals that meet your preliminary considerations but only a limited budget with which to fund new projects. Which projects will you fund?
- You are the vice-president of a retail organization charged with deciding where to locate the company's new stores. How are you going to select among the many possible expansion locations?
- You are on the corporate acquisition staff of a large conglomerate that is interested in acquiring a small- to moderate-sized firm in the oil industry. What firm, if any, are you going to recommend that the company acquire?

What do these situations have in common? Each situation proposes a problem, and each problem has a number of possible alternative solutions. With these scenarios in mind, let us look at six steps that should implicitly or explicitly occur when applying a "rational" decision-making process in each situation.

1. **Define the problem.** The problem has been fairly well specified in each of the five scenarios just listed. However, managers often act without an understanding of the problem to be solved. When this occurs, the manager may solve the wrong problem. It requires accurate judgment to identify the appropriate definition of the problem. Huber (1980) suggests that managers often err by (a) defining the problem in terms of a proposed solution, (b) missing the big problem, or (c) diagnosing the problem in terms of its symptoms. We want to solve the problems, not just eliminate the temporary symptoms.
2. **Identify the Criteria.** Most decisions require the decision maker to accomplish more than one objective. In buying a car, you may want to maximize fuel economy, minimize cost, maximize comfort, and so on. The rational decision maker will identify all relevant criteria in the decision-making process.
3. **Weight the criteria.** The foregoing criteria are of varying importance to a decision maker. Rational decision makers will know the relative value that

they put on each of the criteria identified (for example, the relative importance of fuel economy versus cost versus comfort).

4. **Generate alternatives.** The fourth step in the decision-making process
   requires identification of possible courses of action. An inappropriate amount
   of search time is often spent seeking alternatives, creating a barrier to
   effective decision making. An optimal search continues only until the cost of
   search outweighs the value of the added information.

5. **Rate each alternative on each criterion.** How well will each of the alternative solutions achieve each of the defined criteria? This is often the most
   difficult part of the decision-making process, since this is the stage that
   typically requires forecasting future events. Again, the rational decision
   maker will be able to carefully assess the potential consequences of selecting each of the alternative solutions on each of the identified criteria.

6. **Compute the optimal decision.** Ideally, after all of the first five steps have
   been completed, the process of computing the optimal decision consists of
   multiplying the expected effectiveness of each choice times the weighting
   of each criterion times the rating of each criterion for each alternative solution. The solution with the highest expected value should then be chosen.

The model of decision making just presented assumes that we follow these
six steps in a fully "rational" manner (Friedman, 1957). That is, decision makers
are assumed to (1) perfectly define the problem, (2) know all relevant alternatives, (3) identify all criteria, (4) accurately weigh all of the criteria according
to their preferences, (5) accurately assess each alternative based on each
criterion, and (6) accurately calculate and choose the alternative with the highest perceived value. This rational model provides very good guidance for
thinking about what an optimal decision-making process might look like. In this
book, the term *rationality* refers to the decision-making process that is logically
expected to lead to the optimal result given an accurate assessment of the
decision maker's values and risk preferences.

BOUNDED RATIONALITY

The rational model is based on a set of assumptions that prescribe how a
decision *should* be made rather than describing how a decision *is* made. In his
Nobel Prize–winning work, Simon (1957; March and Simon, 1958) suggested
that individual judgment is bounded in its rationality and that we can better
understand decision making by explaining actual, rather than normative ("what
should be done"), decision processes. While the bounded-rationality framework views individuals as attempting to make rational decisions, it acknowl-
edges that decision makers often lack important information on the definition of
the problem, the relevant criteria, and so on. Time and cost constraints limit the
quantity and quality of available information. Further, decision makers retain
only a relatively small amount of information in their usable memory. Finally,
limitations on intelligence and perceptions constrain the ability of decision

makers to accurately "calculate" the optimal choice from the information that is available. Together, these limitations keep decision makers from making the optimal decisions assumed in the rational model. Instead, March and Simon (1958) suggest that decision makers will forego the best solution in favor of one that is acceptable or reasonable. That is, decision makers *satisfice*. They do not examine all possible alternatives. They simply search until they find a solution that meets a certain acceptable level of performance.

The field of decision making can be loosely divided into two parts: the study of prescriptive models and the study of descriptive models. **Prescriptive** decision scientists are concerned with prescribing methods for making optimal decisions. For example, they might suggest a mathematical model to help a decision maker act more rationally. **Descriptive** decision researchers are concerned with the bounded way in which decisions are actually made. This book relies primarily on a descriptive approach.

Why use a descriptive approach when a prescriptive approach should lead to an optimal decision? Since managers make hundreds of decisions daily, the systematic and time-consuming demands of rational decision making are simply not viable. Most significant decisions are made by judgment, rather than by a defined prescriptive model. This is evident in Mintzberg's (1975) study of managerial behavior. Mintzberg found that the average manager engages in a different activity every nine minutes. In addition, he found that in making decisions, managers tended to avoid hard (that is, systematic, analytical) data and rely more on their intuitive judgment. Thus, we need an alternative approach to improving decision making which addresses the requirements and realities of managerial life.

Although the concepts of bounded rationality and satisficing are important in identifying that judgment deviates from rationality, they do not tell us *how* judgment will be biased. These concepts help decision makers identify situations in which they may be acting on limited information, but they do not help diagnose the specific systematic, directional biases that affect our judgment. Fifteen years after the publication of Simon's work, Kahneman and Tversky (1972, 1973, 1979; Tversky and Kahneman, 1971, 1973, 1974, 1981) continued what March and Simon had begun. They provided critical information about specific systematic biases that influence judgment. Their work, and the work that follows, led to our modern understanding of judgment. Kahneman and Tversky suggest that people rely on a number of simplifying strategies, or rules of thumb, in making decisions. These simplifying strategies are called **heuristics.** They are the standard rules that implicitly direct our judgment. They serve as a mechanism for coping with the complex environment surrounding our decisions. In general, heuristics are helpful, but their use can sometimes lead to severe errors. Identification and illustration of these heuristics and the biases that can result from them in the managerial setting form a central theme of this book. We will use examples of a variety of individual heuristics and biases to explain how individuals deviate from a fully rational decision process in individual and competitive situations.

INTRODUCTION TO JUDGMENTAL HEURISTICS

Consider the following example:

> Sarah Edwards is the director of product marketing for XYZ, Inc., a consumer goods organization. She needs to hire a new MBA for the position of assistant brand manager. The position is very important, since the brand is critical to a new strategic thrust for the organization. Edwards has always followed the heuristic of limiting her search for new MBAs to the top six management schools. How would you evaluate that strategy?

If we evaluate this strategy in terms of the degree to which it follows the rational model outlined earlier, Edwards's heuristic of limiting her search to six schools will be deficient, because her search will not be complete. This heuristic may eliminate the best possible candidates from consideration if they do not attend one of the top schools. However, the heuristic also has some benefits. While the heuristic could eliminate the best choice, the expected time savings of focusing on only six schools may outweigh any potential loss in the expected outcome resulting from Edward's heuristic strategy versus a full search strategy. In addition, this job search heuristic may produce more good decisions than bad decisions. In fact, economists would argue that individuals use heuristics because the benefit that they obtain through the time savings of the heuristic outweighs the costs of any potential reduction in the quality of the decision.

It is critical to realize that heuristics provide time-pressured managers and other professionals with a simple way of dealing with a complex world, producing correct or partially correct judgments more often than not. In addition, it may be inevitable that humans will adopt some way of simplifying decisions. The only drawback is that individuals frequently adopt these heuristics without being aware of them. The misapplication of heuristics to inappropriate situations, unfortunately, leads people astray. If we can make managers aware of the potential adverse impacts of using heuristics, they can then decide when and where to use them, and, if it is to their advantage, to eliminate certain heuristics from their cognitive repertoire.

People use a variety of types of heuristics. The poker player follows the heuristic "never play for an inside straight." The mortgage banker follows the heuristic "people should only spend 35 percent of their income for house expenses." Although an understanding of these specific heuristics is important to the poker player and mortgage banker, our concern in this book is with more generalizable cognitive heuristics that affect virtually all individuals. Thus, the heuristics that are described next are not specific to particular individuals; rather, research has shown that they are generalizable across the population. The three general heuristics that we will focus on throughout the book are (1) the availability heuristic, (2) the representativeness heuristic, and (3) anchoring and adjustment.

The Availability Heuristic   Managers assess the frequency, probability, or likely causes of an event by the degree to which instances or occurrences of that event are readily "available" in memory (Tversky and Kahneman, 1973). An event that evokes emotions and is vivid, easily imagined, and specific will be more "available" from memory than will an event that is an unemotional in nature, bland, difficult to imagine, or vague. For example, the subordinate in close proximity to the manager's office will receive a more critical performance evaluation at year-end, since the manager is more aware of this subordinate's errors (Strickland, 1958). The product manager bases her assessment of the probability of a new product's success on her recollection of the successes and failures of similar products during the recent past. Peter Lynch, the manager of the Fidelity's Magellan Fund (the largest mutual fund in the world) argues in favor of buying stock in firms that are unavailable in the minds of most investors (for example, due to their blandness) because the more available the stock is, the more overvalued it will be. The availability heuristic can be a very useful managerial decision-making strategy, since instances of events of greater frequency are generally revealed more easily in our minds than events of less frequency. Consequently, this heuristic will often lead to accurate judgment. This heuristic is fallible, however, because the availability of information is also affected by other factors that are not related to the objective frequency of the judged event. These irrelevant factors can inappropriately influence an event's immediate perceptual salience, the vividness with which it is revealed, or the ease with which it is imagined.

The Representativeness Heuristic Managers assess the likelihood of an event's occurrence by the similarity of that occurrence to their stereotypes of similar occurrences. As Nisbett and Ross (1980) note, "A botanist assigns a plant to one species rather than another by using this judgment strategy. The plant is categorized as belonging to the species that its principle features most clearly resemble" (p. 7). In this case, the degree to which the unknown plant is representative of a known species of plant is the best information available to the botanist. Managers also use the representativeness heuristic. They predict a person's performance based on the category of persons that the focal individual represents for them from their pasts. They predict the success of a new product based on the similarity of that product to past successful and unsuccessful product types. In some cases the use of the heuristic is a good first-cut approximation. In other cases, it leads to behavior that many of us find irrational and morally reprehensible—like discrimination. A clear problem is that individuals tend to rely on such strategies, even when this information is insufficient and better information exists with which to make an accurate judgment.

Anchoring and Adjustment Managers make assessments by starting from an initial value and adjusting to yield a final decision. The initial value, or starting point, may be suggested from historical precedent, from the way in which a problem is presented, or from random information. For example, managers make salary decisions by adjusting from an employee's past year's salary. In ambiguous situations, a trivial factor can have a profound effect on our decision if it serves as a starting point from which we make adjustments (Dawes, 1988). Frequently, people will realize the unreasonableness of the anchor (for example, "the other firm was *only* paying her $22,000 a year"), yet their adjustment will often remain irrationally close to this anchor. Dawes points out that after having a good meal in a restaurant, we have an unrealistic expectation for future meals at that restaurant as a result of anchoring. (The section on regression to the mean in Chapter 2 will clarify why you might more rationally reduce your expectations in the future.) The key conclusion is that regardless of the basis of the initial value, adjustments from the initial value tend to be insufficient (Slovic and Lichtenstein, 1971; Tversky and Kahneman, 1974). Thus, different values can yield different decisions for the same problem—all depending upon what the initial values are.

AN OUTLINE OF THINGS TO COME

The objective of this book is to improve the reader's judgment. What can the book do to help improve Robert Davis's judgment? The first step is to create an awareness of what is wrong with intuitive judgment. Thus, we can make Davis aware of a number of biases that are likely to affect his decision. However, Lewin (1947) suggests that in order for change to occur and last over time, the individual must do more than simply be aware of imperfections. Lewin argues that for change to be successful, it is necessary to (1) get the manager to "unfreeze" existing decision-making processes, (2) provide the content for change, and (3) create the conditions that allow the change to "refreeze" these processes, thus making the change part of the manager's standard repertoire. This book will attempt to unfreeze your present decision-making processes by demonstrating how *your* judgment systematically deviates from rationality. The content will also be provided to allow you to change your decision-making processes. Finally, the book will discuss methods that you can use to refreeze your thinking to ensure that the changes will last.

Nisbett and Ross (1980, pp. xi–xii) write:

> One of philosophy's oldest paradoxes is the apparent contradiction between the greatest triumphs and the dramatic failures of the human mind. The same organism that routinely solves inferential problems too subtle and complex for the mightiest computers often makes errors in the simplest of judgments about everyday events. The errors, moreover, often seem traceable to violations of the same inferential rules that underlie people's most impressive successes. . . . How can any creature skilled enough to build and maintain complex organizations, or sophisticated enough to appreciate the nuances of social intercourse, be foolish enough to mouth racist cliches or spill its lifeblood in pointless wars?

While Nisbett and Ross refer to the general population, the essence of their question defines a fascinating issue for the field of managerial effectiveness. This book views managers as intelligent employees who have been generally successful, but whose decisions are biased in ways that seriously compromise their potential. The reader will see how habit has forced us into a set of hard-to-break heuristics, imposing constraints on our decision-making effectiveness.

Judgmental limitations can come from at least three sources: (1) emotions, (2) motivations, and (3) cognitions. While all three areas are viable topics of inquiry, this book is primarily concerned with cognitive, judgmental errors. With so much material on the cognitive side, I have plenty to do to cover this topic adequately. In addition, I am prejudiced in the belief that better cognitive decision making reduces emotional and motivational barriers. That is, if one becomes a better cognitive decision maker, emotional barriers that inhibit decision making will break down due to one's increased confidence. Further, motivation will increase, since we tend to be more motivated when our ability allows for a high level of performance.

Before outlining the remainder of the book in more detail, it is critical to clarify its educational philosophy and role. I believe that before managers' decision-making processes can be changed, they must be convinced that elements of their cognitive repertoire could use improvement—that is, unfreezing. "Why should I change my existing decision-making processes when I have been so successful in my managerial career?" To respond to this very appropriate question, this book will include a number of experiential decision-making items that encourage the reader to personally identify with the biases that are discussed. In presenting this material to MBA and executive students in a classroom setting, I have found that many individuals are *initially* offended by being "tricked" by an "ivory-tower" academic. It might be helpful to clarify at the outset that the intent is not to insult, but to help identify and communicate biases that generally affect human judgment. Perhaps the reason for my personal interest in the material lies in my discomfort with the fact that many of these "evil" biases affect my own personal judgment.

Chapters 2 through 5 focus on individual decision making. In these chapters, little attention is given to the fact that many managerial decisions are made in conjunction with other individuals. Instead, the focus is simply on how individuals approach decisions. Chapters 6 through 8 reexamine judgment in a variety of multiparty contexts. These chapters build on the earlier chapters and explore the added considerations that affect judgment when many individuals are involved with a decision. Chapter 9 summarizes the arguments in the book and focuses on how to make the changes suggested throughout the book a lasting part of the reader's decision-making processes. Specifically, the remaining chapters will focus on the following:

Chapter 2. This chapter identifies and illustrates 13 specific biases that affect the judgment of virtually all managers. These biases are the result of the three heuristics described in this chapter. Quiz items and short scenarios demonstrate these biases and emphasize their prevalence.

Chapter 3. Most management students are formally taught about the concept of risk in a microeconomics or statistics course. These courses typically treat risk from a prescriptive perspective, by suggesting rational methods for making decisions involving risk. This chapter extends this prescriptive perspective by examining the psychological factors that explain how managers deviate from "rationality" in responding to uncertainty.

Chapter 4. There is much evidence that managerial decision makers who commit themselves to a particular course of action may make subsequent nonoptimal decisions in order to justify their previous commitment. This chapter examines the research evidence and psychological explanations for this behavior. We will see how escalation has a significant effect in a variety of managerial domains, including new product development, bank loans, and performance appraisal.

Chapter 5. What is managerial creativity? Can you be more creative? These are issues critical to managerial success. This chapter identifies the components of managerial creativity and examines the role of heuristics and biases in limiting creativity. Specific recommendations are made for improving creativity.

Chapter 6. This chapter outlines a framework to help the reader think about two-party negotiations. The focus of attention concerns how you can make decisions to maximize the joint gain available in a two-party decision-making situation, while simultaneously thinking about how to obtain as much of that joint gain as possible for yourself.

Chapter 7. This chapter looks at the judgmental mistakes that we make in two-party negotiations and focuses on the biases that occur in negotiations. The resulting framework shows how consumers, managements, unions, salespersons, and society can simultaneously benefit from debiasing negotiations.

Chapter 8. This chapter looks at the judgment of individuals in multiparty organizational contexts. Specifically, this chapter examines the decision-making processes of individuals in the context of (1) competitive bidding, (2) assisted decision making, (3) group decision making, (4) coalitions, and (5) social dilemmas.

Chapter 9. The final chapter evaluates four explicit strategies for improving judgment, including (1) acquiring expertise, (2) debiasing, (3) using linear models, and (4) adjusting intuitive predictions. Overall, this chapter focuses on how to use the information in this book to create permanent improvements in your future decisions.

TWO
BIASES

The discussion of heuristics in Chapter 1 suggested that individuals develop rules of thumb to reduce the information-processing demands of decision making. These rules of thumb provide managers with efficient ways of dealing with complex problems that produce good decisions a significant proportion of the time. However, heuristics also lead managers to *systematically* biased outcomes. A cognitive bias (or simply *bias* throughout this book) refers to situations in which a heuristic is inappropriately applied by an individual in reaching a decision.

This chapter is written to provide you with the opportunity to audit your own decision making and identify the biases that affect you. A number of problems are presented that allow you to examine your problem solving and learn how your judgments compare to the judgments of others. The quiz items are then used to illustrate 13 predictable biases to which managers are prone, and that frequently lead to judgments that systematically deviate from rationality.

To start out, consider the following two problems:

Problem 1: The following 10 corporations were ranked by *Fortune* magazine to be among the 500 largest United States–based firms according to sales volume for 1987:

Group A: Gillette, Coca-Cola Enterprises, Lever Brothers, Apple Computers, Hershey Foods

Group B: Coastal, Weyerhaeuser, Northrup, CPC International, Champion International

Which group of five organizations listed (A or B) had the larger total sales volume?

Problem 2: (Adapted from Kahneman and Tversky, 1973)
The best student in my introductory MBA class this past semester writes poetry and is rather shy and small in stature. What was the student's undergraduate major:
(A) Chinese studies or
(B) Psychology?

What are your answers? If you answered A for each of the two problems, you may gain comfort in knowing that the majority of respondents choose A. If you answered B, you are part of the minority. In this case, however, the minority represents the correct response. All corporations in group B were ranked in the Fortune 100, while none of the corporations in group A had sales as large. In fact, the total sales for group B was more than double the total sales for group A. In the second problem, the student was actually a psychology major, but more important, selecting psychology as the student's major represents a more rational response given the limited information.

Problem 1 illustrates the availability heuristic discussed in Chapter 1. In this problem, group A contains consumer firms, while group B consists of industrial firms and holding companies. Most of us are more familiar with consumer firms than conglomerates and can more easily generate information in our minds about their size. If we were aware of our bias resulting from the availability heuristic, we would recognize our differential exposure to this information and adjust, or at least question, our judgments accordingly.

Problem 2 illustrates the representativeness heuristic. The reader who responds "Chinese studies" has probably overlooked relevant base-rate information—namely, the likely ratio of Chinese studies majors to psychology majors within the MBA student population. When asked to reconsider the problem in this context, most people change their response to "psychology" in view of the relative scarcity of Chinese studies majors seeking MBAs. This example emphasizes that logical base-rate reasoning is often overwhelmed by qualitative judgments drawn from available descriptive information.

The purpose of problems 1 and 2 is to demonstrate how easily faulty conclusions are drawn when we overrely on cognitive heuristics. In the remainder of this chapter, additional problems are presented to further increase your awareness of the impact of heuristics on your decisions and to help you develop an appreciation for the systematic errors that emanate from overdependence on them. The thirteen biases examined in this chapter are relevant to virtually all individuals. Each of the biases is related to at least one of the three judgmental heuristics introduced in Chapter 1, and an effort has been made to categorize them accordingly. However, it is important to remember that the way our minds work in developing and using heuristics is not straightforward. Often our heuristics work in tandem in approaching cognitive tasks.

The goal of the chapter is to help you "unfreeze" your decision-making patterns and realize how easily heuristics become biases when improperly applied. By working on numerous problems that demonstrate the failures of these heuristics, you will become more aware of the biases in your decision making. By learning to spot these biases, you can improve the quality of your decisions.

Before reading further, please take a few minutes to respond to the problems outlined in Table 2.1. They will be used to illustrate the 13 decision biases presented in the remainder of this chapter.

Table 2.1 Chapter Problems

Respond to the following 11 problems before reading the chapter.

Problem 3: Which is riskier:

    a. driving a car on a 400-mile trip?
    b. flying on a 400-mile commercial airline flight?

Problem 4: Are there more words in the English language

    a. that start with an *r*
    b. for which *r* is the third letter?

Problem 5: Mark is finishing his MBA at a prestigious university. He is very interested in the arts and at one time considered a career as a musician. Is Mark more likely to take a job

    a. in the management of the arts?
    b. with a management consulting firm?

Problem 6: In 1986, two research groups sampled consumers on the driving performance of the Dodge Colt versus the Plymouth Champ in a blind road test; that is, the consumers did not know when they were driving the Colt or the Champ. As you may know, these cars were identical; only the marketing varied.

One research group (A) sampled 66 consumers each day for 60 days (a large number of days to control for weather and other variables), while the other research group (B) sampled 22 consumers each day for 50 days. Which consumer group observed more days in which 60 percent or more of the consumers tested preferred the Dodge Colt:

    a. Group A?
    b. Group B?

Problem 7: You are about to hire a new central-region sales director for the fifth time this year. You predict that the next director should work out reasonably well, since the last four were "lemons," and the odds favor hiring at least one good sales director in five tries. This thinking is

    a. Correct.
    b. Incorrect.

Problem 8: You are the sales forecaster for a department store chain with nine locations. The chain depends on you for quality projections of future sales in order to make decisions on staffing, advertising, information system developments, purchasing, renovation, and the like. All stores are similar in size and merchandise selection. The main difference in their sales occurs because of location and random fluctuations. Sales for 1989 were as follows:

Store	1989	1991
1	$12,000,000	$_____
2	11,500,000	_____
3	11,000,000	_____
4	10,500,000	_____

Table 2.1 (*Continued*)

5	10,000,000	_____
6	9,500,000	_____
7	9,000,000	_____
8	8,500,000	_____
9	8,000,000	_____
TOTAL	$90,000,000	$99,000,000

Your economic forecasting service has convinced you that the best estimate of total sales increases between 1989 and 1991 is 10 percent (to $99,000,000). Your task is to predict 1991 sales for each store. Since your manager believes strongly in the economic forecasting service, it is imperative that your total sales equal $99,000,000.

Problem 9: Linda is 31 years old, single, outspoken, and very bright. She majored in philosophy. As a student, she was deeply concerned with issues of discimination and social justice, and she participated in antinuclear demonstrations.

Rank order the following eight descriptions in terms of the probability (likelihood) that they describe Linda:

_____ **a.** Linda is a teacher in an elementary school.

_____ **b.** Linda works in a bookstore and takes yoga classes.

_____ **c.** Linda is active in the feminist movement.

_____ **d.** Linda is a psychiatric social worker.

_____ **e.** Linda is a member of the League of Women Voters.

_____ **f.** Linda is a bank teller.

_____ **g.** Linda is an insurance salesperson.

_____ **h.** Linda is a bank teller who is active in the feminist movement.

Problem 10: A newly hired engineer for a computer firm in the Boston metropolitan area has four years of experience and good all-around qualifications. When asked to estimate the starting salary for this employee, my secretary (knowing very little about the profession or the industry) guessed an annual salary of $23,000. What is your estimate?

$ _____ per year.

Problem 11: Which of the following appears most likely?
Which appears second most likely?

    a. Drawing a red marble from a bag containing 50 percent red marbles and 50 percent white marbles.

    b. Drawing a red marble seven times in succession, with replacement (a selected marble is put back in the bag before the next marble is selected), from a bag containing 90 percent red marbles and 10 percent white marbles.

    c. Drawing at least one red marble in seven tries, with replacement, from a bag containing 10 percent red marbles and 90 percent white marbles.

Problem 12: Listed below are 10 uncertain quantities. Do not look up any information on these items. For each, write down your best estimate of the quantity. Next, put a lower

Table 2.1   (*Continued*)

and upper bound around your estimate, such that you are 98 percent confident that your range surrounds the actual quantity.

_____   **a.** Mobil Oil's sales in 1987

_____   **b.** IBM's assets in 1987

_____   **c.** Chrysler's profit in 1987

_____   **d.** The number of U.S. industrial firms in 1987 with sales greater than those of Consolidated Papers

_____   **e.** The U.S. gross national product in 1945

_____   **f.** The amount of taxes collected by the U.S. Internal Revenue Service in 1970

_____   **g.** The length (in feet) of the Chesapeake Bay Bridge–Tunnel

_____   **h.** The area (in square miles) of Brazil

_____   **i.** The size of the black population of San Francisco in 1970

_____   **j.** The dollar value of Canadian exports of lumber in 1977

Problem 13:   (Adapted from Einhorn and Hogarth, 1978)

It is claimed that when a particular analyst predicts a rise in the market, the market always rises. You are to check this claim. Examine the information available about the following four events (cards):

Card 1 Prediction: Favorable report	*Card 2* Prediction: Unfavorable report	*Card 3* Outcome: Rise in the market	*Card 4* Outcome: Fall in the market

You currently see the predictions (cards 1 and 2) *or* outcomes (cards 3 and 4) associated with four events. You are seeing one side of a card. On the other side of cards 1 and 2 is the actual outcome, while on the other side of cards 3 and 4 is the prediction that the analyst made. Evidence about the claim is potentially available by turning over the card(s). Which cards would you turn over for the evidence that you need to check the analyst's claim? (Circle the appropriate cards.)

BIASES EMANATING FROM THE AVAILABILITY HEURISTIC

Bias 1—Ease of Recall (based upon vividness and recency)

Problem 3: Which is riskier:

a. driving a car on a 400-mile trip?

b. flying on a 400-mile commercial airline flight?

Many people respond that flying in a commercial airliner is far riskier than driving a car. The media's tendency to sensationalize airplane crashes contributes to this perception. In actuality, the safety record for flying is far better than that for driving. Thus, this example demonstrates that a particularly *vivid* event will systematically influence the probability assigned to that type of event by an individual in the future. This bias occurs because vivid events are more easily remembered and consequently are more available when making judgments.

Consider another example. A buyer of women's wear for a leading department store is assessing her purchasing needs in footwear. To fill the demand for casual shoes, she needs to choose between a proven best-selling brand of running shoes and a newer line of boating shoes. The buyer recalls having seen a number of friends wearing boating shoes at a recent party and concludes that demand for boating shoes is increasing. She decides to order more boating shoes and reduce her order of the historically popular running shoes.

In making this choice, the buyer has biased her ordering decision based upon limited data and the ease with which it came to mind. The buyer judged the demand for boating shoes by the availability of her recollection of a recent party. Under the influence of this bias, she will be consistently less likely to buy popular shoes worn by other groups with whom she tends not to socialize— even though aggregate demand for these alternative styles may be higher.

Tversky and Kahneman (1974) argue that when an individual judges the frequency of an event by the *availability* of its instances, an event whose instances are more easily recalled will appear more numerous than an event of equal frequency whose instances are less easily recalled. They cite evidence of this bias in a lab study in which individuals were read lists of names of well-known personalities of both sexes and asked to determine whether the lists contained the names of more men or women. Different lists were presented to two groups. One group received lists bearing the names of women who were relatively more famous than the listed men, but included more men's names overall. The other group received lists bearing the names of men who were relatively more famous than the listed women, but included more women's names overall. In each case, the subjects incorrectly guessed that the sex that had the more famous personalities was the more numerous.

Many examples of this bias can be observed in the decisions made by managers in the workplace. The following came from the experience of one of my MBA students: As a purchasing agent, he had to select one of several possible suppliers. He chose the firm whose name was the most familiar to him. He later found out that the salience of the name resulted from recent adverse publicity concerning the firm's extortion of funds from client companies!

Managers conducting performance appraisals often fall victim to the availability heuristic. Working from memory, the vivid instances relating to an employee that are more easily recalled from memory (either pro or con) will appear more numerous and will therefore be weighted more heavily in the performance appraisal. Managers also give more weight to performance during the three months prior to the evaluation than to the previous nine months of the evaluation period.

Many consumers are annoyed by repeated exposure to the same advertising message and often wonder why the advertiser doesn't give more useful information, without repeating it so many times. After all, we are smart enough to understand it the first time! Unfortunately, both the frequency and the vividness of the message have been shown to affect our purchasing. This bombardment of repeated, uninformative messages makes the product more easily recalled from memory and is often the best way to get us to buy a product (Alba and Marmorstein, 1987).

Because of our susceptibility to vividness and recency, Kahneman and Tversky suggest that we are particularly prone to overestimating unlikely events. For instance, if we actually witness a burning house, the impact on our assessment of the probability of such accidents is probably greater than the impact of reading about a fire in the local newspaper. The direct observation of such an event makes it more salient to us. Similarly, Slovic and Fischhoff (1977) discuss the implications of the misuse of the availability heuristic on the perceived risks of nuclear power. They point out that any discussion of the potential hazards, regardless of likelihood, will increase the memorability of those hazards and increase their perceived risks.

The stock market provides some telling examples of the tendency to overreact to vivid and recent information in this way. After the April 1986 nuclear accident at Chernobyl in the Soviet Union, U.S. investors sold their nuclear stocks, which caused a dramatic fall in prices. Yet the real safety of the nuclear systems did not change dramatically as a result of the Chernobyl accident. Similarly, the stock of Union Carbide fell 30 percent within three weeks of the December 1984 tragedy at its chemical plant in Bhopal, India. Few investors stopped to realize that Union Carbide might reach an acceptable out-of-court settlement. It was more salient to imagine Union Carbide being hit with a devastating financial penalty. More rational investors who bought the stock at its low point turned a hefty profit—even before the stock moved up higher on an unsuccessful takeover bid (Curran, 1987).

Bias 2—Retrievability (based upon memory structures)

Problem 4: Are there more words in the English language

a. that start with an *r*?
b. for which *r* is the third letter?

If you responded "start with an *r*," you have joined the majority. Unfortunately, this is again the incorrect answer. Kahneman and Tversky (1973) explain that people typically solve this problem by first recalling words that begin with *r* (like *ran*) and words that have an *r* as the third letter (like *bar*). The relative difficulty of generating words in each of these two categories is then assessed. If we think of our mind as being organized like a dictionary, it is easier to find lots of words that start with an *r*. The dictionary, and our minds, are less efficient at finding words that follow a rule that is inconsistent with the organizing structure—like words that have an *r* as the third letter. Thus, words that start with a particular letter are more available from memory, even though most consonants are more common in the third position than in the first.

Just as our tendency to alphabetize affects our vocabulary-search behavior, organizational modes affect information-search behavior within our work lives. We structure organizations to provide order, but this same structure can lead to confusion if the presumed order is not exactly as suggested. For example, many organizations have a management information systems (MIS) division that has generalized expertise in computer applications. Assume that you are a manager in a product division and need computer expertise. If that expertise exists within MIS, the organizational hierarchy will lead you to the correct resource. If they lack the expertise in a specific application, but it exists elsewhere in the organization, the hierarchy is likely to bias the effectiveness of your search. I am not arguing for the overthrow of organizational hierarchies; I am merely identifying the dysfunctional role of hierarchies in potentially biasing search behavior. If we are aware of the potential bias, we need not be affected by this limitation.

Retail store location is influenced by the way in which consumers search their minds when seeking a particular commodity. Why are multiple gas stations at the same intersection? Why do "upscale" retailers want to be in the same mall? Why are the best bookstores in a city often all located within a couple blocks of each other? An important reason for this pattern is that consumers learn the "location" for a particular type of product or store and organize their minds accordingly. To maximize traffic, the retailer needs to be in the location that consumers associate with this type of product or store.

Bias 3—Presumed Associations

People frequently fall victim to the availability bias in their assessment of the likelihood of two events occurring together. For example, consider the following questions: Is marijuana use related to delinquency? Are couples who get married under the age of 25 more likely to have bigger families? How would you respond if asked these questions? In assessing the marijuana question, most people typically remember several delinquent marijuana users and assume a correlation or not based upon the availability of this mental data. However, proper analysis would include recalling four groups of observations: marijuana users who are delinquents, marijuana users who are not delinquents, delinquents who do not use marijuana, and nondelinquents who do not use marijuana. The same analysis applies to the marriage question. Proper analysis would include four groups: couples who married young and have large families, couples who married young and have small families, couples who married older and have large families, and couples who married older and have small families. Indeed, there are always at least four separate situations to be considered in assessing the association between two dichotomous events, but our everyday decision making commonly ignores this scientifically valid fact.

Chapman and Chapman (1967) have noted that when the probability of two events co-occurring is judged by the availability of perceived co-occurring instances in our minds, we usually assign an inappropriately high probability that the two events will co-occur again. Thus, if we know a lot of marijuana users who are delinquents, we assume that marijuana use is related to delinquency. Similarly, if we know of a lot of couples who married young and have had large families, we assume that this trend is more prevalent than it may actually be. In testing for this bias, Chapman and Chapman provided subjects with information about hypothetical psychiatric patients. The information included a written clinical diagnosis of the "patient" and a drawing of a person made by the "patient." The subjects were asked to estimate the frequency with which each diagnosis (for example, suspiciousness or paranoia) was accompanied by various facial and body features in the drawings (for example, peculiar eyes). Throughout the study, subjects markedly overestimated the frequency of pairs commonly associated together by social lore. For example, diagnoses of suspiciousness were overwhelmingly associated with peculiar eyes. In addition, Chapman and Chapman found that conclusions, such as the just noted, were extremely resistant to change, even in the face of contradictory information. Furthermore, the overwhelming impact of this bias toward presumed associations prevented the subjects from detecting other relationships that were, in fact, present.

Summary   A lifetime of experience has led us to believe that, in general, more frequent events are recalled in our minds more easily than less frequent ones, and likely events are easier to recall than unlikely events. In response to this learning, we have developed the availability heuristic for estimating the likelihood of events. In many instances, this simplifying heuristic leads to accurate, efficient judgments. However, as these first three biases (ease of recall, retrievability, and presumed associations) indicate, the misuse of the availability heuristic can lead to systematic errors in managerial judgment. We too easily assume that our available recollections are truly representative of some larger pool of occurrences that exists outside our range of experience.

BIASES EMANATING FROM THE REPRESENTATIVENESS HEURISTIC

Bias 4—Insensitivity to Base Rates

Problem 5: Mark is finishing his MBA at a prestigious university. He is very interested in the arts and at one time considered a career as a musician. Is Mark more likely to take a job

a. in the management of the arts?
b. with a management consulting firm?

How did you decide on your answer? How do most people make this assessment? How *should* people make this assessment? Using the representativeness heuristic discussed in Chapter 1, most people approach this problem by analyzing the degree to which Mark is representative of their image of individuals who take jobs in each of the two areas. Consequently, they usually conclude "in the management of the arts." However, as we discussed in the first part of this chapter, this response overlooks relevant base-rate information. Reconsider the problem in light of the fact that a much larger number of MBAs take jobs in management consulting than in the management of the arts— relevant information that should enter into any reasonable prediction of Mark's career path. With this base-rate data, it is only reasonable to predict "management consulting."

Judgmental biases of this type frequently occur when individuals cognitively ask the wrong question. If you answered "in the management of the arts," you were probably thinking in terms of the question "How likely is it that a person working in the management of the arts would fit Mark's description?" However, the problem necessitates the question "How likely is it that someone fitting Mark's description will choose arts management?" By itself, the representativeness heuristic incorrectly leads to a similar answer to both questions, since this heuristic leads individuals to compare the resemblance of the personal description and the career path. However, when base-rate data is considered, it is irrelevant to the first question listed, but it is crucial to a reasonable prediction on the second question. While a large percentage of individuals in arts management may fit Mark's description, there are undoubtedly a larger absolute number of management consultants fitting Mark's description because of the relative preponderance of MBAs in management consulting.

An interesting finding of the research done by Kahneman and Tversky (1972, 1973) is that subjects do use base-rate data correctly when no other information is provided. For example, in the absence of a personal description of Mark in Problem 5, people will choose "management consulting" based on the past frequency of this career path for MBAs. Thus, people understand the relevance of base-rate information, but tend to disregard this data when descriptive data is also available.

Bias 5—Insensitivity to Sample Size

Problem 6: In 1986, two research groups sampled consumers on the driving performance of the Dodge Colt versus the Plymouth Champ in a blind road test; that is, the consumers did not know when they were driving the Colt or the Champ. As you may know, these cars were identical; only the marketing varied.

One research group (A) sampled 66 consumers each day for 60 days (a large number of days to control for weather and other variables), while the other research group (B) sampled 22 consumers each day for 50 days. Which consumer group observed more days in which 60 percent or more of the consumers tested preferred the Dodge Colt:

a. group A?
b. group B?

Most individuals expect research group A to provide more 60-percent days for the Dodge Colt, because of the larger number of sample days—in other words, there are 60 chances compared to 50. In contrast, simple statistics tells us that it is much more likely to observe more 60-percent days on daily samples of 22 than on daily samples of 66, and the correct answer is group B. This is because a large sample is far less likely to stray from the expected 50-percent preference split between the Dodge Colt and Plymouth Champ—since the cars are identical. (The interested reader can verify this fact with the use of an introductory statistics book.)

While the importance of sample size is fundamental in statistics, Kahneman and Tversky (1974) note that it "is evidently not part of people's repertoire of intuitions" (p. 1126). Why is this? When responding to problems dealing with sampling, people often use the representativeness heuristic. In their minds, they ask the question, Which group is likely to have more days in which the results are skewed to 60 percent for the Dodge Colt instead of the expected 50 percent? From there, the representative heuristic leads them to focus on the number of days as the pertinent variable for comparison. They then conclude that the group covering the greater number of total days will experience the greater number of total deviations. However, this analogy ignores the issue of sample size—which is critical to an accurate assessment of the problem.

Tversky and Kahneman (1974) first discovered this bias toward ignoring the role of sample size, even when these data were emphasized in the formation of the problem, in testing the following research problem:

A certain town is served by two hospitals. In the larger hospital about 45 babies are born each day, and in the smaller hospital about 15 babies are born each day. As you know, about 50 percent of all babies are boys. However, the exact percentage varies from day to day. Sometimes it may be higher than 50 percent, sometimes lower.

For a period of one year, each hospital recorded the days on which more than 60 percent of the babies born were boys. Which hospital do you think recorded more such days?

The larger hospital? (21)
The smaller hospital? (21)
About the same? (53)
(that is, within 5 percent of each other)

The values in parentheses represent the number of individuals who chose each answer. As explained earlier, sampling theory tells us that the expected number of days on which more than 60 percent of the babies are boys is much greater in the small hospital, since a large sample is less likely to stray from the mean. However, most subjects judged the probability to be the same in each hospital, effectively ignoring sample size.

Consider the implications of this bias in advertising, where people trained in market research understand the need for a sizable sample, but employ this bias to the advantage of their clients. "Four out of five dentists surveyed recommend sugarless gum for their patients who chew gum." There is no mention of the number of dentists involved in the survey and the fact that without these data, the results of the survey are meaningless. If only 5 or 15 dentists were surveyed, the size of the sample would not be generalizable to the overall population of dentists.

Bias 6—Misconceptions of Chance

Problem 7: You are about to hire a new central-region sales director for the fifth time this year. You predict that the next director should work out reasonably well, since the last four were "lemons," and the odds favor hiring at least one good sales director in five tries. This thinking is

a. correct.
b. incorrect.

Most people are comfortable with the foregoing logic, or at least have been guilty of using similar logic in the past. However, the performance of the first four sales directors will not directly affect the performance of the fifth sales director, and the logic in problem 7 is incorrect. Most individuals frequently rely upon their intuition and the representativeness heuristic and incorrectly conclude that a poor performance is unlikely because the probability of getting five "lemons" in a row is extremely low. Unfortunately, this logic ignores the fact that we have already witnessed four "lemons" (an unlikely occurrence), and the performance of the fifth sales director is independent of that of the first four.

This question parallels Kahneman and Tversky's (1972) work in which they show that people expect that a sequence of random events will "look" random. They present evidence of this bias in their finding that subjects routinely judged the sequence of coin flips H-T-H-T-T-H to be more likely than H-H-H-T-T-T, which does not "appear" random, and more likely than the sequence H-H-H-H-T-H, which does not represent the equal likelihood of heads and tails. Simple statistics, of course, tell us that each of these sequences is equally likely because of the independence of multiple random events.

Problem 7 moves beyond dealing with random events in recognizing our inappropriate tendency to assume that random *and* nonrandom events will "balance out." Will the fifth sales director work out well? Maybe. You might spend more time and money on selection, and the randomness of the hiring process may favor you this time. But your earlier failures in hiring sales directors will not directly affect the performance of the new sales director.

The logic concerning misconceptions of chance provides a process explanation of the gambler's fallacy. After holding bad cards on ten hands of poker, the poker player believes that he is due for a good hand. After winning $1,000 in the Pennsylvania State Lottery, a woman changes her regular number—because after all, how likely is it that the same number will come up twice? Tversky and Kahneman (1974) note that "Chance is commonly viewed as a self-correcting process in which a deviation in one direction induces a deviation in the opposite direction to restore the equilibrium. In fact, deviations are not corrected as a chance process unfolds, they are merely diluted."

In each of the preceding examples, individuals expected probabilities to even out. In some situations, our minds misconceptualize chance in exactly the opposite way. In sports (basketball specifically), we often think of a particular player as having a "hot hand" or "being on a good streak." If your favorite player has hit his last four shots, is the probability of his making his next shot higher, lower, or the same as the probability of his making a shot without the preceding four hits? Most sports fans, sports commentators, and players believe that the answer is "higher." In fact, there are many biological, emotional, and physical reasons that this answer could be correct. However, it is wrong! Gilovich, Vallone, and Tversky (1985) did an extensive analysis of the shooting of Philadelphia 76ers and Boston Celtics and found that immediately prior shot performance did not change the likelihood of success on the upcoming shot. Out of all of the findings in this book, this is the effect that my managerial students have had the hardest time believing. The reason is that we can all remember sequences of five hits in a row: streaks are part of our conception of chance in athletic competition. However, our minds do not categorize a string of "four in a row" as being a situation in which "he missed his fifth shot." As a result, we have a misconception of connectedness, when, in fact, chance (or the player's normal probability of success) is really in effect.

The belief in the hot hand is especially interesting because of its implication for how players play the game. Passing the ball to the player who is "hot" is commonly endorsed as a good strategy. It can also be expected that the opposing team will concentrate on guarding the hot player. Another player, who is less "hot" but is equally skilled, may have a better chance of scoring. Thus the belief in the "hot hand" is not just erroneous, but could also be costly if you play professional basketball.

Tversky and Kahneman's (1971) work shows that misconceptions of chance are not limited to gamblers, sportsfans, or laypersons. Research psychologists also fall victim to the "law of small numbers." They believe that sample events should be far more representative of the population from which they were drawn than simple statistics would dictate. The researchers put too much faith in the results of initial samples and grossly overestimate the replicability of empirical findings. This suggests that the representativeness heuristic may be so well institutionalized in our decision processes that even scientific training and its emphasis on the proper use of statistics may not effectively eliminate its biasing influence.

Bias 7—Regression to the Mean

Problem 8: You are the sales forecaster for a department store chain with nine locations. The chain depends on you for quality projections of future sales in order to make decisions on staffing, advertising, information system developments, purchasing, renovation, and the like. All stores are similar in size and merchandise selection. The main difference in their sales occurs because of location and random fluctuations. Sales for 1989 were as follows:

Store	1989	1991
1	$12,000,000	$_____
2	11,500,000	_____
3	11,000,000	_____
4	10,500,000	_____
5	10,000,000	_____
6	9,500,000	_____
7	9,000,000	_____
8	8,500,000	_____
9	8,000,000	_____
TOTAL	$90,000,000	$99,000,000

Your economic forecasting service has convinced you that the best estimate of total sales increases between 1989 and 1991 is 10 percent (to $99,000,000). Your task is to predict 1991 sales for each store. Since your manager believes strongly in the economic forecasting service, it is imperative that your total sales are equal to $99,000,000.

Think about the processes used to answer this problem. Consider the following logical pattern of thought: "The overall increase in sales is predicted to be 10 percent ($99,000,000 − $90,000,000/$90,000,000). Lacking any other specific information on the stores, it makes sense to simply add 10 percent to each 1989 sales figure to predict 1991 sales. This means that I predict sales of $13,200,000 for store 1, sales of $12,650,000 for store 2, and so on." This logic, in fact, is the most common approach in responding to this item. Unfortunately, this logic is faulty.

Why was the logic presented faulty? Statistical analysis would dictate that we first assess the predicted relationship between 1989 and 1991 sales. This relationship, formally known as a **correlation,** can vary from total independence (that is, 1989 sales do not predict 1991 sales) to perfect correlation (1989 sales are a perfect predictor of 1991 sales). In the former case, the lack of a relationship between 1989 and 1991 sales would mean that 1989 sales would provide absolutely no information about 1991 sales, and your best estimates of 1991 sales would be equal to total sales divided by the number of stores ($99,000,000 divided by 9 equals $11,000,000). However, in the latter case of perfect predictability between 1989 and 1991 sales, our initial logic of simply extrapolating from 1989 performance by adding 10 percent to each store's performance would be completely accurate. Obviously, 1989 sales are most likely to be *partially predictive* of 1991 sales—falling somewhere between independence and perfect correlation. Thus, the best prediction for store 1 should lie between $11,000,000 and $13,200,000, depending upon how predictive you think 1989 sales will be of 1991 sales. The key point is that in virtually all such predictions, you should expect the naive $13,200,000 estimate to regress toward the overall mean ($11,000,000).

In a study of sales forecasting, Cox and Summers (1987) examined the judgments of professional retail buyers. They examined the sales data from 2 department stores for 6 different apparel styles for a total of 12 different sales forecasts over a 2-week period. They found that sales between the 2 weeks regressed to the mean. However, the judgment of all 31 buyers from 5 different department stores failed to reflect the tendency for regression to the mean. As a result, Cox and Summers argued that a sales-forecasting model that considered regression to the mean could outperform the judgments of all 31 professional buyers.

Many effects regress to the mean. Brilliant students frequently have less successful siblings. Short parents tend to have taller children. Great rookies have mediocre second years (the "sophomore jinx"). Firms that have outstanding profits one year tend to have lesser performances the next year. In each case, individuals are often surprised when made aware of these predictable patterns of regression to the mean.

Why is the regression-to-the-mean concept, while statistically valid, counterintuitive? Kahneman and Tversky (1973) suggest that the representativeness heuristic accounts for this systematic bias in judgment. They argue that individuals typically assume that future outcomes (for example, 1991 sales) will be maximally representative of past outcomes (1989 sales). Thus, we tend to naively develop predictions that are based upon the assumption of perfect correlation with past data.

In some unusual situations, individuals do intuitively expect a regression-to-the-mean effect. In 1980, when George Brett batted .384, most people did not expect him to hit .384 the following year. When Wilt Chamberlain scored 100 points in a single game, most people did not expect him to score 100 points in his next game. When a historically 3.0 student got a 4.0 one semester, her friends did not expect a repeat performance the following semester. When a real estate agent sold five houses in one month (an abnormally high performance), his co-agents did not expect similar performance in the following month. Why is regression to the mean more intuitive in these cases? Because the performance is so extreme that we know it cannot last. Thus, under very unusual circumstances, we expect performance to regress. However, we generally do not recognize the regression effect in less extreme cases.

Consider Kahneman and Tversky's (1973) classic example in which the misconceptions surrounding regression led to overestimation of the effectiveness of punishment and the underestimation of the power of reward. Here, in a discussion about flight training, experienced instructors noted that praise for an exceptionally smooth landing was typically followed by a poorer landing on the next try, while harsh criticism after a rough landing was usually followed by an improvement on the next try. The instructors concluded that verbal rewards were detrimental to learning, while verbal punishments were beneficial. Obviously, the tendency of performance to regress to the mean can account for the results; verbal feedback may have had absolutely no effect. However, to the extent that the instructors were prone to biased decision making, they were prone to reach the false conclusion that punishment is more effective than positive reinforcement in shaping behavior.

How do managers respond when they do not acknowledge the regression principle? Consider an employee with very high performance in one performance period. He (and his boss) may inappropriately expect similar performance in the next period. What happens when his performance regresses toward the mean? He (and his boss) begin to make excuses for not meeting expectations. Obviously, they are likely to develop false explanations and may inappropriately plan their future efforts.

Bias 8—The Conjunction Fallacy

Problem 9: Linda is 31 years old, single, outspoken, and very bright. She majored in philosophy. As a student, she was deeply concerned with issues of discrimination and social justice, and she participated in antinuclear demonstrations.

Rank order the following eight descriptions in terms of the probability (likelihood) that they describe Linda:

____ **a.** Linda is a teacher in an elementary school.
____ **b.** Linda works in a bookstore and takes yoga classes.
____ **c.** Linda is active in the feminist movement.
____ **d.** Linda is a psychiatric social worker.
____ **e.** Linda is a member of the League of Women Voters.
____ **f.** Linda is a bank teller.
____ **g.** Linda is an insurance salesperson.
____ **h.** Linda is a bank teller who is active in the feminist movement.

Examine your rank orderings of descriptions C, F, and H. Most people rank order C as more likely than H and H as more likely than F. The reason for this ordering is that C-H-F is the order of the degree to which the descriptions are *representative* of the short profile of Linda. The description of Linda was constructed by Tversky and Kahneman to be representative of an active feminist and unrepresentative of a bank teller. Recall from the representativeness heuristic that people make judgments according to the degree to which a specific description corresponds to a broader category within their minds.

Linda's description is more representative of a feminist than of a feminist bank teller, and is more representative of a feminist bank teller than of a bank teller. Thus, the representativeness heuristic accurately predicts that most individuals will rank order the items C-H-F.

Although the representativeness heuristic accurately predicts how individuals will respond, it also leads to another common, systematic distortion of human judgment—the **conjunction fallacy** (Tversky and Kahneman, 1983). This is illustrated by a reexamination of the potential descriptions of Linda. One of the simplest and most fundamental qualitative laws of probability is that a subset (for example, being a bank teller and a feminist) cannot be more likely than a larger set that completely includes the subset (e.g., being a bank teller). Statistically speaking, the broad set "Linda is a bank teller" must be rated at least as likely, if not more so, than the description "Linda is a bank teller and a feminist." After all, there is some chance (although it is small) that Linda is a bank teller but not a feminist. Based upon this logic, a rational assessment of the likelihoods of Linda being depicted by the eight descriptions must include a more likely rank for F than H.

While simple statistics can demonstrate that a conjunction (a combination of two or more descriptors) cannot be more probable than any one of its descriptors, the conjunction fallacy predicts and demonstrates that a conjunction will be judged more probable than a single component descriptor when the conjunction appears more representative than the component descriptor. Intuitively, thinking of Linda as a feminist bank teller "feels" more correct than thinking of her as only a bank teller.

The conjunction fallacy can also operate based on greater *availability* of the conjunction than one of the unique descriptors (Yates and Carlson, 1986). That is, if the conjunction creates more intuitive matches with vivid events, acts, or people than a component of the conjunction, the conjunction is likely to be perceived falsely as more probable than the component. For example, Tversky and Kahneman (1983) found experts (in July 1982) to evaluate the probability of

"a complete suspension of diplomatic relations between the USA and the Soviet Union, sometime in 1983"

as less likely than the probability of

"a Russian invasion of Poland, and a complete suspension of diplomatic relations between the USA and the Soviet Union, some time in 1983."

As earlier demonstrated, *suspension* is necessarily more likely than *invasion and suspension.* However, a Russian invasion followed by a diplomatic crisis provides a more intuitively viable story than simply a diplomatic crisis. Similarly, in the domain of natural disasters, Kahneman and Tversky's subjects rated

"a massive flood somewhere in North America in 1989, in which 1,000 people drown"

as less likely than the probability of

"an earthquake in California sometime in 1989, causing a flood in which more than 1,000 people drown."

It is obvious that the latter possibility is a subset of the former, and many other events could cause the flood in North America.

Tversky and Kahneman (1983) have shown that the conjunction fallacy is likely to lead to deviations from rationality in the judgments of sporting events, criminal behavior, international relations, and medical judgments. Our obvious concern with biased decision making resulting from the conjunction fallacy is that if we make systematic deviations from rationality in the prediction of future outcomes, we will be less prepared for dealing with future events.

Summary This discussion concludes our examination of the five biases (insensitivity to base rates, insensitivity to sample size, misconceptions of chance, regression to the mean, and the conjunction fallacy) that emanate from the use of the representativeness heuristic. Experience has taught us that the likelihood of a specific occurrence *is* related to the likelihood of a group of occurrences that that specific occurrence represents. Unfortunately, we tend to overuse this information in making decisions. The five biases we have just explored illustrate the systematic irrationalities that can occur in our judgments when we are not aware of this overreliance.

BIASES EMANATING FROM ANCHORING AND ADJUSTMENT

Bias 9—Insufficient Anchor Adjustment

Problem 10: A newly hired engineer for a computer firm in the Boston metropolitan area has four years of experience and good all-around qualifications. When asked to estimate the starting salary for this employee, my secretary (knowing very little about the profession or the industry) guessed an annual salary of $23,000. What is your estimate?
$ _____ per year.

Was your answer affected by my secretary's response? Most people do not think that my secretary's response affected their response. However, individuals *are* affected by the fairly irrelevant information contained in my secretary's estimate. Reconsider how you would have responded if my secretary had estimated $80,000. On average, individuals give higher salary estimates to the problem when the secretary's estimate is stated as $80,000 than when it is stated as $23,000. Why? Studies have found that people develop estimates by starting from an initial anchor, based upon whatever information is provided, and adjusting from there to yield a final answer. Slovic and Lichtenstein (1971) have provided conclusive evidence that adjustments away from anchors are usually not sufficient to negate the effects of the anchor. In all cases, answers are biased toward the initial anchor, even if it is irrelevant. Different starting points yield different answers. Tversky and Kahneman (1973) named this phenomenon **anchoring and adjustment.**

Tversky and Kahneman (1974) provide systematic, empirical evidence of the anchoring effect. For example, in one study, subjects were asked to estimate the percentage of African countries in the United Nations. For each subject, a *random* number (obtained by an observed spin of a roulette wheel) was given as a starting point. From there, subjects were asked to state whether the actual value of the quantity was higher or lower than this random value and then develop their best estimate for the actual quantity. It was found that the *arbitrary* values from the roulette wheel had a substantial impact on estimates. For example, for groups that received 10 countries and 65 countries as starting points, the median estimates were 25 and 45, respectively. Thus, even though the subjects were aware that the anchor was random and unrelated to the judgment task, the anchor had a dramatic effect on their judgment. Interestingly, paying subjects differentially based upon accuracy did not reduce the magnitude of the anchoring effect.

Salary negotiations represent a very common context for observing anchoring in the managerial world. For example, pay increases often come in the form of a percentage increase. A firm may have an average increase of 8 percent, with increases for specific employees varying from 3 percent to 13 percent. While society has led us to accept such systems as equitable, I believe that such a system falls victim to anchoring and leads to substantial inequities. What happens if an employee has been *substantially* underpaid to begin with? The pay system described does not rectify past inequities, since a pay increase of 11 percent will probably leave that employee still underpaid. Conversely, the system would work in the employee's favor had she been overpaid. It is common for an employer to ask job applicants their current salaries. Why? Employers are searching for a value from which they can anchor an adjustment. If the employee is worth far more than his current salary, the anchoring and adjustment hypothesis predicts that the firm will make an offer below the employee's true value. Does this figure provide fully accurate information about the true worth of the employee? I think not. Thus, the use of such compensation systems accepts past inequities as an anchor and makes inadequate adjustments from that point. Further, these findings suggest that in deciding what offer to make to a potential employee, any anchor that creeps into the discussion is likely to have an inappropriate effect on the eventual offer, even if the anchor is "ignored" as being ridiculous.

There are numerous examples of the anchoring-and-adjustment phenomenon in everyday life.

- In education, children are tracked by a school system that may categorize them into a certain level of performance at an early age. For example, a child who is anchored in the *C* group may meet expectations of mediocre performance. Conversely, a child of similar abilities anchored in the *A* track may strive to meet expectations, which will keep him in the *A* track.

- We have all fallen victim to the first-impression syndrome when meeting someone for the first time. We often place so much emphasis on first impressions that we do not adjust our opinion appropriately at a later date.
- Prior to 1973–1974, the speed limit on most interstate highways was 65 miles per hour (mph), with a normal cruising speed in the left-hand lane of 70 to 75 mph. This did not seem to be an extraordinarily unsafe speed to most people. After 1974, the speed limit was reduced to 55 mph. Most people changed their judgments to view a speed of 70 to 75 mph as extremely unsafe— "something only crazy kids would do." Today, the reinstitution of the 65 mph limit on nonurban highways has rejustified the safety of the 70 to 75 mph speed.

In a fascinating study of anchoring and adjustment in the real estate market, Northcraft and Neale (1987) surveyed an association of real estate brokers, who indicated that they believed that they could assess the value of properties to within 5 percent of their true or appraised value. Further, they were unanimous in stating that they did not factor the listing price of the property into their personal estimate of its "true" value. Northcraft and Neale then asked four groups of professional real estate brokers and undergraduate students to estimate the value of a real house. Both brokers and students were randomly assigned to one of four experimental groups. In each group, all participants were given a 10-page packet of information about the house that was being sold. The packet included not only background on the house, but also considerable information about prices and characteristics of other houses in the area that had recently been sold. The only difference in the information given to the four groups was the listing price for the house, which was selected to be +11 percent, +4 percent, −4 percent, and −11 percent of the actual appraised value of the property. After reading the material, all participants toured the house, as well as the surrounding neighborhood. Participants were then asked for their estimate of the house's price. The final results suggested that *both* brokers and students were *significantly* affected by the listing price (the anchor) in determining the value. While the students readily admitted the role that the listing price played in their decision-making process, the brokers flatly denied their use of the listing price as an anchor for their evaluations of the property—despite the evidence to the contrary. This study provides convincing data to indicate that even experts are susceptible to the anchoring bias. Furthermore, experts are less likely to realize their use of this bias in making decisions.

Joyce and Biddle (1981) have also provided empirical support for the anchoring-and-adjustment effect on practicing auditors of Big Eight accounting firms. Specifically, subjects in one condition were asked the following:

> It is well known that many cases of management fraud go undetected even when competent annual audits are performed. The reason, of course, is that Generally Accepted Auditing Standards are not designed specifically to detect executive-level management fraud. We are interested in obtaining an estimate from practicing au-

ditors of the prevalence of executive-level management fraud as a first step in ascertaining the scope of the problem.

1. Based on your audit experience, is the incidence of significant executive-level management fraud more than 10 in each 1,000 firms (that is, 1 percent) audited by Big Eight accounting firms?

   a. Yes, more than 10 in each 1,000 Big Eight clients have significant executive-level management fraud.

   b. No, fewer than 10 in each 1,000 Big Eight clients have significant executive-level management fraud.

2. What is your estimate of the number of Big Eight clients per 1,000 that have significant executive-level management fraud?
   (Fill in the blank below with the appropriate number.)
   ____ in each 1,000 Big Eight clients have significant executive-level management fraud.

The second condition differed only in that subjects were asked whether the fraud incidence was more or less than 200 in each 1,000 audited, rather than 10 in 1,000. Subjects in the former condition estimated a fraud incidence of 16.52 per 1,000 on average, compared with an estimated fraud incidence of 43.11 per 1,000 in the second condition! Here, even professional auditors fell victim to anchoring and adjustment.

The tendency to make insufficient adjustments is a direct result of the anchoring-and-adjustment heuristic described in the first chapter. Interestingly, Nisbett and Ross (1980) present an argument that suggests that the anchoring-and-adjustment bias itself dictates that it will be very difficult to get *you* to change your decision-making strategies as a result of reading this book. They argue that each of the heuristics that we identify are currently serving as your cognitive anchors and are central to your current judgment processes. Thus, any cognitive strategy that I suggest must be presented and understood in a manner that will force you to break your existing cognitive anchors. Based on the evidence in this section, this should be a difficult challenge—but one that is important enough to be worth the effort!

Bias 10—Conjunctive and Disjunctive Events Bias

Problem 11: Which of the following appears most likely?
Which appears second most likely?

a. Drawing a red marble from a bag containing 50 percent red marbles and 50 percent white marbles.

b. Drawing a red marble seven times in succession, with replacement (a selected marble is put back in the bag before the next marble is selected), from a bag containing 90 percent red marbles and 10 percent white marbles.

c. Drawing at least one red marble in seven tries, with replacement, from a bag containing 10 percent red marbles and 90 percent white marbles.

The most common answer in ordering the preferences is B-A-C. Interestingly, the correct order of likelihood is C (52 percent), A (50 percent), B (48 percent)—the exact opposite of the most common intuitive pattern! This result illustrates a general bias to overestimate the probability of conjunctive events—events that must occur in conjunction with one another (Bar-Hillel, 1973)—and to underestimate the probability of disjunctive events—events that occur independently (Tversky and Kahneman, 1974). Thus, when multiple events all need to occur (problem B), we overestimate the true likelihood, while if only one of many events needs to occur (problem C), we underestimate the true likelihood.

Kahneman and Tversky (1974) explain these effects in terms of the anchoring-and-adjustment heuristic. They argue that the probability of any one event occurring (for example, drawing one red marble) provides a natural anchor for the judgment of the total probability. Since adjustment from an anchor is typically insufficient, the perceived likelihood of choice B stays inappropriately close to 90 percent, while the perceived probability of choice C stays inappropriately close to 10 percent.

How is each of these biases manifested in an applied context? The overestimation of conjunctive events is a powerful explanation of the timing problems in projects that require multistage planning. Individuals, businesses, and governments frequently fall victim to the conjunction-events bias in terms of timing and budgets. Public works projects seldom finish on time or on budget. New product ventures frequently take longer than expected.

Consider the following:

- You are planning a construction project that consists of five distinct components. Your schedule is tight, and every component must be on time in order to meet a contractual deadline. Will you meet this deadline?
- You are managing a consulting project that consists of six teams, each of which is analyzing a different alternative. The alternatives cannot be compared until all teams complete their portion. Will you meet the deadline?
- After three years of study, doctoral students typically dramatically overestimate the likelihood of completing their dissertations within a year. At this stage, they typically can tell you how long each remaining component will take. Why do they not finish in one year?

The underestimation of disjunctive events explains our surprise when an unlikely event occurs. As Tversky and Kahneman (1974) argue, "A complex system, such as a nuclear reactor or the human body, will malfunction if any of its essential component fails. Even when the likelihood of failure in each component is slight, the probability of an overall failure can be high if many components are involved." In *Normal Accidents,* Perrow (1984) argues against the safety of technologies like nuclear reactors and DNA research. He fears that society significantly underestimates the likelihood of system failure because of our judgmental failure to realize the multitude of things that can go wrong in these incredibly complex and interactive systems.

The understanding of our underestimation of disjunctive events also has its positive side. Consider the following:

> It's Monday evening (10:00 P.M.). You get a phone call telling you that you must be at the Chicago office by 9:30 A.M. the next morning. You call all five airlines that have flights that get into Chicago by 9:00 A.M. Each has one flight, and all the flights are booked. When you ask the probability of getting on each of the flights if you show up at the airport in the morning, you are disappointed to hear probabilities of 30 percent, 25 percent, 15 percent, 20 percent, and 25 percent. Consequently, you do not expect to get to Chicago in time.

In this case, the disjunctive bias leads you to expect the worst. In fact, if the probabilities given by the airlines are unbiased, and independent there is a 73 percent chance of getting on one of the flights (assuming that you can arrange to be at the right ticket counter at the right time)!

Bias 11—Overconfidence

Problem 12: Listed below are 10 uncertain quantities. Do not look up any information on these items. For each, write down your best estimate of the quantity. Next, put a lower and upper bound around your estimate, such that you are 98 percent confident that your range surrounds the actual quantity.

_____ **a.** Mobil Oil's sales in 1987

_____ **b.** IBM's assets in 1987

_____ **c.** Chrysler's profit in 1987

_____ **d.** The number of U.S. industrial firms in 1987 with sales greater than those of Consolidated Papers

_____ **e.** The U.S. gross national product in 1945

_____ **f.** The amount of taxes collected by the U.S. Internal Revenue Service in 1970

_____ **g.** The length (in feet) of the Chesapeake Bay Bridge–Tunnel

_____ **h.** The area (in square miles) of Brazil

_____ **i.** The size of the black population of San Francisco in 1970

_____ **j.** The dollar value of Canadian exports of lumber in 1977

How many of your 10 ranges will actually surround the true quantities? If you set your ranges so that you were 98 percent confident, you should expect to correctly bound approximately 9.8 or 9 to 10 of the 10 quantities. Let's look at the correct answers: (a) $51,223,000,000; (b) $63,688,000,000; (c) $1,289,700,000; (d) 381; (e) $212,300,000,000; (f) $195,722,096,497; (g) 93,203; (h) 3,286,470; (i) 96,078; (j) $2,386,282,000.

How many of your ranges actually surrounded the true quantities? If you surround 9–10, we can conclude that you were appropriately confident in your estimation ability. Most people only surround between 3 (30 percent) and 7 (70 percent), despite claiming a 98 percent confidence that each of the ranges will surround the true value. Why? Most of us are *overconfident* in our estimation abilities and do not acknowledge the actual uncertainty that exists.

In Alpert and Raiffa's (1969) initial demonstration of overconfidence based upon 1,000 observations (100 subjects on 10 items), 42.6 percent of quantities fell outside 90% confidence ranges. Since then, overconfidence has been identified as a common judgmental pattern and demonstrated in a wide variety of settings. For example, Fischhoff, Slovic, and Lichtenstein (1977) found that subjects who assigned odds of 1,000 : 1 of being correct were correct only 81 to 88 percent of the time. For odds of 1,000,000 : 1, their answers were correct only 90 to 96 percent of the time! Hazard and Peterson (1973) identified over-confidence among members of the armed forces, while Cambridge and Shreckengost (1980) found extreme overconfidence in CIA agents.

The most well-established finding in the overconfidence literature is the tendency of people to be most overconfident of the correctness of their answers when asked to respond to questions of moderate to extreme difficulty (Fischhoff, Slovic, and Lichtenstein, 1977; Koriat, Lichtenstein, and Fischhoff, 1980; Lichtenstein and Fischhoff, 1977, 1980). That is, as subjects' knowledge of a question decreases, they do not correspondingly decrease their level of confidence (Nickerson and McGoldrick, 1965; Pitz, 1974). However, subjects typically demonstrate no overconfidence, and often some underconfidence, to questions with which they are familiar. Thus we should be most alert to over-confidence in areas outside of our expertise.

There is a large degree of controversy over the explanations of why over-confidence exists (see Lichtenstein, Fischhoff, and Phillips [1982] for an extensive discussion). Tversky and Kahneman (1974) explain overconfidence in terms of anchoring. Specifically, they argue that when individuals are asked to set a confidence range around an answer, their initial estimate serves as an anchor which biases their estimation of confidence intervals in both directions. As explained earlier, adjustments from an anchor are usually insufficient, resulting in an overly narrow confidence band.

In their review of the overconfidence literature, Lichtenstein, Fischhoff, and Phillips (1982) suggest two viable strategies for eliminating overconfidence. First, they have found that giving people feedback about their overconfidence *based on their judgments* has been moderately successful at reducing this bias. Second, Koriat, Lichtenstein, and Fischhoff (1980) found that asking people to explain why their answers might be wrong (or far off the mark) can decrease overconfidence by getting subjects to see contradictions in their judgment.

Why should you be concerned about overconfidence? After all, it has probably given you the courage in the past to attempt endeavors that have stretched your abilities. However, consider the following:

- You are a medical doctor and are considering performing a difficult operation. The patient's family needs to know the likelihood of his surviving the operation. You respond "95 percent." Are you guilty of malpractice if you tend to be overconfident in your projections of survival?

- You work for the Nuclear Regulatory Commission and are 99.9 percent confident that a reactor will not leak. Can we trust your confidence? If not, can we run the enormous risks of overconfidence in this domain?

- Your firm has been threatened with a multimillion dollar law suit. If you lose, your firm is out of business. You are 98 percent confident that the firm will not lose in court. Is this degree of certainty sufficient for you to recommend rejecting an out-of-court settlement? Based on what you know now, are you still comfortable with your 98 percent estimate?

- You have developed a market plan for a new product. You are so confident in your plan that you have not developed any contingencies for early market failure. The plan of attack falls apart. Will your overconfidence wipe out any hope of expediting changes in the marketing strategy?

In each of these examples, we have introduced serious problems that can result from the tendency to be overconfident. Thus, while confidence in your abilities is necessary for achievement in life, and perhaps to inspire confidence in others, you may want to monitor your overconfidence to achieve more effective professional decision making.

Summary   The need for an initial anchor weighs strongly in our decision-making processes when we try to estimate likelihoods (such as the probability of on-time project completion) or establish values (like what salary to offer). Experience has taught us that starting from somewhere is easier than starting from nowhere in determining such figures. However, as the last three biases (insufficient anchor adjustment, conjunctive and disjunctive events bias, and overconfidence) show, we frequently overrely on these anchors and seldom question their validity or appropriateness in a particular situation. As with the other heuristics, we frequently fail even to realize that this heuristic is impacting our judgments.

TWO MORE GENERAL BIASES

Bias 12—The Confirmation Trap

Problem 13: (Adapted from Einhorn and Hogarth, 1978)

It is claimed that when a particular analyst predicts a rise in the market, the market always rises. You are to check this claim. Examine the information available about the following four events (cards):

Card 1 Prediction: Favorable report	Card 2 Prediction: Unfavorable report	Card 3 Outcome: Rise in the market	Card 4 Outcome: Fall in the market

You currently see the predictions (cards 1 and 2) *or* outcomes (cards 3 and 4) associated with four events. You are seeing one side of a card. On the other side of cards 1 and 2 is the actual outcome, while on the other side of cards 3 and 4 is the prediction that the analyst made. Evidence about the claim is potentially available by turning over the card(s). Which cards would you turn over for the evidence that you need to check the analyst's claim? (Circle the appropriate cards.)

Consider the two most common responses: (1) "Card 1 (only)—that is the only card that I know has a favorable report and thus allows me to see whether a favorable report is actually followed by a rise in the market" and (2) "Cards 1 and 3—card 1 serves as a direct test, while card 3 allows me to see whether they made a favorable report when I know the market rose." Logical? Most people think that at least one of these two common responses is logical. However, both strategies demonstrate the tendency to search for confirming, rather than disconfirming, evidence. Einhorn and Hogarth (1978) argue that 1 and 4 is the correct answer to this quiz item. Why? Consider the following logic:

> Card 1 allows me to test the claim that a rise in the market will add confirming evidence, while a fall in the market will fully disconfirm the claim, since the claim is that the market will *always* rise following a favorable report. Card 2 has no relevant information, since the claim does not address unfavorable reports by the analyst. While card 3 can add confirming evidence to card 1, it provides no unique information, since it cannot disconfirm the claim. That is, if an unfavorable report was made on card 3, then the event is not addressed by the claim. Finally, card 4 is critical. If it says "favorable report" on the other side, the claim is disconfirmed.

If you chose cards 1 and 3, you may have obtained a wealth of confirmatory information and were likely to inappropriately accept the claim. Only by including card 4 is there potential for disconfirmation of the hypothesis. Why do very few subjects select card 4? *Most of us seek confirmatory evidence and exclude the search for disconfirming information from our decision process.* However, it is typically not possible to know something to be true without checking for possible disconfirmation.

The initial demonstration of our tendency to ignore disconfirming information was provided in a series of projects by Wason (1960, 1968a, 1968b). In the first study, Wason (1960) presented subjects with the three-number sequence 2-4-6. The subject's task was to discover the numeric rule to which the three numbers conformed. To determine the rule, subjects were allowed to generate other sets of three numbers that the experimenter would classify as either conforming or not conforming to the rule. At any point, subjects could stop when they thought that they had discovered the rule. How would you approach this problem?

Wason's rule was "any three ascending numbers"—a solution which required the accumulation of disconfirming, rather than confirming, evidence. For example, if you thought the rule included "the difference between the first two numbers equaling the difference between the last two numbers" (a common expectation), you must try sequences that do *not* conform to this rule to find the actual rule. Trying the sequences 1-2-3, 10-15-20, 122-126-130, and so on, will only lead you into the confirmation trap. In Wason's (1960) experiment, only 6 out of 29 subjects found the correct rule the first time that they thought they knew the answer. Wason concluded that obtaining the correct solution necessitates "a willingness to attempt to falsify hypotheses, and thus to test those intuitive ideas which so often carry the feeling of certitude" (p. 139).

This result was also observed by Einhorn and Hogarth (1978) with a sample of 23 statisticians. When that group responded to a problem very similar to problem 13, eleven asked for card 1; one asked for card 1 or 3; one asked for any one card; two asked for card 1 or 4; three asked for card 4 alone; and only five trained statisticians asked for cards 1 and 4. Thus, this group tended to realize the worthlessness of card 3 but failed to realize the importance of card 4. This leads to the conclusion that the tendency to exclude disconfirming information in the search process is not eliminated by the formal scientific training that is expected of statisticians.

It is easy to observe the confirmation trap in your decision-making processes. You make a tentative decision (to buy a new car, to hire a particular employee, to start research and development on a new product line). Do you search for data that support your decision before making the final commitment? Most of us do. However, the existence of the confirmation trap implies that the search for challenging, or disconfirming, evidence will provide the most useful insights. For example, in confirming your decision to hire a particular employee, it is probably easy to find supporting positive information on the individual, but in fact the key issue may be the degree to which negative information on this individual, as well as positive information on another potential applicant, also exists.

Bias 13—Hindsight

Consider the following scenarios:
- You are an avid football fan, and you are watching a critical game in which your team is behind 35–31. With three seconds left, and the ball on the opponent's three-yard line, the quarterback *unsuccessfully* calls a pass play into the corner of the endzone. You immediately respond, "I knew that he shouldn't have called that play."

- You are riding in an unfamiliar area, and your spouse is driving. You approach an unmarked fork in the road, and your spouse decides to go to the right. Four miles and fifteen minutes later, it is clear that you are lost. You blurt out, "I knew that you should have turned left at the fork."
- A manager who works for you hired a new supervisor last year. You were well aware of the choices he had at the time and allowed him to choose the new employee on his own. You have just received production data on every supervisor. The data on the new supervisor are terrible. You call in the manager and claim, "There was plenty of evidence that he (the supervisor) was not the man for the job."
- As director of marketing in a consumer-goods organization, you have just presented the results of an extensive six-month study on current consumer preferences for the products manufactured by your organization. After the conclusion of your presentation, a senior vice-president responds, "I don't know why we spent so much time and money to collect these data. I could have told you what the results were going to be."

Do you recognize yourself? Do you recognize someone else? Each scenario is representative of a phenomenon that has been named "the Monday morning quarterback syndrome" (Fischhoff, 1975b), "the knew-it-all-along effect" (Wood, 1978), "creeping determinism" (Fischhoff, 1975a, 1975b, 1980), and "the hindsight bias" (Fischhoff, 1975a, 1975b). This body of research demonstrates that people are typically not very good at recalling or reconstructing the way an uncertain situation appeared to them *before* finding out the results of the decision. What play would have you called? Did you *really* know that your spouse should have turned left? Was there *really* evidence that the selected supervisor was not the man for the job? Could the senior vice-president *really* have predicted the results of the survey? Perhaps our intuition is sometimes accurate, but we tend to overestimate what we knew and distort our beliefs about what we knew beforehand based upon what we later found out. The phenomenon occurs when people look back on the judgment of others, as well as of themselves.

Fischhoff has provided substantial evidence of the prevalence of the hindsight effect (1975a, 1975b, 1977; Fischhoff and Beyth, 1975; Slovic and Fischhoff, 1977). For example, Fischhoff (1975a) examined the differences between hindsight and foresight in the context of judging historical events and clinical instances. In one study, subjects were divided into five groups and asked to read a passage about the war between the British and Gurka forces in 1814. One group was not told the result of the war. The remaining four groups of subjects were told either that (1) the British won; (2) the Gurkas won; (3) a military stalemate was reached with no peace settlement; or (4) a military stalemate was reached with a peace settlement. Obviously, only one group was told the truthful outcome—(1) in this case. Each subject was then asked what his or her subjective assessments of the probability of each of the outcomes would have been without the benefit of knowing the reported outcome. Based upon this and other varied examples, the strong, consistent finding was that knowledge of an outcome increases an individual's belief about the degree to which he or she would have predicted that outcome without the benefit of that knowledge.

A number of explanations of the hindsight effect have been offered. One of the most pervasive is to explain hindsight in terms of the heuristics discussed in this book (Tversky and Kahneman, 1974). Anchoring may contribute to this bias when individuals interpret their prior subjective judgments of probabilities of an event's occurring in reference to the anchor of knowing whether or not that outcome actually occurred. Since adjustments to anchors are known to be inadequate, hindsight knowledge can be expected to bias perceptions of what one thinks one knew in foresight. Further, to the extent that the various pieces of data on the event vary in terms of their support for the actual outcome, evidence that is consistent with the known outcome may become cognitively more salient and thus more *available* in memory (Slovic and Fischhoff, 1977). This will lead an individual to justify a claimed foresight in view of "the facts provided." Finally, the relevance of a particular piece of data may later be judged important to the extent to which it is *representative* of the final observed outcome.

Claiming that what has happened was predictable based on foresight knowledge puts us in a position of using hindsight to criticize another's foresight judgment. In the short run, hindsight has a number of advantages. In particular, it is very flattering to believe that your judgment is far better than it actually is! However, hindsight reduces our ability to learn from the past and to evaluate objectively the decisions of ourselves and others. Leading researchers in performance evaluation (cf. Feldman, 1981) and decision theory (cf. Einhorn and Hogarth, 1981) have argued that, where possible, individuals should be rewarded based on the process and logic of their decisions, not on the results. A decision maker who makes a high-quality decision that does not work out should be rewarded, not punished. The rationale for this argument is that the results are affected by a variety of factors outside the direct control of the decision maker. However, to the extent that we rely on results and the hindsight corresponding to them, we will inappropriately evaluate the logic used by the decision maker in terms of the outcomes that occurred, not the methods that were employed.

INTEGRATION AND COMMENTARY

Heuristics, or rules of thumb, are the cognitive tools we use to simplify decision making. The preceding pages have described 13 of the most common biases that result when we overrely on these judgmental heuristics. These biases are summarized in Table 2.2, along with their associated heuristics. Again, it should be emphasized that more than one heuristic can be operating on our decision-making processes at any one time. We have attempted to identify only the dominant heuristic affecting each bias. In the last two biases, their effects are so broad that it is difficult to even determine a dominant heuristic.

While the use of quiz items has emphasized the biases that our heuristics

Table 2.2 Summary of 13 Biases Presented in Chapter 2

	Bias	Description
	Biases Emanating from the Availability Heuristic	
1	Ease of recall	Individuals judge events that are more easily recalled from memory, based upon vividness or recency, to be more numerous than events of equal frequency whose instances are less easily recalled.
2	Retrievability	Individuals are biased in their assessments of the frequency of events based upon how their memory structures affect the search process.
3	Presumed associations	Individuals tend to overestimate the probability of two events co-occurring based upon the number of similar associations that are easily recalled, whether from experience or social influence.
	Biases Emanating from the Representativeness Heuristic	
4	Insensitivity to base rates	Individuals tend to ignore base rates in assessing the likelihood of events when any other descriptive information is provided—even if it is irrelevant.
5	Insensitivity to sample size	Individuals frequently fail to appreciate the role of sample size in assessing the reliability of sample information.
6	Misconceptions of chance	Individuals expect that a sequence of data generated by a random process will look "random," even when the sequence is too short for those expectations to be statistically valid.
7	Regression to the mean	Individuals tend to ignore the fact that extreme events tend to regress to the mean on subsequent trials.
8	The conjunction fallacy	Individuals falsely judge that conjunctions (two events co-occurring) are more probable than a more global set of occurrences of which the conjunction is a subset.

(continued)

Table 2.2   (*Continued*)

Bias	Description
Biases Emanating from Anchoring and Adjustment	
9 Insufficient anchor adjustment	Individuals make estimates for values based upon an initial value (derived from past events, random assignment, or whatever information is available) and typically make insufficient adjustments from that anchor when establishing a final value.
10 Conjunctive and disjunctive events bias	Individuals exhibit a bias toward overestimating the probability of conjunctive events and underestimating the probability of disjunctive events.
11 Overconfidence	Individuals tend to be overconfident of the infallibility of their judgments when answering moderately to extremely difficult questions.
Two More General Biases	
12 The confirmation trap	Individuals tend to seek confirmatory information for what they think is true and neglect the search for disconfirmatory evidence.
13 Hindsight	After finding out whether or not an event occurred, individuals tend to overestimate the degree to which they would have predicted the correct outcome.

create, it should be stressed that, overall, the use of these heuristics results in far more adequate than inadequate decisions. Our minds adopt these heuristics because, on average, any loss in quality of decisions is outweighed by the time saved. However, we argue against blanket acceptance of heuristics based upon this logic. First, as we have demonstrated in this chapter, there are many instances in which the loss in the quality of decisions far outweighs the time saved by the use of the heuristics. Second, the foregoing logic suggests that we have voluntarily accepted tradeoffs associated with the use of heuristics. But in reality, we have not: Most of us are unaware of their existence and their on-going impact upon our decision making. The difficulty with heuristics is that we typically do not recognize that we are using them, and we consequently fail to distinguish between situations in which their use is more and less appropriate.

To emphasize the distinction between the legitimate and illegitimate uses of heuristics, reconsider problem 6. In that problem, subjects tend to predict that Mark is more likely to take a job in "management of the arts," despite the fact that the contextual data overwhelmingly favor "management consulting." The representativeness heuristic, in this case, prevents us from appropriately incorporating relevant base-rate data. However, if the choice of "management consulting" were replaced with another less common career path for an MBA from a prestigious university (such as management in the steel industry), then the representativeness heuristic is likely to lead to an accurate prediction. That is, when base-rate data are unavailable or irrelevant (that is, the choices have the same base-rate), the representativeness heuristic provides a reasonably good cognitive tool for matching Mark to his most likely career path. *The key to improved judgment, therefore, lies in learning to distinguish between appropriate and inappropriate uses of heuristics.* This chapter provides a start in learning to make this distinction.

This book's examination of biases and heuristics does not end here. In fact, in the next three chapters we will continue to examine biases and heuristics in the areas of risk, the escalation of commitment, and creativity. The latter part of the book will examine biases in the context of more complicated multiparty decision-making situations.

THREE
JUDGMENT UNDER UNCERTAINTY

In the last chapter, we examined how the inappropriate use of cognitive heuristics can lead to biased decision making. In this chapter, we will examine how subtle aspects in the presentation of information, referred to as the **framing** of information, can significantly impact decision making—particularly when uncertainty is involved. Throughout the literature on decision-making, there is substantial evidence to suggest that intuitions about risk routinely deviate from rationality, because managers do not typically appreciate the nature of uncertainty and the effects of framing. Yet, uncertainty is a managerial fact of life.

This chapter seeks to help you to make better decisions under uncertain conditions. In the first part, a general discussion of perceptions of uncertainty is presented, followed by a normative framework for approaching risk. The second part and core of the chapter identifies the systematic ways in which your risky judgment is biased. This section introduces *prospect theory,* the most comprehensive descriptive theory on how we make risky decisions.

AVOIDING UNCERTAINTY: A COMMON RESPONSE

Consider the following:

- A tough-minded executive has a reputation for rewarding "results." This sounds typical of corporate behavior and is commonly viewed as a positive managerial attribute.
- Edmund S. Muskie, a candidate in the 1972 presidential election, stated (borrowing the words of President Harry Truman) that what this country needed was a "one-armed" economist. When asked why, he responded that he was tired of economists who said "on the one hand . . . , but on the other hand . . ."
- When budget crises hit an organization, a common response is to cut out expenditures that are not expected to increase immediate productivity (such

as management training). This administrative response reflects the belief that money should be allocated only to expenses that are sure to lead to increased short-term profit and productivity.

What is the common element in these scenarios? In each case, the decision makers are grasping for certainty in an uncertain world. They want to know what *will* happen, not what *may* happen. Like these decision makers, most of us fail to accept that many decisions must be made in the face of uncertainty. Instead, we tend to wish it away and believe that if we work hard enough, we can control outcomes. Dawes (1988) has observed that a common way of dealing with uncertainty is to ignore it. Langer (1975) has documented that this tendency frequently translates into an inappropriate belief that chance events involve skill and are controllable. Gamblers tend to throw dice harder when they are attempting to roll high numbers (Dawes, 1988). Lottery ticket buyers believe that their ability to choose their numbers increases their likelihood of winning. Dawes argues that humans have a pathological need to "know now" in situations containing inherent uncertainty. He asserts that the need to do away with uncertainty frequently leads people to take too much credit for successes and too much blame for failures.

Despite this tendency to minimize the effects of uncertainty, it is common for people to attempt to identify themselves and others according to degrees of risk aversion and risk seeking. Fischhoff, Slovic, and Lichtenstein (1981) have argued that risk taking is one of the first dimensions we think of in describing someone's personality. For instance, some people place value judgments on risk-seeking behavior: "You won't get very far in life if you don't take risks."

In reality, most people are not consistent in their approach to risk. When Slovic (1972) compared the scores of 82 people on nine different measures of risk taking, he found no evidence to suggest that a generalizable risk-taking trait exists. The correlations between the nine dimensions ranged from -0.35 to 0.34, with a mean of $+0.006$. People who are aggressive in one situation may be conservative in another. The person who gambles with money for a living may be conservative in caring for his/her health or making rules for his/her children. The conservative financial analyst may let "all hell break loose" on weekends. In addition, Slovic found that intelligence was not related to a general risk-taking level.

As managers, we are constantly faced with decisions that will lead to uncertain outcomes (MacCrimmon and Wehrung, 1986). Many of these risky decisions are crucial, involving issues like jobs, safety, product reliability, and organizational existence. We must frequently ask questions like: How risky would it be to build one more nuclear power plant? How risky is it to expose assembly line employees to the chemicals necessary to make animal flea collars?

At some point, our decisions are reduced to basic questions like: What level of risk is acceptable? How much is safety worth? Some people answer "any price." Yet that implies that we should devote *all* of our efforts to highway improvement and cures for cancer, to the exclusion of productivity. Throughout our lives, dealing with risk requires trading off outcomes and costs. If we do not deal rationally with these choices, or only respond in a superficial manner, unfortunate inconsistencies occur. Fischhoff, Lichtenstein, and colleagues (1981) note:

> Our legal statutes are less tolerant of carcinogens in our food than in our drinking water or our air. In the United Kingdom, 2,500 times more money per life saved is spent on safety measures in the pharmaceutical industry than in agriculture (Sinclair, Marstand, and Newick, 1972).

> According to some calculations, U.S. society spends about $140,000 in highway construction to save one life and $5 million to save a person from death due to radiation exposure (R. A. Howard, Matheson, and Owen, 1978, p. 2).

As these examples demonstrate, perceptions of risk are often faulty, frequently resulting in misdirected risk-reduction efforts by public and private decision makers (Fischhoff, Slovic, and Lichtenstein, 1981). The result is that we may be saving fewer lives at greater costs. We can protect ourselves from such errors only through the improvement of managers' judgments.

This chapter helps managers to understand risk, which will enhance their ability to make and evaluate decisions in uncertain situations. If you understand the nature of risky decisions, you are more likely to evaluate these decisions based on the quality of the decision process rather than on the capriciousness of their outcomes. Our perspective is that managers can make better decisions by accepting that uncertainty exists and learning how to think systematically in risky environments. After all, risk is not bad; it is simply unpredictable. Consider the insightful perspective of Dawes (1988, p. 267):

> Imagine a life without uncertainty . . . Imagine how dull life would be if variables assessed for admission to a professional school, graduate program, or executive training program really *did* predict with great accuracy who would succeed and who would fail. Life would be intolerable—no hope, no challenge.

A NORMATIVE BACKGROUND TO RISK

While this book is primarily descriptive, it is critical to consider some basic normative concepts for two reasons. First, we know that individuals are typically neither rational nor consistent in making judgments under uncertainty. Thus, it is useful to outline a "rational" structure for approaching risky problems. Second, this normative structure provides a background for illustrating the systematic deviations from rationality that we are prone to when making decisions under uncertain conditions. (Readers with some background in statistics and economics may find this section trivial, while others will find it necessary for understanding the material that follows.)

Returning to Chapter 1, you will recall that a rational decision-making process includes: (1) specifying the problem, (2) identifying all factors, (3) weighting factors, (4) identifying all alternatives, (5) rating alternatives on each factor, and (6) choosing the optimal alternative. Up until this point, the rational model has not told us how to rate alternatives when the outcome on a particular factor or factors is uncertain. It also has not provided rules for determining the optimal alternative under uncertainty. These are central topics to a normative theory of preferences under risky conditions. We must begin by understanding two concepts: probability and expected value.

Probability   This concept of probability conveys the likelihood that any particular outcome will occur. A probability of 1.0 represents certainty that an event will occur. A probability of zero represents certainty that an event will *not* occur. Any value in between represents uncertainty—the degree to which we believe that an event will occur. As discussed earlier, the outcomes of most events and decisions are uncertain. Through probability, we can assign values to the likelihood that each potential outcome associated with an event or decision will occur. For example, assume that you flipped four quarters (A, B, C, D). The possible combinations of *equally likely* outcomes can be represented by the following sixteen events:

Event	A	B	C	D	Event	A	B	C	D
1	T	T	T	T	9	T	H	H	T
2	T	T	T	H	10	H	T	H	T
3	T	T	H	T	11	H	H	T	T
4	T	H	T	T	12	H	H	H	T
5	H	T	T	T	13	H	H	T	H
6	T	T	H	H	14	H	T	H	H
7	T	H	T	H	15	T	H	H	H
8	H	T	T	H	16	H	H	H	H

Based on the specification of all possible outcomes, we can now observe the probability of various combinations of events. For example, the probability of two or more heads appearing is equal to 11/16 (including events 6 through 16). Or, the probability of getting exactly two heads is 6/16 (including events 6 through 11).

This presentation treats probability in a very simple way, but probability can be very complex, both mathematically and psychologically. For example, it is much more difficult to assess the probability of a democratic presidential candidate's being elected in the year 2000 or the prime rate falling below 6 percent before the year 2010. Why? We are now forecasting the future, without being able to specify the likelihood of all possible outcomes. Unfortunately, most real decisions (excluding the worlds of gambling, cards, games, and the like) take this more complex form.

Expected Value   Calculating the expected value of any alternative involves weighting all potential outcomes associated with that alternative by their probabilities and summing them. For example, if we were going to calculate the expected number of heads occurring from four flips of a coin (the answer is obviously 2), we would weight all possible combinations of the number of heads occurring in four flips of a coin by their likelihood of occurrence (see the combinations listed previously):

Expected value = 1/16(0) + 4/16(1) + 6/16(2) + 4/16(3) + 1/16(4) = 2

Again, the actual calculation of expected value becomes more complicated when we cannot specify the objective likelihood of all possible outcomes. For example, in assessing the expected value of your salary 18 months from now, you have to assess the likelihood of holding various positions and calculate the associated expected pay for each of the possible positions. As problems become more complex, this assessment can become very demanding, with a great potential for bias.

One simple rule for making decisions is to always select the alternative with the highest expected value. The argument for an expected-value decision rule is that in the long run, decisions made according to this rule will, in the aggregate, be optimal; that is, good and bad random errors will cancel out over time. That logic sounds rational, but consider the following scenarios:

- You can (a) have $10,000,000 for sure (expected value = $10,000,000) or (b) flip an honest coin where you get $22,000,000 if a heads occurs but get nothing if a tails occurs (expected value = $11,000,000). An expected-value decision rule would pick b. What would you do?
- You are being sued for $5,000 and estimate a 50 percent chance of losing the case (expected value = −$2,500). However, the other side is willing to accept an out-of-court settlement of $2,400 (expected value = −$2,400). Ignoring attorney's fees, court costs, aggravation, and so on, would you

  a. fight the case?
  b. settle out of court?

An expected-value decision rule would lead you to settle out of court.

Most people would take (a) in both cases. This suggests that a number of situations exist in which people do not follow an expected-value rule. Understanding when and how people deviate from expected value brings the concept of risk into the problem.

Risk Considerations   The final prerequisite to the discussion of risk is the concept of a **certainty equivalent.** A certainty equivalent establishes the certain value that would make a decision maker indifferent between an uncertain event and that certain value. For example, if you had an opportunity to accept a 50 percent chance of obtaining $1,000,000, what would be the certain amount that would make you indifferent between the 50 percent chance of $1,000,000 and that amount? $100,000? $300,000? This is your certainty equivalent to a 50 percent chance of $1,000,000. For most people, this amount is far less than the expected value of the bet of $500,000. Returning to Robert Davis's dilemma in Chapter 1, before engaging in any negotiation on the amount of an out-of-court settlement, he may want to assess the amount that would make him indifferent between that payment and a 50 percent chance of paying the $50,000,000. That amount is defined as his certainty equivalent.

An individual who has a certainty equivalent for an uncertain event that is equal to the expected value of the uncertain payoff is **risk neutral** with regard to that decision. For example, if your certainty equivalent in the previous paragraph was $500,000, you would be risk neutral concerning that choice. The benefit of a certain outcome is no more valuable to you than the benefit of an uncertain outcome with the same expected value. Thus, risk neutrality is synonymous with using an expected-value decision rule. An individual with a certainty equivalent for an uncertain event that is less than the expected value of that uncertain payoff is **risk averse** with regard to that decision. If your certainty equivalent in the foregoing problem was $400,000, then you are risk averse, since you are willing to take an expected value reduction of $100,000 to avoid the risk associated with the uncertain event. Although it is unlikely in this context, an individual with a certainty equivalent for an uncertain event that is more than the expected value for that uncertain payoff is **risk seeking** with regard to that decision. If your certainty equivalent was $550,000, you are risk seeking, since you are demanding extra expected value of $50,000 to forego the risk. Thus, you seek risk, holding the expected value constant.

The concepts of risk-averse and risk-seeking behavior will become crucial as we continue our discussion of judgment under uncertainty. When decision makers act in a risk-averse or risk-seeking manner, they make decisions that often exclude the maximizing of expected value. To explain departures from the expected-value decision rule, Daniel Bernoulli (1738) first suggested replacing the criterion of expected monetary value with the criterion of expected utility. Expected-utility theory suggests that each level of an outcome is associated with some degree of pleasure or net benefit, called *utility*. The expected utility of an uncertain choice is the weighted sum of the utilities of its outcomes, each multiplied by its probability. While an expected-value approach to decision making would treat $1,000,000 as being worth twice as much as $500,000, a gain of $1,000,000 does *not* always create twice as much expected utility as a gain of $500,000. Most individuals do not obtain as much utility from the second $500,000 as they did from the first $500,000. Thus, under expected-utility theory, the decision maker is predicted to select the option with the highest expected utility, regardless of whether that choice has the highest expected value.

Further, according to expected-utility theory, individuals identify outcomes in terms of their overall wealth and the additional wealth they would have as a result of each alternative outcome. That is, each choice that we make is viewed within the context of the overall utility that we are currently experiencing and of what that choice would mean to our overall utility in the future. As we will see in the next section, Kahneman and Tversky's (1979) prospect theory refutes this aspect of expected-utility theory. They argue that each decision is approached independently.

THE FRAMING OF INFORMATION

Consider the following problem (adapted from Bazerman [1983], and replicated by Miller and Fagley [1988]):

Problem 1: A large car manufacturer has recently been hit with a number of economic difficulties, and it appears as if three plants need to be closed and 6,000 employees laid off. The vice-president of production has been exploring alternative ways to avoid this crisis. She has developed two plans:

Plan A: This plan will save one of the three plants and 2,000 jobs.

Plan B: This plan has a 1/3 probability of saving all three plants and all 6,000 jobs, but has a 2/3 probability of saving no plants and no jobs.

Which plan would you select?

There are a number of things that we might consider in evaluating these options. For example, what will be the impact of each action on the union? What will be the impact of each plan on the motivation and morale of the retained employees? How do the values of the vice-president of production differ from those of the larger corporation? While all of these questions are important, a more fundamental question underlies the subjective situation and the resulting decision. Reconsider this problem, replacing the choices just provided with the following choices:

Plan C: This plan will result in the loss of two of the three plants and 4,000 jobs.

Plan D: This plan has a 2/3 probability of resulting in the loss of all three plants and all 6,000 jobs, but has a 1/3 probability of losing no plants and no jobs.

Which plan would you select?

Close examination of the two sets of alternative plans finds them to be *objectively* the same. For example, saving one of three plants and 2,000 of 6,000 jobs (plan A) offers the same objective outcome as losing two of three plants and 4,000 of 6,000 jobs (plan C). In addition, plans B and D are objectively identical. However, informal empirical investigation demonstrates that *most* individuals (over 80 percent) choose plan A in the first set and plan D in the second set. While the two sets of choices are objectively identical, changing the description of the outcomes from jobs and plants *saved* to jobs and plants *lost* is sufficient to shift prototypic choice from risk-averse to risk-seeking behavior.

This shift is consistent with a growing body of literature (Kahneman and Tversky, 1986; Thaler, 1980; Bazerman, 1984) that shows that individuals treat risks concerning perceived gains (for example, saving jobs and plants—plans A and B) differently from risks concerning perceived losses (losing jobs and plants—plans C and D). In an attempt to explain these common and systematic deviations from rationality, Kahneman and Tversky (1979) developed **prospect theory.** This theory suggests the following:

1. Rewards and losses are evaluated relative to a neutral reference point.
2. Potential outcomes are expressed as gains (such as jobs and plants saved) or losses (jobs and plants lost) relative to this fixed, neutral reference point.
3. The choices that people make are formed based on the resulting change in asset position as assessed by an S-shaped value function (see Figure 3.1).

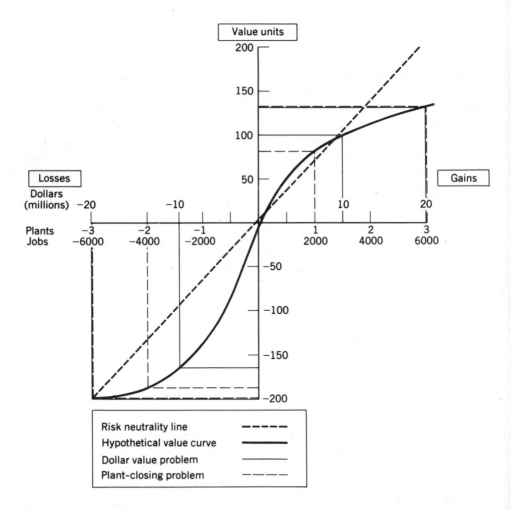

Figure 3.1 Hypothetical value function accounting for framing. *(Source:* Adapted from Kahneman and Tversky (1979). Reprinted by permission of the Econometric Society.)

On this graph, the X axis represents the nominal units gained or lost, and the Y axis represents the units of utility associated with varying levels of gain or loss. Overall, Figure 3.1 suggests that decision makers tend to avoid risk concerning gains and seek risk concerning losses. For example, the S-shaped value function implies that most individuals would choose a $10,000,000 sure gain over a 50 percent chance of getting a $20,000,000 gain, since the utility placed on $20,000,000 is *not* twice as great as the value placed on $10,000,000, but that most individuals would choose a 50 percent chance of a $20,000,000 loss over a sure loss of $10,000,000, since the negative value placed on $20,000,000 is *not* twice as great as the negative value placed on $10,000,000.

An important outcome of this theory is that the way in which the problem is "framed," or presented, can dramatically change the perceived neutral point of the question. In problem 1, *if the problem is framed in terms of losing jobs and plants* (plans C and D), the current position of having three plants open forms the neutral reference point. The choices that both involve losses of plants and jobs are evaluated on the lower part of the curve in Figure 3.1, and risk-seeking behavior results. The negative value placed on the loss of three plants and 6,000 jobs is usually perceived as not being three times as negative as losing one plant and 2,000 jobs. However, *if the problem is framed in terms of saving jobs and plants* (plans A and B), the potential disaster of losing everything becomes the neutral reference point. The choices are then evaluated on the upper part of the curve, and risk-averse behavior results. Figure 3.1 indicates that the gain placed on saving three plants and 6,000 jobs is frequently viewed as not being three times as great as saving one plant and 2,000 jobs.

Thus, one of the most important outcomes of prospect theory is that it identifies a *systematic* pattern of how the framing of the problem causes decision-making behavior to deviate from both expected-value and expected-utility theory. Both of these theories posit that the rational decision makers should be immune to the framing of choices. A second characteristic of our decision-making processes identified by prospect theory is that our response to loss is more extreme than our response to gain. According to Figure 3.1, the pain associated with losing X dollars is generally greater than the pleasure associated with winning the same amount. Tversky and Kahneman (1981) cite "people's reluctance to accept fair bets on a toss of a coin" as evidence of this effect.

Finally, prospect theory identifies a third way in which our decision-making processes deviate from expected-utility theory, which we will discuss only briefly here. It concerns our treatment of probabilities. While expected-utility theory weights a risky option by its probability, prospect theory states that we tend to overweight the probability of low-probability events and underweight the probability of moderate- and high-probability events. Further, underweighting is strongest for high-probability events. Thus, Kahneman and Tversky (1979) also incorporate systematic deviations from rationality in probability assessments as part of their decision model.

THE FRAMING OF RISKY PROBLEMS:
EIGHT QUESTIONS TO CONSIDER

The preceding paragraphs have presented the logic of prospect theory and identified the ways in which its conclusions depart from the normative tenets of expected-utility theory. Broadly, these concepts include the impact of the framing of information on our decisions, our differential response to gains and losses, and our tendency to systematically misrepresent probabilities. Because of its descriptive power, prospect theory has caused a great deal of excitement in the fields of decision theory, psychology, marketing, organizational behavior, and economics over the past ten years. The theory has been responsible for helping researchers to develop a more complete understanding of errors and inconsistencies in our judgment.

Based upon the findings of prospect theory and subsequent research derived from it, this section develops eight general questions to be considered in approaching uncertain situations:

1. How are your decisions affected by the framing of choices?
2. How are your decisions affected by the framing of outcomes?
3. How are your decisions affected by the framed pseudocertainty and certainty of choices?
4. How do you differentially respond to the framing of "paying premiums" versus accepting sure losses?
5. How is your evaluation of the quality of a transaction affected by the frame in which it is presented?
6. How are your decisions affected by summing gains and losses?
7. How does the frame of the problem affect how much your time is worth?
8. How rational are your intertemporal choices?

The answers to these questions build on each other and are not meant to provide a taxonomy of framing effects. Rather, these questions organize much of what is known about the framing of risky decisions and our differential responses to different types of risk. A detailed discussion of each question follows. The eight questions and the description of how individual behavior typically responds to these questions are summarized in Table 3.2, at the end of the chapter.

1. How Are Your Decisions Affected
by the Framing of Choices?

Tversky and Kahneman (1981) asked 150 subjects the following questions:

Problem 2: Imagine that you face the following pair of concurrent decisions. First examine both decisions, and then indicate the options you prefer.

Decision i

Choose between:

a. A sure gain of $240

b. A 25 percent chance to gain $1,000, and a 75 percent chance to gain nothing

Decision ii

Choose between:

c. A sure loss of $750

d. A 75 percent chance to lose $1,000, and a 25 percent chance to lose nothing

In decision *i*, 84 percent of the subjects chose (a), while only 16 percent chose (b). In decision *ii*, 87 percent of the subjects chose (d), while only 13 percent chose (c). The majority chose "a sure gain of $240" in decision *i* because of our tendency to be risk-averse concerning gains and positively framed questions. In contrast, the majority chose "a 75 percent chance to lose $1,000" in decision *ii* because of our tendency to be risk-seeking concerning losses and negatively framed questions. In terms of Figure 3.1, the value associated with a gain of $240 is greater than 24 percent of the value associated with a gain of $1,000, while the negative value associated with a loss of $750 is less than 75 percent of the negative value associated with a loss of $1,000. Combining the responses to the two problems, 73 percent of the respondents chose (a) and (d), while only 3 percent chose (b) and (c).

Now consider the following problems presented by Tversky and Kahneman (1981) to 86 subjects (who were not previously exposed to problem 2):

Problem 2a: Chose between:

e. A 25% chance to win $240, and a 75% chance to lose $760

f. A 25% chance to win $250, and a 75% chance to lose $750

Not surprisingly, all 86 subjects took (f) over (e). In fact, (f) dominates (e) in all respects. Why is this problem interesting? When you combine (a) and (d) (the preferred choices) in problem 2, (e) results, whereas when you combine choices (b) and (c) (the choices not preferred), (f) results.

	Adding choices (a) and (d)			Adding choices (b) and (c)	
	(75%)(−$1000)		(75%)(−$760)	(25%)(+$1000)	(25%)(+$250)
+$240+		=	&	+(−$750)=	&
	(25%)(0)		(25%)(+$240)	(75%)(0)	(75%)(−$750)

The sum of the undesirable choices *dominates* the sum of the desirable choices! Thus, the framing of the combined problem in two parts results in a reversal of preferences. Prospect theory's preference curve (Figure 3.1) accounts for this finding, but that does not imply that the choices are rational. In fact, this inconsistency violates the fundamental requirements for rational decision making: consistency and coherence.

Why is this finding interesting to managers? Many interconnected decisions in the real world, such as portfolio selection, budgeting, and funding for new projects, can be framed as separate or joint decisions. The findings suggest that the subdivision of decision making throughout an organization is likely to enhance the potential for inconsistency and nonrational choice, like that exhibited in problem 2. Sales departments are encouraged to think in terms of the acquisition of corporate gains, while credit offices are encouraged to frame decisions in terms of avoiding corporate losses. To arrive at a coherent strategy for making judgments under uncertainty, individuals and organizations need to become more aware of this bias and develop procedures for identifying and integrating risky decisions across organizations.

2. How Are Your Decisions Affected by the Framing of Outcomes?

As previously suggested in our discussion of prospect theory, outcomes are evaluated relative to a neutral reference point. Consequently, the location of the reference point is critical to whether the decision is positively or negatively framed and affects the resulting risk preference of the decision maker. The plant-closing problem (problem 1) illustrates the importance of reference points. In the positively framed case, the question is, how many plants (and jobs) can be saved? Saved from what? Saved from the possible loss of three plants. Thus, the loss of three plants is the neutral reference point. In contrast, in the negatively framed case, the question is, how many plants (and jobs) will be lost? Lost from what? Lost from the existing three operating plants. Here, three open plants is the neutral reference point. As we showed earlier, after shifting the reference point, most individuals move from evaluating the choice on the upper part of the curve (Figure 3.1) to the lower part.

For other examples of the importance of this reference point shift, consider the following scenarios:

Problem 3: You were given 100 shares of stock in XYZ corporation two years ago, when the value of the stock was $20 per share. Unfortunately, the stock has dropped to $10 per share during the two years that you have held the asset. The corporation is currently drilling for oil in an area that may turn out to be a big "hit." On the other hand, they may find nothing. Geological analysis suggests that if they hit, the stock is expected to go back up to $20 per share. If the well is dry, however, the value of the stock will fall to $0 per share. Do you want to sell your stock now for $10 per share?

Problem 4: (Adapted from Tversky and Kahneman [1981]):
You are spending the afternoon at the racetrack. You have lost $90 and are considering a $10 bet on a 10 : 1 long shot in the last race. Are you going to bet on the long shot?

In problem 3, what is your reference point? Is it the amount that you can gain (the amount that you receive for the stock above $0 per share), or is it the amount that you can lose (the amount that the stock has fallen from $20 per share when you sell the stock)? Figure 3.1 suggests that if you cognitively adopt $0 per share as your reference point, you will be risk averse and will take the sure "gain" by selling the stock now. If your reference point is $20 per share, however, you will be risk seeking and will hold onto the stock rather than accept a sure "loss."

In problem 4, as you consider the tenth race, what is your reference point? Are you considering the race independent of the first nine races, or are you thinking about this race from the perspective of "$90 in the hole." Prospect theory predicts that the latter frame will lead to more risk-seeking behavior. Interestingly, if people do not adjust their reference points as they lose, they may take risks that they would ordinarily find unacceptable. Tversky and Kahneman (1981) argue that this analysis is supported by the popularity of long shots on the last race of the day.

What should you do about your decisions in light of the impact of reference points? Identify your reference point when making a risky decision, and find out whether other reference points are just as reasonable. If the answer is yes, think about your decision from multiple perspectives and see whether there is a contradiction. Then you will be prepared to respond to the problem with a full awareness of the alternative frames in which the problem could have been presented.

3. How Are Your Decisions Affected by the Framed Pseudocertainty and Certainty of Choices?

Prospect theory suggests that people underweight high-probability events but appropriately weight events that are certain. Thus, if an event has a probability of 1.0 or zero, we tend to accurately evaluate the event's probability. However, if the event has a probability of .99, we tend to respond as the expected-utility framework would expect us to respond to a probability of something less than .99. Slovic, Lichtenstein, and Fischhoff (1982) note that "any protective action that reduces the probability of harm from, say, .01 to zero will be valued more highly than an action that reduces the probability of the same harm from .02 to .01" (p. 24).

Interestingly, the *perception* of certainty (that is, the perception that the probabilities of an event are zero or 1.0) can be easily manipulated. Slovic, Lichtenstein, and Fischhoff (1982) provide an example concerning an insurance policy that covers fire but not flood. This insurance can be accurately advertised either as "full protection" against fire or as a reduction in the overall probability of loss. The logic of prospect theory presented in the previous paragraph predicts that the policy will be more attractive to potential buyers with the full-protection advertisement. This is because the full-protection option reduces perceived uncertainty for loss from fire to zero, whereas the overall policy reduces uncertainty some incremental amount to a value still above zero. Obviously, the insurance is the same in both cases. The perceived certainty that results through the full-protection framing of this advertisement has been labeled **pseudocertainty** (Slovic, Fischhoff, and Lichtenstein, 1982; Tversky and Kahneman, 1981).

Slovic and colleagues (1982) provided empirical evidence of the strength of the pseudocertainty effect in the context of disease vaccination. Two forms of a questionnaire were created. Form 1 described a disease that was expected to afflict 20 percent of the population. Subjects in this condition were asked if they would receive a vaccine that protected half of the individuals vaccinated. Form 2 described two mutually exclusive and equiprobable strains of the disease, each of which was expected to afflict 10 percent of the population. Vaccination in the latter case was said to give complete protection (certainty) against one strain and no protection against the other. Would you take the vaccine described in form 1? What about the vaccine described in form 2? In either case, the vaccine would objectively reduce one's overall risk from 20 percent to 10 percent. Slovic and colleagues predicted that form 2 (pseudocertainty) would be more appealing than form 1 (probabilistic), and they found that they were right. Some 57 percent of subjects who were given form 2 said that they would get the vaccination, compared to only 40 percent of the subjects who received form 1.

Tversky and Kahneman (1981) simultaneously investigated the impact of certainty and pseudocertainty on judgmental choice. Consider the following problems (excerpted from Tversky and Kahneman [1981]):

Problem 5: Which of the following options do you prefer?

a. A sure win of $30
b. An 80% chance to win $45

Problem 6: Consider the following two-stage game. In the first stage, there is a 75 percent chance to end the game without winning anything, and a 25 percent chance to move into the second stage. If you reach the second stage you have a choice between

c. a sure win of $30
d. an 80% chance to win $45

Your choice must be made before the game starts—that is, before the outcome of the first stage is known. Please indicate the option you prefer (c or d).

Problem 7: Which of the following options to you prefer?

e. A 25% chance to win $30
f. A 20% chance to win $45

Tversky and Kahneman (1981) presented each of these problems to a different group of subjects. In problem 5, 78 percent of the subjects chose (a), and 22 percent chose (b). In problem 6, 74 percent of the subjects chose (c), and 26 percent chose (d). In problem 7, 42 percent of the subjects chose (e), and 58 percent chose (f). Some interesting contrasts result. Consider problem 6: By combining the first and second parts of the problem, it becomes evident that (c) offers a .25 chance to win $30 and (d) offers a .25 × .80 = .20 chance to win $45. The same choice offered in problem 7! Yet the modal choice has shifted. In problem 6, if you lose in the first stage, it does not matter what choice you made. If you win in the first stage, problem 6 reduces to problem 5. Consequently, there seems to be no reason to respond differently to problem 5 and 6. Since problem 6 is equivalent to problem 5 and problem 7, it can be inferred that problems 5 and 7 should also be treated similarly. However, subjects responded similarly to problems 5 and 6, but differently to problem 7. Why this discrepancy in response to problem 7?

The difference between problems 5 and 7 illustrates a phenomenon that Tversky and Kahneman (1981) call the **certainty effect.** "A reduction of the probability of an outcome has more importance when the outcome was initially certain than when it was merely probable" (p. 455). The discrepancy, in response to objectively identical problems 6 and 7, illustrates the **pseudocertainty effect** (Slovic, Fischhoff & Lichtenstein, 1982; Tversky and Kahneman, 1981). The prospect of winning $30 is more attractive in problem 6 than in problem 7 because of the *perceived* certainty ("a sure win") associated with choice (c). However, this potential "certainty" is contingent upon reaching the second stage of the game, which still makes the outcome uncertain.

The certainty and pseudocertainty effects lead to judgmental inconsistencies. Under the certainty effect, we are more apt to be interested in reducing the likelihood of certain events than uncertain events. Under the pseudocertainty effect, we are more likely to favor options that assure us certainty than those that only reduce uncertainty. Rationally, any constant reduction of risk in an uncertain situation should have the same value for the decision maker. For example, reducing the risk of cancer from 20 percent to 10 percent should have the same value as a reduction from 10 percent to 0 percent. But prospect theory tells us that perceived certainty, or "pseudocertainty," has a special value to most people. Manipulations of pseudocertainty have important implications for the design of communications about medical treatments, personal insurance, corporate liability protection, and a variety of other forms of protection. The data presented suggest that individuals may buy insurance not only to protect against risk, but also to eliminate the worry caused by *any* amount of uncertainty (Tversky and Kahneman, 1981).

4. How Do You Differentially Respond to the Framing of "Paying Premiums" versus Accepting Sure Losses?

What is an insurance premium? It is the certain loss (the premium) that you accept in exchange for the reduction of a small probability of a large loss. Interestingly, Schoemaker and associates (Hershey and Schoemaker, 1980; Schoemaker and Kunreuther, 1979) and Slovic and co-workers (1982) have found that certain losses are more attractive when *framed* as insurance premiums than when framed as monetary losses. In the study conducted by Slovic's group, the situations involving different levels of certain and uncertain loss were constructed and presented under two conditions—one framing a certain loss as an insurance premium and the other framing it as a straight loss. In one situation, Slovic and colleagues asked people to choose between a .001 chance of losing $5,000 and a certain loss (or insurance cost) of $5. In another situation, subjects were asked to choose between a .25 chance of losing $200 and a certain loss (or insurance cost) of $50. Each subject responded to only one of the two situations under only one of the conditions. The results in Table 3.1 demonstrate that the certain loss was more likely to be selected in the insurance context, for both of the two gambles.

This framing effect can be explained in a number of ways. Prospect theory would suggest that in the monetary loss condition, people use the status quo as a reference point. In contrast, in the insurance condition, the reference point already incorporates the loss of the premium (Slovic, Fischhoff, and Lichtenstein, 1982). It is easy to use Figure 3.1 to determine how these reference points lead to differing decisions.

Table 3.1 Proportions of Subjects Choosing the Certain Loss in Insurance and Preference Contexts

	Probability of Loss	
Context	.001	.25
Insurance premium	37/56	26/40
	66%	65%
Monetary loss	28/72	8/40
	39%	20%

Adapted from Slovic, Fischoff, and Lichtenstein (1982), p. 27.

Kahneman and Tversky (1979) and Hershey and Schoemaker (1980) also argue that "insurance" triggers social norms. "How can you not carry insurance?" "All good citizens carry insurance." Buying insurance is an activity that most of us do without considering an alternative strategy. When was the last time you considered dropping your car insurance (assuming that you live in a state where it is legal to be uninsured)?

Regardless of the cause of this framing effect, it is critical to realize the implications of the framing of decisions concerning insurance versus accepting certain losses. Empirical data suggest that people are more likely to accept a certain loss if it is viewed as insurance rather than as a sure monetary loss.

5. How Is Your Evaluation of the Quality of a Transaction Affected by the Frame in which It Is Presented?

The term **transactional utility** was recently introduced by Thaler (1985) and can be best seen in terms of the following scenario:

(Read this scenario twice—first with the words in parentheses and excluding the words in brackets, and second with the words in brackets and excluding the words in parentheses.)

> You are lying on the beach on a hot day. All you have to drink is ice water. For the last hour you have been thinking about how much you would enjoy a nice cold bottle of your favorite brand of beer. A companion gets up to go make a phone call and offers to bring back a beer from the only nearby place where beer is sold (a fancy resort hotel) [a small, run-down grocery store]. He says that the beer might be expensive and asks how much you are willing to.pay for it. He says that he will buy the beer if it costs as much as or less than the price you state. But if it costs more than the price you state, he will not buy it. You trust your friend, and there is no possibility of bargaining with the (bartender) [store owner]. What price do you tell him?

Notice some of the features of this dual problem. First, in both the hotel and the grocery story versions, you get the same product. Second, there is no possible negotiation on price. Third, there will be no advantage to the resort hotel "atmosphere," since you are going to drink the beer on the beach. According to expected-utility theory, people should be willing to pay the same amount in both versions of the scenario. In fact, Thaler found that participants in an executive development program were willing to pay significantly more if the beer was purchased from the "fancy resort hotel." The results were medians of $2.65 for the resort and $1.50 for the store. Why does this occur?

Thaler suggests that the reason for this contradiction is that while "paying $2.50 for a beer at a fancy hotel would be an expected annoyance, paying $2.50 at a grocery store would be an outrageous 'rip-off.'" This leads to the conclusion that something else matters besides the value you place on the commodity acquired. Did you ever buy something because it was "too good a deal to pass up," despite the fact that you had no need for the commodity? Thaler explains this by suggesting that purchases are affected by both acquisition utility and transactional utility. **Acquisition utility** is associated with the value you place on the commodity (in this case, the beer). **Transactional utility** refers to the quality of the deal that you receive, evaluated in reference to "what the item should cost." Obviously, paying $2.50 for a beer at a grocery store leads to a greater negative transactional utility than paying $2.50 at the fancy resort hotel. One can argue that the inclusion of transactional utility in decision making is not rational, but it does describe our behavior.

6. How Are Your Decisions Affected by Summing Gains and Losses?

Would you rather receive two checks in the mail (on different days) for $100 each, or a single check for $200? Would you rather be forced to pay two gambling/investment losses of $250 each or a single loss of $500? You are probably thinking that it obviously makes no difference, but most people behave in a manner that suggests that perceived differences exist.

The argument for perceived differences follows logically from the S-shaped curve identified by prospect theory (Figure 3.1). Prospect theory argues that we value initial gains from a reference point more highly than we value subsequent gains. Thus, the first $100 gained is valued more than half of the value associated with a $200 gain. When you receive $100 on each of two different days, you are likely to evaluate each in reference to the neutral reference point of neither gaining nor losing anything. Prospect theory also argues that we value initial losses more negatively than subsequent losses, as evaluated in terms of a neutral reference point. Thus, an initial loss of $250 causes more than 50 percent of the loss in value caused by the $500 loss. Of course, if choices were presented as described at the beginning of the previous paragraph, you would realize that the choices were identical.

In giving presents, should you give all the presents to one person at once? Prospect theory suggests that the recipient's comparatively strong valuation of the initial gain would lead to giving gifts independently; thus each gift will be evaluated separately, maximizing the *value* received. In recruiting a key executive, should you display all of the benefits of the company at once, or let them be seen and evaluated one at a time? In negotiating with another party, should you give in on a number of issues at once, or let the opposition feel each "victory" independently? Should the company give the workforce a lot of "fringes" (bonuses, parties, and so on) at Christmas or spread them out throughout the year? Thaler asserts that the received value can be maximized by not wrapping "all the Christmas presents in one box."

Conversely, prospect theory also suggests that we lose less value by one large loss than by an identical loss suffered in multiple parts. Thaler suggests that one of the many desirable properties of credit cards is that they pool many small losses (debts) into one larger loss. Financial agencies also use this preference to their advantage by "allowing" you to pay off "all of your debt, and owe just one payment every month." This transaction often increases your overall debt (because of the higher interest rate that goes along with the consolidation), yet it is attractive to many consumers.

The positive perceived impact of summing losses can also be seen in the context of summing probabilistic losses. In Slovic, Fischhoff, and Lichtenstein's (1978) analysis of seat belt use, it is argued that the resistance to seat belts is largely due to the extremely small probability of an accident on a single trip. A fatal accident occurs only once in every 3,500,000 person trips, and a disabling injury only once in every 100,000 person trips (Slovic et al., 1978). Based on the rarity of these events, it is easy to argue that refusing to buckle seems reasonable. Slovic and colleagues point out, however, that the risks of not using seat belts can be framed very differently—by summing across multiple probabilistic losses. They summed the probabilities of fatality and disabling injury across a 50-year lifetime of driving—on average, 40,000+ trips. Based upon this summation analysis, Slovic's group concluded as follows: "The probability that one of these trips will end in a fatality is .01, and the probability of experiencing at least one disabling injury during this period is .33. It is as appropriate to consider these cumulative probabilities of death or disability as it is to consider the odds on a single trip." Slovic et al. (1978) investigated this framing contradiction empirically by inducing subjects to adapt either a lifetime or trip-by-trip perspective. Ten percent of the subjects exposed to single-trip risk statistics claimed that they would increase their use of seat belts, while 39 percent of those exposed to lifetime statistics said that they would increase their use. Further, 54 percent of the subjects exposed to single-trip statistics favored mandatory protection, while 78 percent of those exposed to lifetime statistics favored such a law. Thus, by summing probabilistic losses, significant changes in preference and intended behavior were observed.

7. How Does the Frame of the Problem Affect How Much Your Time is Worth?

So far, this chapter has dealt exclusively with decisions involving risk. An area that is clearly related to risk, yet conceptually different, is the way in which people deal with decisions about time.

Before reading further, answer the following question: How much is your time worth per hour?

Now consider the following problems:

Problem 8: Assume that you are planning to clean your apartment/ house/condominium next Saturday morning for four hours. What is the *most* that you would pay someone to do the same amount of cleaning for you, so that you could relax for those four hours? (Assume that the quality of cleaning will be the same, that security is not a problem, and so on.)

Problem 9: Assume that you were planning to relax next Saturday morning.

What is the *least* that you would accept to clean an apartment/house/condominium for four hours?

In recent years, professionals have become very explicit in viewing time as being their most valuable commodity, and thinking rationally about the value of our time has become increasingly important. Each of the foregoing questions attempts to identify the value that you place on your relaxation time (in comparison to cleaning). Interestingly, it turns out that most people demand far more to clean than they are willing to pay to avoid cleaning. In fact, it is common for individuals to demand 5 to 20 times as much in problem 9 than they are willing to pay in problem 8.

Economic and other normative frameworks suggest that the responses should be similar, or at least not off by a factor of 5, between these two problems. Why the discrepancy? Through the use of prospect theory, Thaler (1980) explains the empirical difference by arguing that a certain degree of inertia exists in the consumer process, such that goods (and free time) that you possess will be more highly valued than goods (and free time) that you do not possess. That is, you will demand more for giving up your free time (a loss) than you would pay for receiving additional free time (a gain).

The following problems, adapted from Tversky and Kahneman (1981), further illustrate contradictions in the way people value their time.

Problem 10: Imagine that you are about to purchase a calculator for $50. The calculator salesperson informs you that the calculator that you wish to buy is on sale at the store's other branch, located a 20-minute drive away. What is the *highest* price that the calculator could cost at the other store such that you would be willing to travel there for the discount?

Problem 11: Imagine that you are about to purchase a color television for $500. The television salesperson informs you that this television is on sale at the store's other branch, located a 20-minute drive from where you are now. What is the *highest* price that you would be willing to pay at the other store to make the "discount" worth the trip?

How much is 20 minutes of your time plus the cost of travel worth? The answer to this question in comparison to the amount saved at the sale prices should determine whether or not you will make the trip in each case. However, most people demand a greater discount in absolute dollars to make the television trip than to make the calculator trip. Why? The issue of transactional utility enters into your evaluation of the worth of your time. You are wiling to travel the 20 minutes only to get a "very good deal." A $25 (5 percent) savings is not a big discount on the television, but it is an outstanding deal on the calculator (you would be saving 50 percent). Normatively, however, the difference in percentage reduction is irrelevant to considering these problems. One should simply compare the savings obtained versus the value of the time spent, and this value should be consistent across decisions.

8. How Rational Are Your Intertemporal Choices?

Another aspect in the study of decision making related to the value we place on our time is the value that we place on the differential timing of outcomes. Loewenstein (1987, 1989) calls these types of decisions **intertemporal choices.** Many of the most important decisions that we make have an intertemporal component: how much education to obtain, when to get married, how much to save for retirement, when to buy a house, and so on (Loewenstein and Thaler, in press). Standard decision models generally assume that we act to maximize expected utility at a single, constant discount rate (Loewenstein and Thaler, in press). That is, these models portray individuals as acting consistently in terms of the value of time.

While we are entitled to any discount rate that we like, the reality that the future is something inherently uncertain leads many individuals to bring biases to intertemporal choice that are similar to those made in assessing risky choice. While we all know that there is a time value of money (a bank will pay you interest in a very safe account), many of us behave in ways that are inconsistent with this basic fact. A large majority of U.S. taxpayers receive refunds from the Internal Revenue Service each year (Loewenstein and Thaler, in press). These taxpayers could be earning interest on this money by simply having less money withheld from their paychecks.

An interesting aspect of intertemporal choice concerns the difference in value that we place on identical good/bad nonmonetary outcomes when they differ only in when we get the outcome. We would rather have a desirable commodity (food, for example, or a piece of clothing) today than two months from now. Conversely, we would rather delay receiving a negative outcome for two months than get it today. In general, we also evaluate time delays differently now than in the future. For example, waiting an extra two weeks for a good or bad outcome feels very different than waiting an extra two weeks a year from now for the same outcome.

Consider the following set of problems (adapted from Loewenstein, 1989):

Problem 11: Which would you prefer? (Circle a or b.)

a. A lobster dinner at a nice restaurant in two weeks
b. A lobster dinner at a nice restaurant in six weeks

If you prefer (a), then how much would you need to be paid at the time of dinner (b) so that you would be indifferent between (a) and (b)?
        $_____

Problem 11a: Which would you prefer? (Circle c or d.)

c. A lobster dinner at a nice restaurant in one year

d. A lobster dinner at a nice restaurant and $2 less than the amount of money you just specified, both to be received a year and four weeks from now

Loewenstein found that 88 percent of the MBA students and 81 percent of the undergraduates in his sample preferred (a) over (b) by an amount greater than $2. Of this group that preferred (a) over (b) by more than $2, 70 percent preferred (d) over (c). Since the absolute delay in the dinner between (a) and (b) is the same as that between (c) and (d) (four weeks), the key question in both cases is how much you would have to be paid to accept a delay of four weeks. If you consistently valued this four-week delay across time, you would end up answering (c) to the second question, since (d) offers you $2 less than the amount that you suggested that you require to accept the same delay in problem 11.

Why do people choose (d) instead of (c)? An intuitive explanation of this inconsistency is that people discount the future more when the nondelayed outcome is more proximate. That is, the difference between getting a good outcome now versus a month from now is larger than the difference between getting a good outcome 12 months versus 13 months from now. This implies that we become more impatient when we can "taste" the good outcome. Interestingly, we can infer that many people would accept a delay (for a fee) and receive a good outcome 13 months from now, rather than 12 months from now. When the 12 months is up, however, their preference is likely to change such that they will wish that they could reverse the initial choice. The proximity to the good outcome creates an "I want it now" mentality that most of us do not acknowledge as a bias in our decision-making scheme.

This dynamic inconsistency between proximate decision making and more distal decision making results in behavior that is not explainable from a rational model. "Who is sovereign, the self who sets the alarm clock to rise early, or the self who shuts it off the next morning and goes back to sleep?" (Loewenstein and Thaler, in press). Similarly, when a pregnant woman tells her doctor that "regardless of the circumstances, I want to be awake for the delivery of my baby" and then changes her mind when she experiences the pain, what should the doctor do? We all experience situations in which we have internal disagreements. These struggles between multiple selves occur partially as a result of our inconsistencies in dynamic decision making (Schelling, 1984; Thaler and Shefrin, 1981).

Intertemporal choices, like risky choices, are also affected by framing—particularly differences in the summing of outcomes. Loewenstein (1989) explored this by asking individuals to answer the questions in problems 12 and 13. Half were first asked problem 12 and a week later were asked problem 13. The other half answered the questions in the reverse order.

Problem 12: Imagine that your current job gives you 30 vacation days a year. As a reward for your excellent work, your manager gives you a 14-day vacation bonus. You have the following choice:

a. take 14 days extra off this year
b. take 7 days extra off this year and 7 days extra next year

Problem 13: Imagine that your current job gives you 30 vacation days a year. As a reward for your excellent work, your manager gives you a 14-day vacation bonus. You have the following choice:

a. take 44 days off this year and 30 days off next year
b. take 37 days off this year and 37 days off next year

Although both questions are objectively identical, many people's preferences shift as a result of the differences in framing. The majority choose answer (a) in problem 12 but answer (b) in problem 13. Since the same individuals answered both questions, many remained consistent across the two questions. However, among those who were inconsistent, 90 percent favored lumping the extra days into the current year in the version that focused on the allocation of extra days (problem 12) and favored the equal division of days in the version that focused on the total portfolio of vacation days (problem 13). It seems that when individuals focus only on a specific element of a positive outcome, they focus on "I want it now." However, when those same individuals think in terms of a total portfolio of a positive outcome, they tend to think beyond "I want it now" and are more willing to space out the benefits of that outcome and say, "I want some good things now and some good things later."

INTEGRATION OF VARIOUS FRAMING EFFECTS

As we have just discussed, prospect theory represents the most important advance in our understanding of behavioral decision-making processes in the last 20 years. The previous questions have attempted to demonstrate some of the key findings of that work—namely, the critical importance that the framing of information has on how we make decisions in uncertain situations. These questions are summarized in Table 3.2, at the end of this chapter. In general, people tend to respond differently when risky outcomes are defined in terms of losses versus gains or in terms of certainty versus uncertainty. The context in which outcomes occur also affects our views of transactional utility and leads to inconsistencies in how we interpret outcomes. Similarly, the summing, or aggregation, of a number of outcomes evokes different responses from us than we would give if we were to approach the same outcomes separately. In responding to temporal choices, particularly when they do not necessarily involve risk, we put a higher value on losing personal time than we do on gaining more personal time. Similarly, we respond differently to the timing of good and bad outcomes. We want good outcomes now but bad outcomes later. Postponing a good outcome results in a greater loss of perceived utility than not postponing an equivalent bad outcome. Like risky outcomes, the summing of temporal choices affects us differentially.

From the information presented, you should now be able to identify situations in which you currently adopt a particular frame to the exclusion of other perspectives. If you can understand and apply this knowledge, the consistency and quality of your decisions will be greatly improved. The concept of framing has enormous potential for expanding our understanding of applied managerial problems. Consider how these effects can be applied in a variety of organizational contexts. For instance, in the area of job choice:

> An employee with five years of experience since obtaining his MBA has a reasonable job, security, and an average salary for someone with his background. He now has the option to abandon his current, safe position and commit himself to a high-risk, high-opportunity start-up firm. Will he make the job change?

According to the careers literature, common considerations include his family situation, his current salary, his promotion potential, his lifestyle, and so on. Prospect theory suggests, however, that the reference point from which he evaluates the options will be a critical factor. A low reference point (where he thinks he should be at this point in his career) will lead to an evaluation on the gain part of the utility curve (see Figure 3.1) and a risk-averse choice (not switching jobs). A high reference point, however, will lead to an evaluation on the loss part of the curve and a risk-seeking choice (switching jobs). This analysis is critical to identifying the inappropriate impact that false career expectations can have on employees. Graduate schools and employers frequently create unrealistic career expectations as part of their marketing strategy. This type of analysis is not unique to issues of job choice; rather, it is intended to highlight the potential of applying the framing concept to better analyze managerial situations.

INDIVIDUAL RISK TAKING IN ORGANIZATIONS

This chapter has focused primarily on risk taking by individuals. Organizations have an even more difficult task. How can an organization get employees to follow a rational risk-taking strategy? For example, having a sales department that tries to make risky decisions while the credit department tries to make conservative decisions is inconsistent. There is probably a risk-taking strategy between the strategies pursued by these two departments that more closely resembles the appropriate strategy for the overall organization, and the stockholders would probably prefer to have all divisions following a *consistent* overall approach. Swalm (1966) has suggested that division and lower-level managers are typically more risk averse than top managers in the same organizations. Further, Swalm (1966) has found that managers readily acknowledge that they make many decisions using a risk strategy that responds to their own best career interests, rather than to the best interests of their organization. Why do departments have different risk strategies? Why do managers use risk strategies that are different from their organizational's risk strategy? Two factors contribute to such inconsistency in managerial risk taking: communication and incentives.

One reason that managers may not make decisions that are consistent with an organization's overall risk strategy is that they may not *know* the organization's risk strategy. If an organization does not make clear the degree of risk that it is willing to accept in providing customer credit, for example, then fighting between the sales and credit department is predictable. The organization must develop and *communicate* the company's overall perspective concerning risk.

In addition, managers may not make decisions that are consistent with the organization's overall risk strategy because the organization provides incentives that go *against* its best interests. Organizations tend to reward results: "If your decision turns out disastrously, then you made a terrible decision." As we argued earlier, this should not be the case. Most decisions are probabilistic, and even the best decisions may not work out well. To the extent that the organization rewards results, however, some managers will behave conservatively to avoid making the "mistake" that leads to dismissal, while others will make unusually risky decisions in the hope that an unexpected success will lead to a promotion! How can the organization change such behavior? By rewarding the *quality* of the decisions rather than the results of the decisions! A second strategy to get managers to make decisions in the best interests of the organization is to reward based on the organization's, rather than the individual's, success. This is a primary tenet of organization-wide incentive systems. These plans link the individual's rewards to the success of the organization. The individual is no longer rewarded or punished based on personal success (which leads to differing risk strategies). The goals of the individual and of the organization no longer conflict.

SUMMARY

This chapter has provided an analytical framework that increases your awareness of the nature of uncertainty and risky decisions, identifies systematic ways in which judgment deviates from rationality in uncertain conditions, and puts this information into a context that will allow you to generalize the material presented to broader managerial applications. Most important, a key purpose of the chapter has been to create an awareness (that is currently missing in many individuals) of the inherently probabilistic nature of most decisions. This is critical for the development of the managerial ability to make effective decisions and to properly evaluate the decisions of others. As Dawes (1988) reminds us:

> . . . [T]here is much uncertainty in the world, and one of our most basic choices is whether we will accept that uncertainty as a fact or try to invent a stable world of our own. Such people's natural desire to reduce uncertainty, which may be basic to the whole cognitive enterprise of understanding the world, runs amok to the point that they come to believe uncertainty does not exist (p. 273).

Table 3.2 Summary Descriptions of the Eight Effects of Framing Presented in Chapter 3

Organizing Question	Description of How Most People Are Affected
1. How are your decisions affected by the framing of choices?	Individuals tend to be risk averse to positively framed choices and risk seeking to negatively framed choices.
2. How are your decisions affected by the framing of outcomes?	After individuals gain or lose some commodity, future decisions (in the short term) are evaluated in terms of Figure 3.1, in reference to the current sure loss or gain position.
3. How are your decisions affected by the framed pseudocertainty and certainty of choices?	Individuals value the reduction of uncertainty more when the outcome was initially certain than when it was merely probable.
4. How do you differentially respond to "paying premiums" versus accepting sure losses?	Certain losses are more attractive when *framed* as insurance premiums than when *framed* as monetray losses.
5. How is your evaluation of the quality of a transaction affected by the frame in which it is presented?	Individual purchasing behavior is affected by acquisition utility and transactional utility. *Acquisition utility* is associated with the value that the individual places on the commodity. *Transactional utility* refers to the quality of the deal, in reference to what the item "should" cost
6. How are your decisions affected by summing gains and losses?	Individuals value a series of small gains more than a single gain of the same summed amount. In addition, individuals lose less value by one large loss than by an identical loss suffered in multiple smaller parts.
7. How does the frame of the problem affect how much your time is worth?	Individuals value their time at extremely different rates, depending on social norms, transactional utility, anchor points based on market values, and expectations of how much "work" they should do in a given time period.
8. How rational are your intertemporal choices?	Individuals show a number of inconsistencies in making decisions about whether to take a good thing now or delay, as well as about whether to accept a bad outcome now or delay this negative event.

FOUR
THE NONRATIONAL ESCALATION OF COMMITMENT

If at first you don't succeed, try, try again. Then quit. No use being a damn fool about it.

W. C. Fields

In the previous chapters, we have examined single decisions and the way in which judgmental biases and the framing of information can influence our responses to them. However, many critical managerial decisions concern a series of choices rather than an isolated decision. Management research suggests that we are prone to a particular type of bias when decisions are approached serially—namely, a tendency to escalate committment.

This chapter will introduce you to a specific aspect of this phenomenon—the nonrational escalation of commitment. In the first three sections, research into the individual (or unilateral) components, the competitive components, and other factors affecting this behavior are reviewed. In the final section, a taxonomy of explanations for the psychological tendency to escalate is developed, and recommendations for eliminating nonrational escalation behavior are offered.

To start out, consider the following examples:

You personally decided to hire a new middle-level manager to work for you. Although you had expected excellent performance, early reports suggest that she is not performing as you had hoped. Should you fire her? Perhaps you really can't afford her current level of performance. On the other hand, you have invested a fair amount in her training. Furthermore, she may just be in the process of learning the ropes. So you decide to invest in her a bit longer and provide additional resources so that she can succeed. But still she does not perform as expected. Although you have more reason to "cut your losses," you now have even more invested in this employee. When do you give up on your "investment"?

You take a position with a well-known firm with an excellent reputation. You believe that it offers an excellent career opportunity in a firm that you can grow with. After two years you are not progressing as rapidly as you had expected. You decide to invest large amounts of unpaid overtime in demonstrating your contribution to the company. You still do not get the recognition that you expect. By now, you have been with the organization for several years and would lose numerous benefits, including a vested interest in the company's pension plan, if you decide to leave. You are in your late 30s and feel that you have invested your best years with this company. Do you quit?

You are a bank loan officer. A seemingly good credit risk comes to you and asks for a $50,000 business start-up loan. After a careful review of the application, you personally make the decision to grant the loan. Six months later, the same applicant shows up in your office and says: "I have bad news, and I have good news. The bad news is that the company is having problems. In fact, without additional help, we are going to go under, and you will lose the $50,000. The good news is that I am quite confident that if you lend us an additional $50,000, we can turn the whole thing around." Do you lend him an additional $50,000? (This scenario was inspired by a study of bank loan decision making by Lewicki [1980]).

You have spent the last three years working on a doctorate in Victorian history—a field with very poor job prospects. You choose to invest more time to finish the degree, rather than quit the program and shift fields. After all, you have already invested a lot in your doctoral program. You stick with it, and two years later you have your degree. You take a job as a part-time instructor at a low-quality institution—it's the best job available in your field. Now you are dissatisfied with the way the school treats part-timers, and, quite frankly, you think you deserve more recognition than you are receiving. You can stick with this position, but the prospects for improvement are poor. When do you shift to a different field?

Although each of these decisions represents a very different situation, they share a number of common elements. In each case, you have a decision to make as a result of a previous decision. You hired the employee. You took the job. You made the loan. You decided to pursue a doctorate in a field with poor job prospects. In each case, you have invested a great deal of time, effort, and resources in your selected course of action, and now things are not working out in an optimal way.

We are frequently faced with similar decisions of varying levels of importance. Do you put more money into that old wreck that you call a car? You call the airline and are put on hold. How long do you stay on hold? If you think about your own career and life, you will probably come to the conclusion that situations of this type are common. Inertia frequently leads us to continue on our previously selected course of action. After all, we often feel that we have "too much invested to quit." Is continuing the course of action irrational? How do you know when to quit? To the extent that continuing the course of action is irrational, why is such behavior so common? These are the central questions of this chapter.

The key to making intelligent decisions in dynamic contexts, like those just discussed, is being able to discriminate between situations in which persistence will pay off and situations in which it will not. Misdirected persistence can lead you to waste a great deal of time, energy, and money (Tyler and Hastie, 1990). However, directed persistence can lead to commensurate payoffs. After all, we are taught from an early age to "try, try again."

A variety of authors from different fields have presented ideas relevant to the four problems just listed, and a number of different terms (such as escalation, entrapment, and persistence) and related definitions have been used to describe commitment to a previously selected course of action. Without presenting the diversity of definitions used in the literature, this chapter defines **nonrational escalation** as the degree to which an individual escalates commitment to a previously selected course of action to a point beyond that which a rational model of decision making would prescribe.

Accountants and economists provide insight into how to handle these scenarios. Experts from these areas tell us that in each of these situations we need to recognize that the time and expenses already invested are "sunk costs." That is, these costs are historical costs that are *not* recoverable and should *not* be considered in any future course of action. Our reference point for action should be our current state, and we should consider all alternative courses of action by evaluating only the *future* costs and benefits associated with each alternative. For example, it does not matter whether it took you six months or four years to get to a particular point in the doctoral program; the key decision involves the future costs of exiting versus the future benefits of continuing.

While accountants teach their students to recognize sunk costs in an accounting context, the decisions of managers trained in accounting suggest that the textbook training to ignore sunk costs is seldom translated to real-world problems. Why is it so hard for managers to absorb the sunk-cost concept in a lasting manner? A key deficiency in this training is a descriptive identification of why we intuitively tend to include sunk costs in our calculations. To eliminate escalatory behavior—beyond the accounting textbook problem—we need to identify the existing nonrational behavior within ourselves, "unfreeze" that behavior, and prepare for change.

Psychologists bring a perspective to the escalation problem that is very different from that of the accountants and economists. Psychologists begin by describing what decision makers actually do, rather than prescribing what they should do. In general, psychologists (Bazerman, Giuliano, and Appelman, 1984; Brockner and Rubin, 1985; Staw, 1976, 1981; Teger, 1980) have demonstrated that decision makers who commit themselves to a particular course of action have a tendency to make subsequent decisions that continue that commitment beyond the level suggested by rationality. As a consequence, resources are often allocated in a way that justifies previous commitments, whether or not those initial commitments now appear valid. The earlier problems provide meaningful examples of this phenomenon—the hiring decision, the job choice decision, the loan decision, the professional field decision. The following section examines the components of this behavior in more detail.

THE UNILATERAL ESCALATION PARADIGM

To introduce this paradigm, reconsider the previously specified problem of the bank loan officer. The way we have just described the escalation situation has probably biased your impression toward assuming that it is "bad" to escalate your commitment to the loan. However, it might be economically rational to continue. After all, we are not always expected to quit at the first sign of failure. In fact, many would argue that such behavior would be a sign of a serious psychological deficiency.

How do you separate the rational from the nonrational tendency to escalate? One body of knowledge suggests that you should try to determine the rational course of action, excluding the fact that you personally made the initial loan commitment, and a number of studies have attempted to pull out the effect of being the person who made the initial commitment. These studies have investigated the difference between how two groups of decision makers make a second decision that follows an initial failure. One group has already made the initial decision, while the other group inherits the initial decision.

In Staw's initial (1976) study of this type, one group of subjects (labeled the high-responsibility subjects) was asked to allocate research and development funds to one of two operating divisions of an organization. The subjects were then told that, after three years, the investment had either proven successful or unsuccessful and that they were now faced with a second allocation decision concerning the same division. A second group (labeled the low-responsibility subjects) was told that another financial officer of the firm had made a decision that had been either successful or unsuccessful (the same content information about success or failure was provided to this group as to the previous group) and that they were to make a second allocation of funds concerning that division. When the outcome of the previous decision was negative (an unsuccessful investment), the high-responsibility subjects allocated significantly more funds to the original division in the second allocation than the low-responsibility subjects. In contrast, for successful initial decisions, the amount of money allocated in the second decision was roughly the same across subjects. Given that the greater escalation of commitment occurred only for the subjects who had made a previously unsuccessful decision, Staw concluded that the mechanism underlying escalation is cognitive dissonance (Festinger, 1957) or self-justification (Aronson, 1968). That is, once an individual makes an initial decision to embark on a course of action, negative feedback is dissonant with having made the initial decision. One way to eliminate this dissonance is to escalate commitment to the initial action in the belief that eventual success in that course of action will now be obtained. This explanation of escalation parallels Festinger's (1957) argument that once a person commits to a course of action, there will be "less emphasis on objectivity . . . and more partiality and bias in the way in which the person views and evaluates the alternatives." An important conclusion from Staw's (1976) study is that the responsibility felt by the decision maker for the initial decision significantly biases the subsequent decision toward escalation.

A number of other studies have identified additional factors that predict whether or not escalatory behavior is observed. For example, Staw and Ross (1978) showed that the tendency to escalate commitment by high-responsibility subjects was particularly pronounced when an explanation could be developed for the initial failure that was unpredictable and unrelated to the decision maker's action (for example, the economy suffered a severe setback). Bazerman, Giuliano, and Appelman (1984) found escalation to occur in groups as well as individuals. Here, using the Staw (1976) methodology, groups that made an initial unsuccessful decision allocated significantly more funds to the division than groups that inherited the initial decision. In addition, we found escalation to be related to the degree to which individuals and groups experienced dissonance as a result of the feedback from the initial decision. Bazerman, Schoorman, and Goodman (1980) also found that the tendency to escalate was significantly affected by (1) the degree of disappointment felt by the decision maker when the negative feedback from the initial decision was provided, (2) the perceived importance of the decisions, and (3) the perceived relationship between the two decisions.

Bazerman, Beekun, and Schoorman (1982) found that the tendency to escalate generalized from the financial resources context (used in all previous studies) to a performance appraisal domain. Specifically, we found that individuals who had made the initial decision to hire an employee subsequently evaluated that employee more favorably, provided larger rewards, and made more optimistic projections of future performance than did evaluators who had not made the initial decision to hire the employee. Thus, in the performance appraisal dilemma that was presented at the beginning of the chapter, you are not only likely to nonrationally escalate your commitment to keep the employee, but your performance reviews, salary reviews, and expectations of her future performance are also likely to be distorted accordingly. In a more recent study, Schoorman (1988) found that supervisors who participate in a hiring *or* promotion decision and agree with the eventual decision to hire or promote positively bias subsequent performance appraisals for that employee. In addition, supervisors who participate in a hiring or promotion decision and disagree with the eventual decision to hire or promote bias subsequent performance appraisals for that employee in a negative direction.

Taken together, the foregoing evidence suggests that managers have difficulty separating previous decisions from related future decisions. The consequence is that we tend to bias our decisions by our past actions, and we have a natural individual tendency to escalate commitment, particularly after receiving negative feedback. Why does this tendency to escalate occur? Northcraft and Wolf (1984, p. 3) offer the following explanation:

> The decision maker may, in the face of negative feedback [about the consequences of his or her decision], feel the need to reaffirm the wisdom of time and money already sunk in the project. Further commitment of resources somehow "justifies" the initial decision (Staw, 1976), at least provides further opportunities for it to be proven correct. The decision maker may also treat the negative feedback as simply a learning experience—a cue to redirect efforts within a project, rather than abandon it (Connelly, 1978). Or perhaps the decision maker will rationalize away the negative

feedback as a whim of the environment—a storm to be weathered, rather than a message to be heeded.

We will examine the psychological factors underlying escalation behavior in more detail later in the chapter.

THE COMPETITIVE ESCALATION PARADIGM

In the unilateral escalation paradigm just described, all the justification forces that lead to nonrational escalation lie within the individual. We escalate because of *our own* previous commitments. However, in the competitive escalation paradigm, additional competitive forces feed the escalatory process. This section examines the process of escalation in competitive situations.

Imagine yourself in a room with 30 other individuals. The person at the front of the room takes a $20 bill out of his/her pocket and announces the following:

I am about to auction off this $20 bill. You are free to participate or just watch the bidding of others. People will be invited to call out bids in multiples of $1 until no further bidding occurs, at which point the highest bidder will pay the amount bid and win the $20. The only feature that distinguishes this auction from traditional auctions is a rule that the second-highest bidder must also pay the amount that he/she bid, although he/she will obviously not win the $20. For example, if Bill bid $3 and Jane bid $4, and bidding stopped, I would pay Jane $16 ($20 − $4) and Bill, the second-highest bidder, would pay me $3.

Would you be willing to bid $2 to start the auction? (Make this decision before reading further.)

I have run this auction with undergraduate students, graduate students, and executives. The pattern is always the same. The bidding starts out fast and furious until the bidding reaches the $12-to-$16 range. At this point, everyone except the two highest bidders drops out of the auction. The two bidders then begin to feel the trap. One bidder has bid $16 and the other $17. The $16 bidder must either bid $18 or suffer a $16 loss. The uncertain option of bidding further (a choice that might produce a gain if the other guy quits) seems more attractive than the current sure loss, so the $16 bidder bids $18. This continues until the bids are $19 and $20. Surprisingly, the decision to bid $21 is very similar to all previous decisions: You can accept a $19 loss or continue and reduce your loss if the other guy quits. Of course, the rest of the group roars with laughter when the bidding goes over $20—which it virtually always does. Obviously, the bidders are acting irrationally. But what are the irrational bids?

(Skeptical readers should try out the auction for themselves. It is very common to have final bids in the range of $30 to $70. In total, I have earned over $10,000 running these auctions in classes over the last four years.)

The dollar-auction paradigm was first introduced by Shubik (1971), an economist and game theorist. (I have adjusted the auction from $1 to $20 to account for inflation and to earn a little extra cash.) More recently, Teger (1980) has used the paradigm extensively to investigate the question of why individuals escalate their commitment to a previously selected course of action. Teger argues that subjects naively enter the auction not expecting the bidding to exceed $1 (or $20); "after all, who would bid more than a dollar for a dollar?" The potential gain, coupled with the possibility of "winning" the auction, are enough reason to enter the auction. Once the subject is in the auction, it takes only a few extra dollars to stay in the auction rather than accept a sure loss. This "reasoning," along with a strong need to justify the bidder's entering the auction in the first place, is enough to keep most bidders bidding for an extended period of time.

Thoughtful examination of the dollar-auction game suggests that individuals who bid create a problem for themselves. It is true that one more bid may get the other guy to quit. But if both bidders feel this way, the result can be catastrophic. Yet, without knowing the expected bidding patterns of the opponent, we cannot conclude that continued bidding is clearly wrong. So what is the bidder's solution? Successful decision makers must learn to identify traps, and the key to the problem lies in identifying the auction as a trap and never making even a very small bid. One cognitive strategy for identifying competitive traps is to try to consider the decision from the perspective of the other decision maker(s). In the dollar auction, this strategy would quickly tell you that the auction looks just as attractive to other bidders as it does to you. With this knowledge, you can accurately predict what will occur and stay out of the auction.

We can find similar traps in business, war, and our personal lives. Teger concludes that the Vietnam War was a clear application of the dollar-auction paradigm. Two gasoline stations staging a price war can also produce the dollar-auction trap. The price of gasoline is $1.20 per gallon. Your competitor decides to drive you out of business. You would also like to drive her out of business. She drops the price to $1.13 per gallon. You drop the price to $1.10 per gallon—your break-even point. She drops her price to $1.07 per gallon. What's your next move? Both parties may suffer tremendous costs in an effort to win the price war, and like the dollar auction, neither side is likely to actually win the competition.

Two highly visible applications of escalation can be seen in the airline industry and the car industry. Perhaps the most innovative marketing program in the history of the airlines was American Airline's introduction of the Frequent Flyer program in 1981. The idea was that business flyers (or anyone else who flew frequently) could earn miles for the flights that they took and use these miles for travel awards. The logic was to provide an incentive to the traveler to be loyal to American. Soon every airline in the industry had its own program, and they began to increase the competition by offering double miles to their most frequent passengers, miles for hotel stays and car rentals, and so on. By 1987, analysts estimated that the airlines owed their passengers between $1.5 and 3 *billion* dollars in free trips.

How could the airlines get out of this mess? (Remember that antitrust regulations barred discussion among the airlines.) Delta had also identified an additional problem—namely, United and American were picking up market share from these programs because passengers had an incentive to be a member of a program with an airline that flew to the largest number of cities. Since United and American served the largest number of cities, they were getting the largest number of frequent flyers. What could Delta do? On December 15, 1987, they announced that all passengers who charged their tickets to American Express would get *triple* miles for all of 1988. Presumably, passengers would switch their loyalty for triple miles. What happened instead was that all major airlines announced triple miles, and a number of other benefits were added that kept dramatically escalating a bad situation throughout the remainder of 1988. Airline debt increased geometrically.

What could the airlines have done instead? How could American or United have stopped Delta from escalating the Frequent Flyer war? One answer comes from a similar war that existed in the auto industry during 1986. All three U.S. auto companies were engaged in an escalatory war of rebate programs that was eliminating their profits. Then they added the option of discount financing as an alternative to a rebate. The competition was fierce. How could any company stop without losing market share to the other two? Lee Iacocca, the chief executive officer (CEO) of Chrysler, came up with a solution. He communicated to the press that all the companies had programs scheduled to expire in the near future and that he had no plans of continuing with the program. However, if either of the other two announced a continuation of their plans, he would be forced to meet or beat any promotion that was offered. What was his message? He was announcing an opportunity to end the war if the others cooperated, but threatened retaliation if the others continued the war. The other two car companies got the message, and the rebate/financing program stopped for a significant period of time. What would have happened if United or American made the announcement that Iacocca made before Delta announced triple miles?

The competitive dollar-auction paradigm has much in common with the unilateral Staw paradigm. In both cases the decision maker makes an initial decision that he or she feels a need to justify through future decisions, and the decision maker feels that he or she has "too much invested to quit." However, there is one major difference between the two paradigms. In the dollar auction, the competition with the other party—that is, the desire to "win"—serves as added motivation to escalate commitment.

OTHER FACTORS CONTRIBUTING TO ESCALATION

The unilateral and competitive paradigms illustrate escalation behavior in two different types of entrapping situations. Rubin and Brockner (1975; Brockner et al., 1982; Brockner et al., 1984; Brockner and Rubin, 1985; Brockner, Rubin, and Lang, 1981; Brockner, Shaw, and Rubin, 1979; Nathanson et al., 1982; Rubin et al., 1980) have examined the escalation problem in a different manner. Rather than developing one specific escalation scenario, they have conducted an extensive series of studies using a wide variety of situations to identify factors that contribute to the tendency to escalate commitment.

In general, they have found that the belief that one is very close to the goal, and thus has too much invested to quit, is a leading contributor to remaining in an escalatory situation. In addition, they found that individuals are far more likely to quit if remaining in the escalatory situation requires an active, rather than a passive, response. That is, many individuals escalate, not because they have made a clear choice, but because they have done nothing to stop a previous course of action. For example, many individuals escalate their commitment to a job or career not because they make a conscious choice, but because they never actively confront the decision to stay or leave, which leads to maintaining the status quo. Rubin and Brockner also found that the presence of a "competitive other" (for example, the competing bidder in the dollar-auction game) provides an added source of motivation to escalate commitment to a previous course of action. Further, they found that the salience of the costs necessary to continue the investment is an important predictor of the decision to continue. Finally, they found that the behavior of role models has a very strong influence on the focal decision maker's behavior. Individuals seem to learn whether or not to escalate commitment by observing the behavior of other individuals. This last finding is particularly important in an organizational context, where we are constantly surrounded by potential role models.

Based on these studies, Rubin (1980) summarized the results of the group's research in terms of a set of recommendations on how to avoid escalation. These are the major points:

1. **Set limits on your involvement and commitment in advance.** In addition, once you set a limit, stick with it. Decision makers who set limits are eliminating the subsequent escalation bias that results from the need to justify a previous decision. At the time of limit setting, the individual has not yet been trapped.

2. **Avoid looking to other people to see what you should do.** Since escalation is a commonly observed behavior, it is easy to look around for examples of others escalating, which allow you to falsely justify your tendency to escalate.

3. **Actively determine why you are continuing.** Many of us escalate not because we believe that it is the best decision, but to manage the impression of others, such as a boss or a friend.

4. **Remind yourself of the costs involved.** When people become committed to a course of action, they often fail to consider the added costs of continuing. Rather, they assume that the costs must be minor in comparison to the overall costs of the project.

5. **Remain vigilant.** Escalation sneaks up on us. As was suggested earlier, escalation is often a passive response. We must constantly reassess the costs and benefits of continuing.

WHY DOES ESCALATION OCCUR?

Each of the previous sections has provided some clues about the conditions under which escalation occurs. However, the key to eliminating nonrational escalation is the ability to identify the psychological factors that feed escalation behavior. The existing literature clearly suggests that there are multiple reasons that escalation occurs. Building upon findings in earlier chapters, this section provides a taxonomy of these reasons. The first three classes of explanations, including perceptual biases, judgmental biases, and impression management, are general to all of the examples of escalation presented. The fourth class of explanations, competitive irrationality, differentiates the unilateral escalation paradigm from the competitive escalation paradigm. After presenting each class of explanations of the escalation phenomenon, the implications for the elimination of escalation are examined.

Perceptual Biases Consider the case at the beginning of this chapter, in which you made the decision to hire the employee who was subsequently not performing at the level expected. The evidence presented earlier in this chapter suggests that your perception of the employee's performance may be biased by your previous decision. That is, you may notice information that supports your hiring decision, while ignoring information that stands against your initial decision. Similarly, in the bank loan case, you may have a greater tendency to notice positive information about the company than negative information about the company after making the initial loan decision. This can be predicted from the suggestion in Chapter 2 that we pay more attention to confirming than disconfirming information. Similarly, Staw (1980) and Caldwell and O'Reilly (1982) suggest that trapped administrators often protect their initial decisions by actively seeking out information that supports these decisions—for example, information that suggests that the employee is performing well. Caldwell and O'Reilly empirically show that subjects who freely choose a particular course of action subsequently filter information selectively to maintain commitment to that course of action.

The perceptual biases that result after we make a commitment to a particular course of action suggest a number of corrective procedures. As recommended in Chapter 2, in making decisions, we need to search vigilantly for disconfirming information, as well as for the confirming information that we intuitively seek. This need is particularly pronounced in serial decisions, where we have a natural tendency toward escalation. In addition, establishing monitoring systems that help us check our perception before a subsequent judgment or decision is made could prove useful. For instance, if an objective outsider could evaluate our openness to disconfirming information, this perceptual barrier to nonescalatory behavior could be reduced or eliminated.

Judgmental Biases   Once we have filtered the information that we will use in making a subsequent decision, we still have to make the decision. The central argument of this section is that any loss from the initial investment (such as bidding more than $20 in the competitive-escalation paradigm, or the initial research and development funding in Staw's unilateral escalation paradigm) will systematically distort judgment toward continuing the previously selected course of action. The logic of this prediction lies in the framing concepts developed in Chapter 3.

Recalling the central thesis of the framing concept, individuals tend to be risk averse to positively framed problems and risk seeking to negatively framed problems. Assume that you are the bank loan officer from the beginning of the chapter. You made an initial investment of $50,000 to the start-up venture. After a short period of time, you are faced with the decision of accepting a loss of that $50,000 or risking an added $50,000 in the hope that this added investment will eliminate the loss entirely. The risk-averse response is to accept the sure loss of $50,000, while the risk-seeking action is to try to recover the initial funds by allocating an additional $50,000. From Chapter 3, we know that most of us prefer a 50 percent chance of a loss of $100,000 over a sure loss of $50,000—even if they have the same expected value. Based upon this systematic preference, we would expect most individuals to give the additional loan if the expected success of that added loan was at least 50 percent. Now reconsider the problem assuming that you did not make the initial investment. You are now likely to evaluate the potential benefit of the second loan from a different reference point. From this reference point, the decision is either to quit now with no gain or loss or to take a 50:50 chance of winning or losing $50,000. Most individuals would quit, choosing not to accept the gamble. Following this line of reasoning, high- and low-responsibility subjects in Staw's paradigm may have simply been responding to the framing of the allocation problem (Arkes and Blumer, 1985; Bazerman, 1984; Northcraft and Neale, 1986).

The framing explanation of the escalation phenomenon suggests the same solution as the approach argued by accountants. We need to get individuals to assess the new decision from a neutral reference point that eliminates the extreme risk-seeking behavior observed among high-responsibility subjects (that is, decision makers who have already committed funds or resources to a course of action). This reference-point shift can be accomplished by convincing the decision maker that the initial investment has proven to be a loss, and that the second decision represents a new problem to be examined objectively. If this is not feasible, we need to introduce a new decision maker to make the subsequent decision.

Impression Management   Returning to the hiring decision from the beginning of this chapter, even if your perception and judgment led to the conclusion that that employee should be fired, you might not fire the employee. Why? Firing the employee would be tantamount to a public announcement that you made a mistake in your earlier decision. Keeping the employee might be the preferred alternative in order to "save face." Thus, managing the impression of others serves as a third reason for escalating your commitment to a previously selected course of action. This is consistent with Caldwell and O'Reilly's (1982) work that shows that individuals not only selectively perceive information, but also selectively provide information to others. Specifically, individuals who make an initial commitment to a particular course of action are more likely to provide confirming, rather than disconfirming, information to others.

In addition to not wanting to admit failure to others, we also try to appear consistent, and the consistent course of action is to increase our commitment to our previous actions. Staw and Ross (1980) have found evidence to suggest that our society perceives that administrators who are consistent in their actions are better leaders than those who switch from one line of behavior to another. They offer the following excerpts from the press's evaluation of Jimmy Carter as support for their position:

> Carter has exacerbated many of the difficulties he has faced. His most damaging weakness in his first two years has been a frequent indecisiveness . . . ("The State of Jimmy Carter," 1979).

> A President must, plainly, show himself to be a man made confident by the courage of his clear convictions . . . The American people find it easy to forgive a leader's great mistakes, but not long meanderings (Hughes, 1978).

Indecisiveness was also cited as the second most common reason for dissatisfaction with Carter in the Gallup poll collected after Carter's first year in office (Staw, 1981). Similarly, John F. Kennedy's book *Profiles in Courage* suggests that one of the most courageous decisions that politicians ever have to make are those favoring an action that they believe to be in the best interests of the constituency, yet that they know will be disfavored by that very same constituency. As Staw and Ross's findings suggest, that conflict is particularly severe if this action consists of turning one's back on a previously supported direction.

Thus, an interesting paradox results: To make the best choice suggests making the best decision for your organization based on future costs and benefits—ignoring any previous commitments. Yet, empirical evidence (Ross and Staw, 1986; Staw and Ross, 1980) shows that you are more likely to be rewarded for escalating your commitment to previously selected courses of action. From an organizational standpoint, this suggests that we need to create systems that reward making good decisions over managing impressions. Otherwise, as the bank loan officer who made the initial loan, you would have the incentive to escalate commitment (in order to be a consistent decision maker and "save face"), in comparison to a loan officer who had not made the initial decision. First, managers must convey throughout the organization that impression management at the expense of high-quality decisions within the firm will not be tolerated. Second, organizations should strive to make the employees' values closer to those of the organization through reward systems. The organization wants the best decision. Managers want to make decisions that will be best for managing their future careers. To the extent that rewards are based on results, employees will hide a bad result by escalating commitment. To the extent that rewards are based on the quality of the decision, the loan employees are motivated to make the best possible decisions at subsequent decision points, whether or not their initial decisions have been adjudged correct (Staw and Ross, 1987).

The view expressed in the previous paragraph that decisions should be evaluated based on process rather than outcome is consistent with Peters and Waterman's (1982) discussion of Heinz's experimentation with "perfect failures." The perfect-failure concept recognizes that many decisions are inherently risky. In fact, the system suggests that management recognize the learning that is acquired through failures and celebrate when failures occur! The central point that Peters and Waterman convey to the managerial world is that we must recognize good choices, not just good outcomes.

Competitive Irrationality The previous three explanations of escalation are generalizable to both the unilateral and competitive paradigms. Competitive irrationality, however, offers an explanation that distinguishes between the two paradigms. Specifically, competitive irrationality refers to a situation in which two parties (there is only one actor in the unilateral Staw paradigm) engage in an activity that is clearly irrational in terms of the expected outcomes to both sides, yet in which it is hard to identify specific irrational actions by either party. Many people would argue that getting involved in the dollar auction is irrational, and while this is a very reasonable perspective, the argument is not completely valid. If it makes sense for you not to play, then it does not make sense for anyone else to play. If no one else plays, then you can bid a small amount and get a bargain. This reasoning sounds logical, but once you make the initial bid, another individual bids, and the bind that we have already described appears. It was earlier argued that continuing to bid then depends on your estimation of the likelihood of the other party quitting. Obviously, the same reasoning applies to the other party. If it is possible for someone to get a very cheap $20 (for $1, for example), then it must be rational for one individual to be able to bid. Yet we know what happens when multiple individuals adopt this attitude. Thus, in many ways, competitive irrationality presents an unresolved paradox, rather than an explanation of escalation. The only recommendation that can be derived from the competitive irrationality explanation of escalation is that many situations may look like opportunities but prove to be traps unless the actions of others are fully considered.

Integration This section has suggested four additive causes that contribute to our tendency to escalate commitment to a previously selected course of action. By referring to the four causes as additive, we are suggesting that they are not mutually exclusive. Each one can independently cause escalation, but they more often act together to increase a decision maker's nonrational tendency to continue a previous mistake. The four causes of escalation are graphically presented in Figure 4.1. To reduce escalation, we must attack each cause at the individual and organizational levels. In trying to reduce escalation, we must remember that we are trying to counter the *nonrational* commitment to a course of action. Rational commitment remains a valuable attribute.

Overall, the findings on the tendency to escalate suggest that managers need to take an "experimenting" approach to management (Campbell, 1969). That is, as a manager, you should make a decision and implement it, but be open to dropping your commitment and shifting to another course of action if the first plan does not work out. This means constantly reassessing the rationality of future commitments and learning to identify failures early.

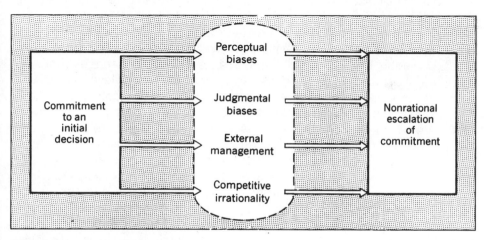

Figure 4.1. Four causes of escalation.

FIVE
CREATIVITY AND JUDGMENT

Innovative. Clever. Unique. Insightful. Illogical. Different. These words are connected to the alluring topic of creativity. These words can be used to describe the products of creative individuals. They can also be used to describe the traits commonly associated with creative individuals. Many people think of creativity as a stable characteristic of individuals. Some have it and others don't! While this may be partially true, this view distracts managers from the more useful perspective that all of us can improve our current level of creativity.

For the purpose of this chapter, creativity is defined as a cognitive process concerned with the development of an idea, commodity, concept, or discovery that is novel to its creator or some targeted audience—a process distinct from, yet compatible with, the logical processes of decision making identified in Chapter 1. The central thesis of this chapter is that the lack of creativity that exists in most individuals is a result of the judgmental biases discussed earlier in the book, and the key to creativity lies in breaking many of the previously described heuristics. Interestingly, the importance of creativity has not been ignored by corporate America. A 1983 study of large corporations found that a majority had undertaken some form of formal training in creativity in the last two years.

To begin the chapter, attempt to solve the following classic creativity problem (used without original reference by many previous authors):

Problem 1: Without lifting your pencil (or pen) from the paper, draw four (and only four) straight lines that connect all nine dots shown here:

•   •   •

•   •   •

•   •   •

Most people come up with unsuccessful attempts that look something like one of the following:

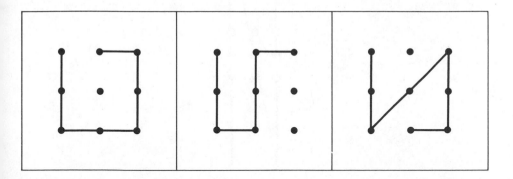

Why are most people unsuccessful? Most people attempt to use their *logical* decision-making skills on the *perceived* problem: connecting all nine dots without going outside the boundaries imposed by the nine dots. They make assumptions that frame the problem and constrain them from finding a solution. The most critical barrier to creative decisions is our assumptions. *Individuals make false assumptions about problems in order to fit the problems into their previously established decision-making processes.* When our logical processes fail, creative solutions often lie outside our self-imposed assumptions.

Back to the problem. Once the assumption about the barrier around the nine dots is broken, the following solution is fairly easy to achieve:

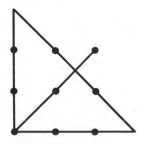

This solution is not achievable by trying additional alternatives within our commonly perceived assumptions. Yet the problem is easily solved after the assumption is removed. Adams (1986) claims that at least 27 solutions exist. For example, the problem can be solved with three lines:

Viewing creativity as an assumption-breaking process is a central perspective of this chapter. However, this perspective is not unique to this book (see, for example, Adams, 1986; DeBono, 1971; Winklegren, 1974), and we will make no attempt to fully review the literature on creativity. Instead, this chapter uses this perspective to examine the assumptions that limit creativity and show *why* individuals are often not as creative as they could be. This exploration follows from the limitations to rationality introduced in the first four chapters of this book.

Returning to the rational decision-making process described in Chapter 1, recall that a perfect decision-making process would have a clear definition of the problem, all alternatives would be known, all relevant factors would be identified and properly weighted, and so on. Since this rational model always leads to the optimal decision, all decisions would be fully creative as well. In contrast to this idealistic view, we have documented that our decisions are better explained by bounded rationality and guided by a set of heuristics and biases. These are the same processes that inhibit our creativity. This chapter starts with an examination of potential assumptions at each step in the logical decision-making process. We will then go on to explore how the specific deviations from rationality described in earlier chapters create assumptions at these various stages. Finally, we will discuss a number of heuristic-breaking tools for eliminating the assumptions that result from these limitations to rationality.

ASSUMPTIONS AT VARIOUS STAGES
OF THE DECISION-MAKING PROCESS

Assumptions manifest themselves at various points in the decision-making process. In this section we will explore the impact of these assumptions on multiple steps in the rational decision-making process introduced in Chapter 1.

Specifically, we will examine the limiting effect of assumptions in defining the problem, identifying alternatives, and weighting and identifying factors.

Definition of the Problem　Individuals are quick to define the problem. Defining the task allows us to use our standard logical processes. However, as the nine-dot problem demonstrated, false assumptions at this stage can prevent us from finding the best solution. Similarly, a manager who writes a job description (defining the problem) in a constrained manner may succeed in reducing the number of résumés that she needs to review, but she may also succeed in defining away the individual who was best for the job but lacked some unimportant "requirement."

Alternative Generation　Where do we look for alternatives? Do we just search for the standard alternatives? Are we making assumptions about the requirements necessary to view an alternative as viable? Frequently, the creative solution lies in identifying an alternative that most people would have excluded from consideration due to their assumptions. A vivid example of this limitation affected me (and many others) in the famous hedge maze at Hampton Court in England. The hedge maze consists of very tall hedges that form a human maze (a real highlight of a trip to England for a game player). As you enter the maze, signs implicitly lead you to walk to the left to "begin the maze." In actuality, turning to the left leads you to a complex set of dead ends. However, if you simply walk to the right (which is set up to be counterintuitive) and turn a corner, you're out. I walked to the left and tried to solve the maze quickly (to beat my spouse) by logically eliminating the various dead ends. Unfortunately, I did not even consider the idea that my initial turn may have been wrong. After 75 minutes, I was frustrated and convinced that I had negated all possible alternatives. I gave up and decided to go out the way I came in, which led me to find the solution to the problem (and my laughing spouse, who claimed to have been waiting for most of the time that I spent in the maze).

Criteria Identification and Weighting　What criteria are relevant in selecting among alternatives? What assumptions do we make in criteria identification? Again, creatively choosing between alternatives may result from breaking our assumptions about which criteria are important and what weights to attach to each factor. Consider the recent MBA selecting between multiple job offers. She eventually chooses a job with a well-know consulting firm that offers the highest starting salary and a great deal of prestige. (After all, the criteria that are salient to graduating students are firm prestige and salary. Note that these are the factors that can be easily compared to the jobs accepted by other students.) Over time, she realizes that the job was never consistent with her true values. What she wanted was a job with little travel that only demanded a 40- to 50-hour work week. Why did she take the wrong job? When she made the decision, she considered the criteria that were the most salient: money and prestige. The more appropriate and creative choice required that she examine more carefully the assumptions that she was making concerning her preferences.

This section demonstrates that most decisions have more than one point at which creativity, and assumption breaking, may be necessary. The next section explores the psychological bases of these assumptions.

THE PSYCHOLOGICAL BASES OF CREATIVITY-LIMITING ASSUMPTIONS

The contention in this section is that the judgmental biases identified in the first four chapters of this book create assumptions that limit creativity. Because these limitations to rationality lead the decision maker to simplify the optimal decision-making process, the opportunity for creativity becomes blocked in subsequent decisions. Specifically, we examine the framing of problems, anchoring and adjustment, the representativeness heuristic, the availability heuristic, the tendency to escalate commitment, and cultural and environmental blocks.

The Framing of Problems   In Chapter 3, it is shown that individual choice is systematically affected by the way in which problems are framed. Individuals tend to be risk averse to positively framed problems and risk seeking to negatively framed problems. In addition, we tend to make the implicit false assumptions that the frame in which the problem is presented is the only perspective for the problem. Most problems are framed with a variety of connotations, expectations, and so on. Each time we choose a single frame, we limit our view of the decision. This suggests that one basis of the assumptions that block creativity emanates from the framing of information.

The potential negative impact of framing on creativity can be illustrated by the often-repeated story of the manager who asks "How can I get my employees to work harder?" If the manager is trying to increase performance, his frame on the problem is likely to eliminate the possibility of increasing performance by finding the answer to the question "How can I get my employees to work smarter?" Obviously, the nature of the framing concept suggests that framing is most likely to inhibit creativity in the problem-definition stage.

A skilled salesperson can use our limited frame and creativity against us. In trying to sell you a home protection system, she asks you whether or not your spouse and children are worth $2,000. This is a very different frame than "How can you efficiently and effectively make your home safe?" The salesperson is using the fact that most of us look at a problem from only a single frame, and it is in her best interest to provide us with the frame that is optimal for selling the product. Looking at purchases from multiple frames eliminates a barrier to creativity and can improve the quality of the purchases that we make.

Anchoring and Adjustment   You have a problem to solve. You remember how you solved a similar problem once before. You use that strategy and try to make the appropriate adjustment. Unfortunately, this problem had a fundamental difference from the former problem that was disguised by your focus on their similarity. The result is an unsuccessful solution. What happened? You were anchored by an initial strategy for solving the problem. Thus, the anchoring-and-adjustment heuristic can lead to problem-solving short-cuts that inhibit a full search for alternatives. Time is not spent exploring options. The anchor keeps you from considering alternatives that lie outside its boundaries. Obviously, anchors can come from a variety of places. The key is to notice how the creativity of your search is anchored in a particular situation.

Representativeness Representativeness affects judgment by leading individuals to assess an occurrence by the correspondence of that occurrence to a similar set of known occurrences. If we are evaluating alternatives to a problem, we are likely to select alternatives that are similar to successful decisions in similar past problems. While this strategy is often successful, the creative alternative is likely to be one that the representativeness heuristic would lead us to ignore. Thus, although the representativeness heuristic serves most of us fairly well on a day-to-day basis, being creative often consists of going beyond our existing heuristics.

The creativity-blocking effect of the representativeness heuristic can be illustrated in the context of selecting new employees. A manager who bases the selection on the degree to which applicants are representative of previously selected employees is likely to replicate past levels of success. However, the use of this heuristic will also destroy the opportunity to find a new creative employee profile that might be equally or more successful in that work environment or that would bring a different perspective to the organization. In an era in which the lack of creativity in management is a critical concern, the use of the representativeness heuristic is a barrier to busting out of an old mold.

Availability Availability affects judgment by leading individuals to assess an event by the degree to which similar occurrences are readily available in memory. All of us have standard ways of approaching problems; we have available decision-making strategies. We are especially affected by very vivid memories. Under the availability heuristic, an individual is likely to select a decision-making approach that has previously led to a very vivid success, even though further consideration may have led to a better alternative. While the use of the availability heuristic enables us to respond to a problem quickly, we may be sacrificing a more creative and less available result. Each of us would be more creative if we searched beyond the intuitive problem-solving strategies that are most readily available to us.

Escalation Creative thinking requires that we remain open to divergent ideas. If the first hole seems to be in the wrong place, what other holes would be appropriate to consider digging? This is the creative strategy. In contrast, the escalation literature predicts that once we dig a hole and obtain negative results, we are likely to nonrationally continue to dig in order to justify the initial decision to dig that hole. The strategy described by the escalation literature is in direct conflict with the need for divergent thinking that is central to the creativity process. Thus, the nonrational tendency to escalate commitment to a previously selected course of action leads us to make implicit assumptions about the rationality of our initial strategy, reducing our potential creativity at future stages of the decision-making process.

Cultural and Environmental Blocks   Most of the previous blocks have been specified at a cognitive level, but many of the cognitive assumptions that we make about how to solve the problems arise from the culture and environment that surround us. This is best illustrated by Adams (1986, p. 54) through the following vivid example:

Problem 2: Assume that a steel pipe is embedded in the concrete floor of a bare room, as shown in Figure 5.1. The inside diameter is .06 inches larger than the diameter of a ping-pong ball (1.5 inches) that is resting gently at the bottom of the pipe. You are one of six people in the room, along with the following objects:

100 feet of clothesline
A carpenter's hammer
A chisel
A box of Wheaties
A file
A wire coat hanger
A monkey wrench
A light bulb

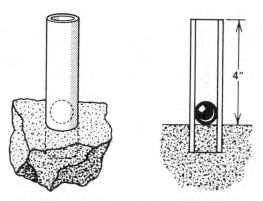

Figure 5.1   The ping-pong ball problem.

List as many ways as you can think of (in 5 minutes) to get the ball out of the pipe without damaging the ball, tube, or floor.

Adams argues that a creative person can come up with a number of solutions. Solutions include (1) filing the wire hanger in two, flattening the resulting ends, and making a large pair of tweezers to retrieve the ball and (2) smashing the handle of the hammer with the monkey wrench and using the splinters to retrieve the ball. However, Adams suggests that it takes an unusually creative individual to identify the solution: Have everyone in your group urinate in the pipe. Why is this solution so difficult to develop? Because our society has a taboo against solutions like these. As Adams notes, "urinating is somewhat of a closet activity." The important message is that we often make assumptions about problem solving based on the organization, culture, and society that surround our behavior.

A general pattern that emerges from examining these blocks to creativity is that each of them leads us to seek a single or limited set of right answers, which causes us to abbreviate our decision-making process prematurely. Our assumptions may make the decision-making process more time efficient, but each also has the potential to stifle creativity.

This section has offered an approach for specifying why we make assumptions that block creativity. We have argued that the heuristics and frames that govern our decision-making process also govern our creative abilities. This suggests that creativity and decision making are not separate topics. In fact, many of the factors that explain our bounds to decision-making rationality also explain our lack of creativity. Thus, *we conceptualize the lack of creativity under the rubric of bounded rationality, with a particular focus on problems that require novel solutions.*

STRATEGIES FOR BREAKING BLOCKS TO CREATIVITY

Until now, the focus of this chapter has been to describe why most individuals are insufficiently creative. The foregoing discussion suggests (1) that lack of creativity limits the quality of our decisions *and* (2) that individuals can be trained to improve their judgment by learning how to be more creative. This conclusion implies that creativity is trainable—which I believe—but contradicts popular wisdom, which suggests that creativity is something that one is born with. While there are individual differences in creativity, it is also true that we all sometimes neglect creative solutions because of the assumptions we make. Thus, the lack of creativity is similar to other heuristics: (1) It affects all of us, and (2) we can improve our judgment by reducing our lack of creativity. Strategies are proposed in this section for overcoming the limitations identified in the previous sections and enhancing our creativity. We will begin with a general discussion of the four stages of the creative process and then identify specific strategies for attacking our limitations to creativity at each stage.

The Four Stages of the Creative Process

Wallas (1926) proposed that creative thinking was a four-stage process: (1) preparation, (2) incubation, (3) illumination, and (4) verification. This four-stage model, along with other similar models, has been used by many authors to describe what creative individuals typically do and to prescribe what they should do to be creative. A general conclusion is that while following these four stages cannot guarantee creativity, the stages point out a number of useful ingredients for developing creativity.

Preparation (or Problem Definition)   Getzel (1975, p. 15) provides the following example concerning the importance of preparation before going on to the "action" part of problem solving:

> An automobile is traveling on a deserted country road and blows a tire. The occupants of the automobile go to the trunk and discover that there is no jack. They define the dilemma by posing the problem: Where can we get a jack? They recall that several miles back they had passed a service station, and decide to walk to the station for a jack. While they are gone, another automobile coming from the other direction also blows a tire. The occupants of this automobile go to the trunk and, by happy coincidence needed for our example, they too discover that there is no jack. They define the dilemma by posing the problem: How can we raise the automobile? They look about and see that adjacent to the road is an old barn with a pulley for lifting bales of hay to the loft. They push the car to the barn, raise it on the pulley, change the tire, and drive off, while the occupants of the first car are still trudging toward the service station.

This example shows how the preparation (problem identification) of one group led to a significantly superior decision than that made by another group. Preparation consists of obtaining a broader perspective on the problem through a wider search for information, clarifying the problem that needs to be solved, analyzing the resources that you have to address the problem, identifying missing resources, gathering additional resources, and assessing the assumptions that are being made about the problem. To the extent that the decision maker tries to move beyond the preparation prematurely (known as "ready–fire–aim"), the following problem-solving deficiencies are likely to result:

- You solve a problem, but it turns out to be the wrong problem. That is, you did not clearly understand the question and came up with a solution that does not solve the real problem. Rather, it solves the mythical problem that you thought existed.
- You make assumptions that keep you from finding the solution to the problem. We saw this in the nine-dot problem.
- You begin to work on the problem with insufficient physical resources, knowledge, and so on. A common result is that by the time you realize that added resources are needed, you have invested a significant amount of time, money, and energy in directions that are not productive. Many researchers find

themselves in the middle of research projects that they wonder why they ever started. Insufficient problem definition may be the answer.

- You solve the short-term problem but not the long-term problem. That is, you identify the problem according to the existing symptoms. Your answers eliminate the symptoms, but not the fundamental cause of the symptoms. Frequently, a broader perspective would have allowed for specifying the fundamental, long-term problem, rather than the superficial, short-term problem.

Finally, a critical part of preparation can consist of finding interesting problems to solve. This may sound confused: Why solve a problem that does not exist? Getzel (1975) asks and answers:

Is not the world already teeming with dilemmas at home and in business, in economics and technology, in science and in art? The world is, of course, teeming with dilemmas. But the dilemmas do not present themselves as problems capable of resolution or even of sensible contemplation. They must be posed and formulated in fruitful and often radical ways if they are to be moved toward solution.

Similarly, Einstein argued that

The formulation of a problem is often more essential than its solution, which may be merely a matter of mathematical or experimental skill. To raise new questions, new possibilities, to regard old questions from a new angle, requires creative imagination . . .

Incubation   Once the problem has been defined, the next step in a logical, but uncreative, decision-making process is to converge toward a solution. Such logical decision-making processes are typically sequential, moving in a planned direction, conservative, and built on established patterns. The process typically consists of identifying the immediately apparent alternatives, using obvious factors to evaluate the alternatives, and logically determining the best solution. Unfortunately, we often develop an early impression of the best solution, and most of our decision-making process consists of collecting confirmatory information for that decision (see Chapter 2).

In contrast, incubation is defined as a stage in the creativity process in which the individual explores unusual alternatives, eliminates assumptions that may hide alternatives, elaborates on the definition of the problem, and, in general, thinks about the problem in divergent ways. Unlike the logical pattern of decision making, incubation will lead the individual to focus on low-probability (high-payoff) alternatives and to think creatively and flexibly. DeBono (1971) describes incubation as a lateral thinking process, which he contrasts with logical (vertical) thinking, by comparing the problem-solving process to the digging of a hole. Logic digs bigger and deeper holes and escalates commitment to digging a particular hole. However, if the hole is in the wrong place, no amount of high-quality digging is going to put it in the right place. Lateral thinking explores different locations first and then determines the right place to dig.

Many areas of research are criticized for studying the obvious. While the research may be extensive and of high quality, it may also be guilty of vertical thinking—digging the wrong hole very well. Like the manager, the researcher must consider the benefits of additional incubation. On the other hand, however, incubation taken to an extreme becomes a rationalization for procrastination.

Illumination   This is the "aha" in problem solving. In its purest form, new ideas appear in a flash of insight. However, a more common, and still valid, form of illumination occurs when all of the pieces fall into place. While Wallas describes illumination as a stage in the creativity process, it is really the climax of the incubation stage.

Verification   This is the stage in which many highly "creative" people fail to be creative. After preparation, incubation, and illumination, we are ready to celebrate. All too often, however, we fall victim to the confirmatory trap and the overconfidence bias. We try only to confirm, but not disconfirm, that the innovation works, and we approach this task with a degree of overconfidence that is great for morale, but potentially destructive to the innovation. Verification is the stage in which traditional logic and reason (the logical steps in decision making) are applicable for rigorously testing the validity of the innovation. An important aspect of this stage is to search for disconfirming evidence—the true test of an innovation.

Specific Strategies for Enhancing the Creative Process

Until now, this section has focused on describing a set of stages that are intended to help to organize your thinking about the creative process. Now we will draw from the creativity literature and identify some specific strategies for enhancing creativity at each point in the process. Overall, the strategies focus on how to break the blocks to creativity specified in the previous section. These strategies can be viewed as a partial checklist to refer to in developing creative solutions to a particular problem. As before, the presentation is accompanied by a number of problems, which you are encouraged to solve before continuing your reading.

Assumption Breaking   Attempt to solve the following problem:

Problem 3: (Adapted from Winklegren, 1974)
You are given 4 separate pieces of chain that are each 3 links in length (see left diagram of Figure 5.2). It costs $100 to open a link and $150 to close a link. All links are closed at the beginning of the problem. Your goal is to join all 12 links of chain into a single circle (see right diagram of Figure 5.2). Your total budget for forming the single circle is $750.

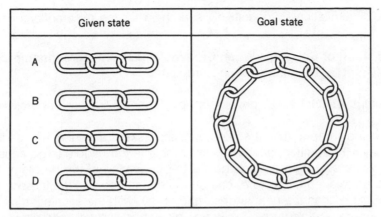

	Given state	Goal state

Figure 5.2 Given and goal states for the necklace problem.

This problem is quite similar to the nine-dot problem that introduced the chapter. Most people fail to solve the nine-dot problem because of the false assumption that you cannot go outside the boundaries of the nine dots. In this problem (called the "necklace"), most people fail to connect the chain because they falsely assume that after you open one link, you can insert only one closed link into the opened link. For example, they try opening a link at the end of chain A, inserting an end link of chain B, and closing the joining link. They then open one end of the six-link chain and insert one of the other three-link chains, and so on. Unfortunately, this strategy will lead to the need to spend $1,000—which is beyond your budget. There are a number of action sequences that are essentially identical to this strategy, and all of them cost $1,000.

In contrast, a few people have the insight to break the assumption that when you open one link, you are limited to inserting only one link into the opening. This leads to a variety of very similar successful solutions. For example, open all three links in chain A (cost, $300). Use one of them to combine chains B and C (cost, $150), use the second one to combine the free end of chain C to either end of D (cost, $150), and use the final open link to combine the remaining free end of chains B and D (cost, $150). The total cost is $750.

As you can see, the solution is simple. However, very bright people can look at this problem for hours and not find the solution. Why? Because we make assumptions about the problem that eliminate the solution. Frequently, we miss the optimal solution to a problem not because we actively chose a different alternative over the optimal choice, but because we never considered the optimal choice as feasible. The reason for this oversight is typically due to the assumptions that we make. Thus, the first proposed heuristic-breaking tool is to make the examination of your assumptions about a problem and its potential solutions a standard part of your decision-making process.

This first strategy is a direct response to the argument that our limited rationality leads to assumptions that block creativity. We simply suggest that an awareness of the assumption-formation process can lead a decision maker to reduce this limitation by cognitively searching for the assumptions behind a decision.

Identification of Subgoals When the Whole Task Appears Incomprehensible Attempt to solve the following problem:

> **Problem 4:** (Originally developed by François-Edouard-Anatole Lucas, 1883)
>
> There are three identical spikes and six disks. Each disk has a different diameter. In addition, each disk has a hole in the middle large enough for any of the spikes to go through. At the beginning of the problem, the six disks are placed on spike A, one on top of another, with the largest disk on the bottom, then the next largest, and so on, with the smallest disk on top (see Figure 5.3). You are permitted to move one and only one disk at a time from one spike to another, with the restriction that a larger disk must never be moved on top of a smaller disk. The goal is to transfer all six disks from spike A to spike C (without a larger disk ever resting on a smaller disk). Note: You can use three pencils and six pieces of different-size paper as a readily available substitute for the equipment shown in Figure 5.3.

Most people find this task overwhelming, or they immediately start moving the disk on a trial-and-error basis—a strategy that is not very successful. (If you find it easier than I describe, think about the problem with eight disks rather than six.) A more useful strategy consists of considering the problem in terms of a sequence of actions to be solved, similar to a long computer program.

Your ultimate goal is to get all six disks stacked up on the C spike. Since disk 6 has to be on the bottom, you have to get all of the other disks off of disk 6, so that it is free to move. Also, you have to make sure that spike C is empty, so that disk 6 can be moved there. Fulfilling these requirements necessitates getting

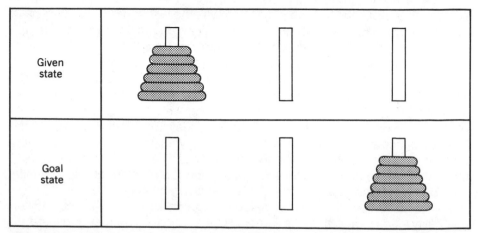

Figure 5.3 Given and goal states for the Tower of Hanoi problem.

the five smallest disks on spike B (the five-disk problem)—a useful subgoal. In reaching this subgoal, it should become apparent that you must first get disks 1 through 4 on spike C (the four-disk problem), so that you can move disk 5 to spike B. To solve this four-disk problem, you need to get disk 1 through 3 on spike B (the three-disk problem), so that disk 4 can be moved to spike C. I am sure that you can easily solve this three-disk problem.

Once you solve the three-disk problem, an interesting pattern emerges. You move disk 4 to spike C, and you want to move disks 1 through 3 on disk 4. Interestingly, you already know from your experience how to move disks 1 through 3 from one spike to another. Now that you have disks 1 through 4 on spike C, you move disk 5 to spike B. And now you know from your recent experience how to move disks 1 through 4 from one spike to another. Once this is done, you are free to move disk 6 to spike C and repeat your knowledge of how to move disks 1 through 5 from one spike to another. Notice that you have now solved a problem that seemed quite difficult without performing any operation that was truly difficult. By breaking the problem into subgoals, a difficult challenge turns into a series of fairly simple procedures.

Of course, you are not typically called upon to solve Tower of Hanoi puzzles as part of your managerial life. Instead, you are faced with a variety of problems that *do* require subgoals. Computer programs have already been mentioned. The rationale for a subgoal approach generalizes to any problem that has multiple stages. The interesting task is to identify multistage problems that may not be presented as such.

Finally, a word of warning is in order. The subgoal approach will not work on all problems. Some problems require a single, unique insight. Other problems have no subgoals. In either case, the subgoal approach will not lead to a solution. Thus, it is critical to identify whether or not a particular problem is in the domain of a subgoal approach.

Process Analysis   Consider the following problems:

Problem 5: (Adapted from Bartlett, 1978)
A hobo can make 1 whole cigar from every 5 cigar butts he finds. How many cigars can he make if he finds 25 cigar butts?

Problem 6: (Adapted from *Omni* magazine, 1981)
Ten male senators are on their way to the Inaugural Ball. A crowd of disgruntled taxpayers attacks them with a volley of snowballs, knocking each senator's top hat to the ground. A helpful page retrieves the hats and hands one to each senator—but without checking to see who owns which one. What is the *exact* probability that *exactly* nine senators will receive their own hats? (Do not use a statistics book to help you solve this problem.)

Both of these problems are fairly simple using the heuristic-breaking tool called **process analysis.** By thinking about the processes, or actions, associated with each actor, a problem solver can gain unique insights into the problem. Consider the hobo problem. The obvious answer is 5. Unfortunately, this answer is wrong! Imagine the hobo on the park bench working with the 25 butts. What will he do with them? Create 5 cigars. Then why is 5 the wrong answer? The right answer lies in continuing to think about the bum in this situation. What will he do with the cigars? Smoke them. What will happen after he smokes the 5 cigars? He will get 5 butts and create a 6th cigar!

Similarly, consider the senator problem. Imagine the scene. Ten senators all lose their hats. How likely is it that exactly nine get the right hat? Try to imagine the return of the hats. If nine out of ten senators get the right hat back, what about the tenth hat and the tenth senator? If nine have the right hat, then there is only one senator and one hat left, meaning that the tenth senator must also have the right hat. Thus, the probability of exactly nine senators getting the right hat is zero.

Now that you have had some practice with process analysis, try the following problem. (It's a tough one!)

Problem 7: (Adapted from Bartlett, 1978)
A conversation took place between two friends, a philosopher and a mathematician, who had not seen or heard from each other in years. The mathematician, who had an exceedingly good memory, asked the philosopher how many children he had. The philosopher replied that he had three. The mathematician then asked how old the children were. His friend, who knew how much most mathematicians enjoy puzzles, said that he would give him a number of clues to the children's ages.
The philosopher's first clue: "The product of the children's ages is 36." The mathematician immediately replied that this was insufficient information.
The philosopher's second clue: "All of the children's ages are integers; none are fractional ages, such as 1 and ½ years old." Still, the mathematician could not deduce the correct answer.
The philosopher's third clue: "The sum of the three children's ages is identical to the address of the house where we played chess together often, years ago." The mathematician still required more information.
The philosopher then gave his fourth clue: "The oldest child looks like me."
At this point, the mathematician was able to determine the ages of the three children. Here is your problem: What were the ages of the three children?

This could be the hardest problem in this book. In trying to solve it, think about the information available to the mathematician after each clue. Why was he unable to solve the problem after the first three clues, but able to solve it after the fourth?

Let's analyze the likely thought processes of the mathematician. After the first clue, he knows that if you multiply the three numbers together, they will equal 36. There are an infinite number of possible combinations; thus the mathematician cannot solve the problem at this point. After the second clue, the mathematician knows that all the ages are integers. This reduces the possibilities from an infinite number of possible solutions to the following eight:

a. $1 \times 1 \times 36$
b. $1 \times 2 \times 18$
c. $1 \times 3 \times 12$
d. $1 \times 4 \times 9$
e. $1 \times 6 \times 6$
f. $2 \times 2 \times 9$
g. $2 \times 3 \times 6$
h. $3 \times 3 \times 4$

After the second clue, however, the mathematician has no way of deciding between these possibilities (although alternative (a) seems a bit unlikely). The third clue tells the mathematician that the sum of the ages is equal to the address where they used to play chess, so the mathematician probably considers the sums of the eight possible combinations:

a. $1 + 1 + 36 = 38$
b. $1 + 2 + 18 = 21$
c. $1 + 3 + 12 = 16$
d. $1 + 4 + 9 = 14$
e. $1 + 6 + 6 = 13$
f. $2 + 2 + 9 = 13$
g. $2 + 3 + 6 = 11$
h. $3 + 3 + 4 = 10$

Even after doing this, however, the mathematician, who has an extremely good memory (which suggests that he remembers the address where they used to play chess), still cannot determine the answer. Why not? There must be more than one answer that fulfills the requirements of multiplying to 36 and adding to the address where they used to play chess. Thus, the answer must be (e) or (f). After the first three clues, however, the mathematician still has no way of choosing between the two alternatives. After the fourth clue, that the *oldest* looks like the philosopher, the mathematician learns that there is an oldest! In choice (e), there is no oldest child, since the two oldest are twins. Thus, the answer must be alternative (f)—2,2, and 9.

This problem is clearly very difficult. Yet even if you did not solve it, you should realize the potential insights that can be obtained by considering the actions and decision-making processes of the actors in the problem. We are often faced with situations in which we cannot understand how a particular circumstance arose. Process analysis suggests that we can often gain a number of insights by separately thinking about the processes that are involved. Most of us, in contrast, tend to use a rational model based on surface evidence to understand our world.

All of the heuristic-breaking tools presented up to this point have represented strategies that are likely to be counterintuitive to most readers. There are a number of other heuristic-breaking strategies that are commonly acknowledged in the creativity literature but are underused by decision makers. These strategies tend to appear obvious, but they can be very effective in enhancing creativity.

Brainstorming   Brainstorming is probably the most well-known method of idea generation. The objective is to generate the greatest number of alternative ideas from uninhibited cognition. "Free wheeling" is encouraged; nothing is held back. Initially, no idea is rejected or criticized. Any attempt to analyze, evaluate, or reject ideas is prohibited. Brainstorming breaks our tendency to quickly eliminate any solution that appears outside the boundaries of our assumptions. While brainstorming is typically presented as a group problem-solving strategy, the logic of brainstorming is clearly extendable to individual problem solving. Get all of your wildest ideas out without prejudgment.

One of the problems with brainstorming is the development of many shallow, poor-quality ideas—especially if the ideas are taken too seriously. Thus, a useful companion strategy is "reverse brainstorming," which consists of specifying everything that might be wrong with an idea. Just as brainstorming increases the likelihood of finding the hidden great idea, reverse brainstorming allows us to find the hidden flaw that renders the proposed solution useless.

The Scientific Method   In many ways, the scientific method seems to be the antithesis of creativity. It is logical. It is orderly. It tends to be vertical. Yet, for many of us it helps to identify solutions that we would never have considered. While many forms of the scientific method have been proposed, the steps generally include the following: (1) define the problem, (2) develop alternatives based on the existing information, (3) hypothesize the most likely solution, (4) gather data on the hypothesis, (5) incorporate the data into a proposed solution, (6) create an independent test of the solution, and (7) make a final determination. The scientific method leads people to follow a logical process—which may not occur based on intuitive strategies. More important, the scientific process builds in the potential to disconfirm what you thought would be true. As argued in Chapter 2, we tend to seek only anecdotal evidence that supports our position. The scientific method leads us to question exhaustively the accuracy of our ideas.

Integration   While a number of strategies have been proposed in the creativity literature for enhancing our creativity, most of them overlap with the ideas presented here. What have been presented are a set of strategies that directly attack the bases of our blocks to creativity. In addition, this chapter has argued that these prescriptions respond to the specific limits to creativity that are triggered by our heuristics and biases. These techniques are a mere sampling of heuristic-breaking tools. Other techniques have been, and should continue to be, identified. To illustrate this point, simply consider the following additions to the strategies previously presented: explore analogies, "sleep on it," produce at least two solutions, be playful, explain it to someone else, call in a consultant. There are many strategies, and we should attempt to match the strategies to the cause of our lack of creativity—namely, the assumptions that we are most prone to make. We should constantly assess which strategy is most likely to eliminate the assumptions of a particular situation.

At this point, you should be aware of the reasons that we make assumptions and are often insufficiently creative, and you should be equipped with some strategies for overcoming these barriers. But we have developed our intuitive processes over many years. How can we change to become more creative in the ways specified? First, we must be vigilant. Stay alert to situations in which (1) assumptions are likely, (2) subgoals exist, (3) you can think about the process of the situation, (4) additional ideas may exist, (5) convergent thinking seems to have occurred quickly, or (6) you are failing to "test" the designated solution. Second, actively use some or all of the strategies suggested. By incorporating these strategies into your decision-making processes, you will make them second nature. Finally, learn to evaluate your decision-making processes in order to obtain feedback on your use of creative strategies. We will continue to explore the issue of improving creativity in Chapter 6, which deals with improving judgment.

SOME CONCLUDING COMMENTS

The relevance of our assumption-breaking approach to creativity can be further understood by considering its implications in a specific domain. Because of my biases and professional background, these concluding comments will briefly consider this approach to creativity in the research process. Davis (1971) suggests that "interesting" research is developed by breaking the "assumption ground" of the reader. That is, research will be interesting (or creative) to the reader to the extent that the researcher demonstrates some piece of knowledge that contradicts the assumptions that the reader imposes on the world. Many people question the value of research that confirms what they have already assumed to be true. But clear evidence that *contradicts* what you thought was true—"*that's* interesting!" The difference between the nine-dot problem and Davis's arguments lies in the target of the assumption breaking. In the nine-dot problem, the focus of the creativity lies in breaking your assumptions, while in Davis's definition of creativity, the focus lies in breaking the assumptions of the readers to whom the work is targeted.

In a related stream of thought, Kuhn (1970) argues that science is incremental (or normal) until a revolution comes that contradicts the assumptions of a field of inquiry. Revolution formation is viewed as an unusually creative process in science and as a very rare occurrence. Further, Kuhn presents revolutions as an activity for a few lucky and gifted scientists, rather than as a teachable scientific process. While Kuhn's classic work has been a worthy development in training researchers to understand the scientific process, it may have also hindered the development of creativity. This book argues (1) that "revolutions" can be developed at varying levels of aggregation and (2) that researchers can be trained to create "revolutions" by questioning the assumptions that surround their research.

This chapter has suggested that we need to break more of our assumptions. It is also true that (like other heuristics) our assumptions have benefits in our decision-making processes. Specifically, they allow us to provide closure to a particular part of a problem and get on with solving the problem. Taken to an extreme, attempting to be infinitely creative can be counterproductive, keeping us from ever making a decision. This issue can be viewed on the following continuum:

"Normal" decision-making processes-----------Creativity-----------Absurdity

The central argument developed in this chapter is that most of us are insufficiently creative; we are too far to the left on the continuum. If we think about the research domain, most would agree that there is too much research that lacks creativity. This leads to admirable cries for more "interesting" research. Frequently, the most vocal of these critics are those who are doing research that much of the field perceives as bordering on the absurd. We argue that researchers should be aware of the continuum, and the definition of creativity in various fields of inquiry should be openly debated.

This chapter encourages a movement toward creativity, but not an overreaction that leads to absurdity. In addition, some individuals are very creative (or even absurd) in some domains, yet make too many assumptions that limit their decision-making processes in other domains (for example, the logical decision maker at work who breaks all assumptions on the weekends). I hope that this chapter has provided you with some descriptions and prescriptions that are useful for thinking about creativity and for deciding where you lie on the continuum depicted here.

SIX
MAKING RATIONAL DECISIONS IN TWO-PARTY NEGOTIATIONS

In negotiation, as in life, we tend to end up with less than our wildest dreams, but with a great deal more than is provided by the next best alternative.

Jeffrey Z. Rubin, 1983

When two or more parties need to reach a joint decision but have different preferences, they negotiate. They may not be sitting around a bargaining table; they may not be making explicit offers and counteroffers; they may even be making statements suggesting that they are on the same side. But as long as their preferences concerning the joint decision are not identical, they have to negotiate to reach a mutually agreeable outcome.

Many managerial decisions are made in conjunction with other organizational actors who have preferences different than our own. Thus, negotiation is central to organizational life. Yet, just as our individual decisions are subject to irrationalities, so, too, are negotiated, multiparty decisions—only here the opportunities for bias and error are more complex because of the multiplicity of individual judgments and potential outcomes that are involved. Negotiations can result in impasse or agreement, and when agreement is reached, better and worse outcomes can be obtained for each party and for the agreement as a whole.

While the first five chapters of this book have focused on biases and irrationalities affecting individual decision making, this chapter and the next two examine judgment in multiparty contexts. These chapters draw selectively from information presented in the first five chapters, as well as from information in the multiparty decision-making literature, including negotiation, competitive bidding, third-party intervention, group decision making, coalition behavior, social dilemmas, and competitive bidding. In Chapters 6 and 7, two-party negotiations are the focus. This chapter outlines a framework for thinking rationally in two-party negotiation contexts. Chapter 7 uses this framework to examine how our individual biases and heuristics are manifested in the negotiation context. It also provides new information on cognitive biases that are created by the competitive environment. In Chapter 8, we move beyond the face-to-face, two-party negotiation context of Chapters 6 and 7 to consider more complex, multiparty competitive environments.

The goals of this chapter are to give you a framework for thinking about two-party negotiations and to introduce prescriptive suggestions for improving decision making within this context. First, this chapter seeks to improve the quality of your outcomes as the "focal" negotiator. Second, this chapter seeks to improve the total outcomes for all parties and, hence, the effectiveness to society in dealing with conflict. This is achieved by learning how to reduce the likelihood of impasse when it is in the interest of all parties for a settlement to be reached and by expanding the total range of benefits that both parties receive.

Like the topic of decision making, the topic of negotiation has been of increasing interest during the 1980s. One reason for this is the expectation that we can provide useful prescriptions to make negotiators more successful. As the next three chapters highlight, it is my contention that, indeed, we can!

The earliest attempts to provide prescriptive advice to negotiators were made by economists. The most well-developed component of this economic school of thought is game theory. In game theory, mathematical models are developed to analyze the outcomes that will emerge in multiparty decision-making contexts if all parties act rationally. To analyze a game, specific conditions are outlined that define how decisions are to be made—for example, the order in which players get to choose their moves—and utility measures of outcomes for each player are attached to *every* possible combination of player moves. The actual analysis focuses on predicting whether or not an agreement will be reached, and if one is reached, what the specific nature of that agreement will be. The advantage of game theory is that, given absolute rationality, it provides the most precise prescriptive advice available to the negotiator. The disadvantages of game theory are twofold. First, it relies upon being able to completely describe all options and associated outcomes for every possible combination of moves in a given situation—a tedious task at its best, infinitely complex at its worst. Second, it requires that *all* players act consistently rationally. Yet, as we have seen in earlier chapters, individuals often behave irrationally in systematically predictable ways that are not easily captured within rational analyses.

A DECISION ANALYTIC APPROACH TO NEGOTIATIONS

As an alternative to game theoretical analyses of negotiations that take place in a world of "ultrasmart, impeccably rational, supersmart people," Raiffa (1982) has developed a **decision analytic approach** to negotiations—an approach more appropriate to how "erring folks like you and me actually behave" rather than "how we should behave if we were smarter, thought harder, were more consistent, were all knowing" (p. 21). Raiffa's decision analytic approach focuses on giving the best available advice to negotiators involved in real conflict with real people. His goal is to provide guidance for you as the focal negotiator given the most likely profile of the expected behavior of the other party. Thus, Raiffa's approach is prescriptive from the point of view of the party receiving advice but descriptive from the point of view of the competing party.

Raiffa's approach offers an excellent framework for approaching negotiations. The analytical structure of this approach is based upon three key sets of information. These include the assessment of:

- Each party's alternative to a negotiated agreement
- Each party's set of interests
- The relative importance of each party's interests

Together, these three sets of information determine the structure of the negotiation game (Sebenius, 1989).

Alternatives to a Negotiated Agreement Before we begin any important negotiation, we should consider what we will do if no agreement is reached. That is, what is our *best alternative to a negotiated agreement*, or BATNA (Fisher and Ury, 1981)? Why is this important? Because the subjective expected utility of a negotiator's BATNA provides a lower bound for determining the minimum outcome we require of a negotiated agreement. Any negotiated agreement that provides more value to us than our BATNA does is preferred over impasse; any negotiated agreement that provides less is declined. This assessment logically determines the negotiator's **reservation point** (also called an **indifference point**)—the point at which the negotiator is indifferent between a negotiated agreement and impasse.

Alternatives to agreement take a variety of forms. For example, rather than buy a specific new car, you may decide to continue to use mass transit. Alternatively, your BATNA may be to buy the same car from another dealership at a price that you have been offered in writing. Notice that in the second situation, it is far easier to determine your reservation price. However, whether you have an easy-to-assess reservation price, or whether it seems like you're comparing apples and oranges, you should always determine your BATNA and your best estimate of the value of your opponent's BATNA. While this analysis may be difficult, this assessment provides a better basis for negotiation than your intuitive assessments without preparation. Often the critical issue comes down to a decision of whether or not to "walk" when you are in the actual negotiation situation.

The Interests of the Parties To analyze a negotiation, it is necessary to identify all of the interests of the parties. Negotiators are not always fully aware of their interests. How can this be? There is a difference between the parties' underlying interests and their stated positions. **Positions** are the claimed requirements that parties demand from the other side. **Interests** are ancillary or underlying issues behind these positions that could matter to the negotiators if they were made aware of them. As the following sections highlight, sometimes a focus on deeper interests can identify a more useful set of concerns to the parties and form the basis of a more reasonable bargaining platform.

Consider the story of two sisters fighting over an orange (Fisher and Ury, 1981; Follett, 1940). It is the last orange, and each sister wants it. After arguing for several minutes, they finally agree to a compromise and split the orange in half. While the settlement seems reasonable, neither sister is pleased. One sister needed the peel of a full orange to make a cake, and the other sister wanted to make orange juice. One half of an orange does not truly satisfy either sister's interests. A better agreement would have given the peel to one sister and the inside to the other. Yet, because the sisters were too focused on their stated positions of who should get the last orange, they failed to recognize that their true interests were not incompatible and could easily be met.

The Relative Importance of Each Party's Interests Even when we are aware of our interests, we may not have thought through the relative importance of each interest. To be fully prepared to negotiate, we must be aware of how important each issue is to us. The best agreements are reached by trading off relatively less important issues for relatively more important issues. For example, in negotiating a new job offer, it may be more important to you to get more comprehensive benefits than to get an extra three days of personal time. Or you may be more interested in postponing your start date in exchange for fewer vacation days during your first year. Whatever your preferences, you must be prepared ahead of time to recognize which tradeoffs are more and less attractive to you.

Summary Together, these three pieces of information (each party's alternative to a negotiated agreement, each party's set of interests, and the relative importance of each party's interests) provide the building blocks for thinking analytically about a negotiation, and a negotiator should assess this information before entering any important bargaining situation. With this information in hand, the negotiator is prepared for the two primary tasks of negotiation:

- **Integration**—enlargement of the pie of available resources
- **Distribution**—claiming of the pie

We will now discuss both the distributive and integrative elements of negotiation.

DISTRIBUTION IN NEGOTIATION

Consider the following example:

An MBA from a very prestigious school, with a number of unique talents, is being recruited for a highly specialized position. The organization and the employee have agreed on all issues except salary. The organization has offered $40,000, and the employee has counteroffered at $50,000. Both sides believe that they have made fair offers. However, both sides would very much like to see an agreement reached. The student, while not verbalizing this information, would be willing to take any offer over $43,000 rather than lose the offer. The organization, while not verbalizing this information, would be willing to pay up to $47,000 rather than lose the candidate.

Most recent discussions of the positions of parties in negotiations have used Walton and McKersie's (1965) concept of the "bargaining zone." A simplified view of the bargaining zone concept is diagrammed here to describe the recruitment problem:

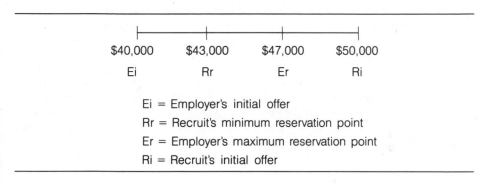

The bargaining zone framework assumes that each party has some reservation point below (or above) which the negotiator would prefer impasse to settlement at that level. These points are represented by the two reservation points in the diagram. Notice that the zone between the two initial offers and their corresponding reservation points overlap. Thus, there are a set of resolutions that both parties would prefer over impasse (in this case, all points between $43,000 and $47,000). This area is known as a positive bargaining zone. When a positive bargaining zone exists, a rational model of negotiation would dictate that the negotiators should reach a settlement—it is the rational thing to do. When the reservation points of the two parties do not overlap, a negative bargaining zone is said to exist. If a negative bargaining zone exists, no resolution should be possible, since there are no settlements that are acceptable to both parties.

Many people find the notion of a bargaining zone to be counterintuitive. After participating in a variety of negotiations during their lives, they conclude that the reservation points of parties never overlap; they simply meet at the point of agreement. This thinking is incorrect. In fact, at the point of agreement, when both parties choose a settlement in comparison to impasse, their actual reservation points are overlapping. This settlement point represents only one of what are often many points within the bargaining zone.

Returning to the previously described recruiting example, we can see that the bargaining zone consists of the range between $43,000 and $47,000. If the employer would convince the recruit that an offer of $43,100 was final, we know the recruit would accept the offer, and the firm would be minimizing its settlement costs. Similarly, if the recruit could convince the employer that $46,900 was the lowest salary that she would accept, we know the employer would accept this figure, and the recruit would be maximizing her settlement benefit. Thus, one of the key skills of negotiation is to determine the other party's reservation point and to aim for a resolution barely acceptable to the other party. This is a delicate process, however. If one or more of the parties misjudge the situation, they may rigidly demand a bargain that is outside the other party's reservation point, and no bargain will be achieved (such would be the case if, for example, the recruit holds to a demand of $46,000 and the employer holds to the offer of $44,000—both believing that the other side will "cave in"). When this behavior occurs, the parties act in ways that prohibit the rational choice of finding a solution within the positive bargaining zone. As Ben Franklin observed:

> Trades [like an employment agreement] would not take place unless it were advantageous to the parties concerned. Of course, it is better to strike as good a bargain as one's bargaining position permits. The worst outcome is when, by overreaching greed, no bargain is struck, and a trade that could have been advantageous to both parties does not come off at all (Raiffa, 1982).

INTEGRATION IN NEGOTIATION

The foregoing analysis dealt with negotiation in a situation in which a single issue (salary) was disputed. In contrast, many negotiations consists of several disputed issues. For example, consider the Camp David talks in 1978 (documented in Pruitt and Rubin [1985]):

> Egypt and Israel tried to negotiate the control of the Sinai Peninsula, a situation in which it appeared that the two sides had directly opposing goals. Egypt wanted the return of the Sinai in its entirety, while Israel, which had occupied the territory since the 1967 war, refused to return this land. Efforts at compromise failed. Neither side found the proposal of splitting the Sinai acceptable.

An initial examination of this conflict suggests that a negative bargaining zone existed and that a negotiated resolution would not be possible. That is, if we mapped the *positions* of the parties onto a single scale, the reservation points would not overlap, and an impasse would be reached.

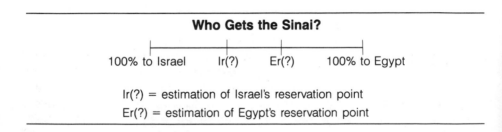

Who Gets the Sinai?

100% to Israel   Ir(?)   Er(?)   100% to Egypt

Ir(?) = estimation of Israel's reservation point
Er(?) = estimation of Egypt's reservation point

In contrast to this pessimistic and false prediction, the existence of multiple issues and the development of **integrative bargaining** explains the resolution that eventually developed at Camp David.

As the Camp David negotiations continued, it became clear that while the *positions* of Egypt and Israel were incompatible, the *interests* of the two countries were compatible. Israel's underlying interest was security from land or air attack. Egypt was primarily interested in sovereignty over land which was part of Egypt for thousands of years. What emerged was the existence of two real issues, instead of one, with differential importance to the two parties: sovereignty and military protection. The solution that emerged traded of these issues. The agreement called for Israel to return the Sinai in exchange for assurances of a demilitarized zone and new Israeli air bases.

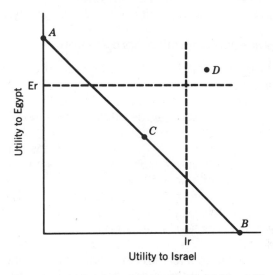

Figure 6.1   Integrating Interests in the Israel-Egypt Dispute.

To analyze this agreement, examine the more complex diagram presented in Figure 6.1. The utility of an agreement to Israel is represented on the horizontal axis, and the utility of an agreement to Egypt is represented on the vertical axis. Point A represents the solution of giving the land and total control to Egypt. Notice that this solution would be completely acceptable to Egypt and completely unacceptable to Israel. Point B represents the solution of Israel keeping the land and maintaining control over the land. This solution would be completely acceptable to Israel and completely unacceptable to Egypt. Point C represents a straight compromise—giving each party control over half of the land. As illustrated in the bargaining zone diagram, this solution fails to meet the reservation points of either Israel or Egypt. It does not give Egypt sovereignty over the Sinai, and it does not give Israel sufficient security guarantees. Point D (the eventual resolution), however, suggests a redefinition of the bargaining zone. In Figure 6.1, a positive bargaining zone exists to the extent that there are solutions that achieve the reservation points of both parties along the dimensions of sovereignty and security. The upper right-hand part of the figure beyond the dotted lines represents the reservation points of the two parties.

What appears to have occurred in the Camp David accords is that the two parties realized the existence of a positive bargaining zone by considering the *interests* of the parties, not just the stated positions. With these interests in hand, it was possible to develop an integrative solution by trading off the issue that each country cared less about for the issue that each country cared more about. Point D allowed both sides to obtain their objectives, while being compatible with the needs of the other party. Israel's utility was determined primarily by the degree to which it obtained security, while Egypt's utility was determined primarily by the degree to which it obtained sovereignty over the land.

The Development of Integrative Agreements

As the foregoing example indicates, integrative behavior can increase the likelihood of a negotiated compromise and improve outcomes for both parties. Integrative solutions to conflicts reconcile the parties' interests to yield higher joint benefit than distributive agreements (Pruitt, 1983). Strictly distributive agreements occur when two parties bargain along a stated dimension in a search for some middle ground. This approach leads to procedures for dividing a fixed pie of resources (for example, "What percentage of the Sinai will be held by Israel and Egypt?" or "Who should get the orange?"). When integrative potential exists, integrative behavior results in greater joint outcomes to the two parties. This approach focuses on how the parties can make tradeoffs or jointly solve problems to the mutual benefit of both parties ("How can the Sinai situation be resolved to maximize the joint utility of Israel and Egypt?" or "How can the orange be divided to maximize the joint benefit of the two sisters?").

Just as we discussed in Chapter 5 that individuals often make assumptions that create barriers to developing creative individual problem solving, these barriers also exist in the multiparty negotiation context. In this sense, the search for integrative bargains can be viewed as the search for creative solutions that lie outside distributive assumptions. As Pruitt (1983) writes:

> Integrative agreements sometimes make use of known alternatives, whose joint value becomes apparent during the controversy. But more often they involve the development of novel alternatives. Hence, it is proper to say that they usually emerge from creative problem solving. Integrative alternatives (those that form the basis for integrative agreements) can be devised by either party separately, by the two of them in joint sessions, or by a third party such as a mediator.

In the following paragraphs, we will be reviewing five strategies that have been developed by Pruitt (1983) for creating integrative agreements. As a context for examining these strategies, consider the following managerial situation:

ABC, Inc., a consumer-oriented manufacturer, has identified an outstanding recruit from a high-caliber competitor. In fact, two departments are interested in hiring this recruit: marketing and sales. Both departments desire this individual's skills as a systems analyst and value her background in consumer goods. Like many organizations, ABC is rapidly computerizing its internal systems. However, the number of individuals trained in both the nature of the industry and computer systems is limited. The immediate problem concerns how to deal internally with the mutual desire of the two departments to hire this recruit. How should the two departments deal with their conflict? (Before continuing to read, identify as many possible solutions as you can.)

From a distributive perspective, a couple of obvious solutions exist. The two departments could use a free-market approach and compete against each other as separate entities in trying to hire the recruit. However, ABC is likely to end up paying more than necessary to hire the recruit, and the process is likely to seem peculiar to her. Another obvious alternative is to compromise. One example would be to split the recruit's time, 50 percent in marketing and 50 percent in sales. This solution leads to a number of administrative problems, and at least one of the departments is likely to feel that 50 percent of the time is insufficient for its objectives. Note that both of these solutions *assume* that the two departments must split a fixed resource. The following paragraphs explore potential integrative solutions that are derived from Pruitt's five alternative strategies.

1. Obtaining Added Resources   The recruiting problem, like many conflicts, results from a resource shortage. One approach to integrating the interests of two parties when the conflict arises due to resource shortages is to expand the available resources. Namely, can the departments use similar recruiting procedures to identify another recruit? If so, the firm can hire two similar individuals, allowing each department to achieve its objective.

This solution lies outside the immediate domain of the conflict. It involves changing the salient question from "How do we allocate this recruit?" to "How do we increase the number of qualified recruits?" Obtaining added resources is a useful strategy when additional resources may exist but premature assumptions about the conflict are blocking the search for these added resources. In addition, this strategy is only viable when the parties' interests are not mutually exclusive. In our example, there is nothing about the marketing department's interest in hiring a consumer-oriented systems analyst that conflicts with the sales department's interests. In many conflicts, however, parties do have mutually exclusive interests. In these cases, obtaining added resources is unlikely to be a successful integrative strategy.

2. Trading Issues   Trading issues consists of having each party concede on low-priority issues in exchange for concessions on higher-priority issues. Each party gets the part of the agreement that it finds to be most important.

In the recruiting example, let's assume that the computerization issues facing both the sales and marketing department are twofold: (1) the long-term need to hire qualified computer professionals and (2) the immediate need to handle its share of the work in a merger of the sales and marketing databases for more effective analyses by both departments. The recruit would be valuable to either department. However, it may be that the primary interests of the two parties are different. For example, the marketing department may be primarily concerned with developing a high-quality group of computer professionals, while sales is primarily interested in handling the immediate database merger with maximum efficiency. In this case, an agreement could be reached that called for the marketing department to hire the recruit and offer to take full responsibility for the database merger, thus reducing the workload of the sales group.

Trading issues can also be facilitated by refocusing the kinds of questions asked by the parties. Appropriate questions would include: Do the parties have different underlying interests? If so, which issues are most important to marketing? Which are most important to sales? Trading issues is a very effective strategy when the parties are blocked by a surface-level statement of the position(s) being disputed. It is also a very effective strategy when the dispute is defined as a multi-issue dispute. To develop issue-trading solutions, it is necessary to fully explore information about the interests of the parties so that exchangeable concessions can be identified.

3. Providing Nonspecific Compensation   In nonspecific compensation, one party gets what it wants and the other party is paid on some *unrelated* issue. Compensation is defined as nonspecific when the "unrelated" issue is external to the main issue being negotiated. For example, assume that the sales and marketing departments had also been arguing about another issue unrelated to the new recruit—for example, which department should pay for acquiring a new database that is relevant for both sales and marketing. Nonspecific compensation might consist of an agreement whereby the two departments agree that the sales department hires the recruit and also agrees to pay the entire bill for acquiring the mutually desired database.

Providing nonspecific compensation is conceptually very similar to trading issues. Under trading issues, two or more issues *within* the domain of the conflict are traded. Under nonspecific compensation, additional issues are brought into the conflict to create the potential to trade issues. Thus, nonspecific compensation can be viewed as trading issues within a broader definition of the conflict.

Nonspecific compensation is also likely to be affected by the kinds of questions asked by the two parties. Useful questions to ask include: What could each party supply to the other party in exchange for favorable terms on the focal issue (for example, the recruit)? How much does each side value the recruit? How much does each side value the additional issues that can be redefined as part of the conflict? Like trading issues, the development of agreements using the nonspecific compensation strategy requires the full exploration of information about the interests of the parties so that exchangeable concessions can be identified.

4. Cost Cutting The cost-cutting strategy calls for one party to get what it wants and for the other party to have its costs associated with the concession reduced or eliminated. The joint benefits are increased not because the party that achieves its focal demand changes its position, but because the conceding party suffers less. Assume that the recruit is a highly priced, highly skilled individual. In addition, assume that the marketing department really values the high level of skill, but the sales department simply needs added personnel with computer skills. An integrative agreement could be arranged that calls for marketing to hire the recruit and to agree to transfer a lower, but adequately skilled, employee to the sales department.

Cost cutting often takes the form of specific compensation, whereby the party who makes the major concession receives something in return that satisfies the precise goals that were frustrated by the concession. Cost cutting is also conceptually similar to trading issues in terms of identifying some tradeoff. However, it is a unique strategy because it concentrates on reducing or eliminating any costs to the conceding party that result from the other party's achieving its objectives.

Like previous strategies, cost cutting is likely to be affected by the kinds of questions asked by the two parties. Useful questions to ask include: What costs would be imposed on sales if marketing hired the recruit (or vice versa)? The development of cost-cutting solutions necessitates an understanding of the costs incurred by each party if the other party achieves its objectives. Like trading issues, the development of agreements using cost cutting requires a full exploration of information about the interests of the parties to identify the salient costs to each side.

5. Bridging Bridging involves the development of a new option that satisfies the most important interests underlying the demands of both parties. Under bridging, neither side achieves its initially stated objective; rather, the parties search for new, creative solutions that are hidden by the original statement of the conflict. For example, assume that both sales and marketing want the following from hiring the recruit: (1) some of the skills of the employee; (2) the ability to continue to use these skills over an extended period of time; and (3) completion of the department's share of the work merging the sales and marketing databases. One bridging solution would consist of hiring the recruit into a staff position in the MIS (Management Information Systems) department with the understanding that the person would initially be assigned to the sales/marketing database merger and that she would then continue to be available for special projects to both sales and marketing.

Bridging involves a reformulation of the conflict by assessing a wider variety of potential solutions that can fulfill the underlying interests of both parties in the focal conflict. Again, bridging necessitates a clear understanding of the underlying interests of the two parties. The search for bridging solutions consists of removing the parties from the immediate definition of the conflict, identifying the underlying interests of the parties, and brainstorming for a variety of potential solutions that can bridge these interests.

Summary   Each of Pruitt's five strategies for identifying integrative agreements requires negotiators to break out of the existing definitions of the conflict. Typically, either side or a third party can use these strategies to develop alternatives that integrate the interests of the parties. Each of these strategies, when successful, results in resolutions of higher joint benefit than simple distributive compromises. While all of Pruitt's strategies for developing integrative agreements are viable, the three that focus on creating mutually beneficial trades—trading issues, nonspecific compensation, and cost cutting—are the most commonly available techniques for increasing the size of the pie of resources to be distributed within the existing context of the situation. Obtaining additional resources expands the agreement context, and bridging reformulates that context to find a new bargaining zone.

AN EXTENDED EXAMPLE OF THINKING RATIONALLY IN NEGOTIATION: THE CASE OF EL-TEK

Virtually all negotiations involve the distribution of outcomes. However, negotiators often overlook the potential for integration. In this section, we develop an example that can be solved distributively and then show the benefit of adding an integrative perspective. Consider the following situation (adapted from Bazerman and Brett's (1988) "El-Tek" simulation):

> El-Tek is a large conglomerate in the electrical industry with sales of over $3.1 billion. El-Tek is a decentralized, product-centered organization, in which the various divisions of the firm are expected to operate autonomously and are evaluated based on their divisional performance. Divisions are chartered to sell their products to specific customer groups outside the company in order to preclude competition among the divisions on sales to external customers.
>
> Recently, the Audio Division (AD) developed a new magnetic material called Z-25. Their corporate charter prevents them from selling the discovery outside the company. Nevertheless, the product is still valuable to AD. They can sell the magnetic material within the corporation and also use this magnet to competitively increase the quality of their own audio products. AD has assessed that under this scenario they would earn $5 million from the magnet over an estimated two-year life. This figure includes $1.75 million from selling magnets internally to El-Tek and $3.25 million from product improvements to their audio components that would not be available to their competitors.
>
> While this $5 million is attractive to AD and El-Tek, the Magnetic Division (MD) could generate far more income for El-Tek if it sold this magnet. MD has much better manufacturing capabilities and could sell the magnet to a vast outside market. In fact, MD projects that it could earn $14 million over the same two-year period from this magnetic material. Without this magnetic material, MD would be using their manufacturing and selling capabilities on an alternative product that is only expected to yield a profit of $4 million.

The parties have agreed to get together to discuss the possibility of AD selling the magnet rights to MD. Both parties already have target prices and reservation points in mind. With this information, the El-Tek situation can be analyzed using the bargaining zone concept diagrammed here:

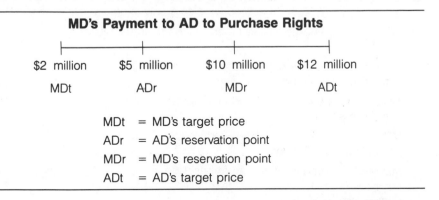

MD's Payment to AD to Purchase Rights

$2 million	$5 million	$10 million	$12 million
MDt	ADr	MDr	ADt

MDt = MD's target price
ADr = AD's reservation point
MDr = MD's reservation point
ADt = AD's target price

Analysis Most people enter into negotiations with some idea of what their target outcomes are. However, most negotiators fail to think hard enough about their reservation prices and the reservation prices of the other negotiators, which are determined by evaluating both parties' BATNAs. In this example, AD can make $5 million without reaching an agreement with MD. MD can make $4 million without the magnet and thus is indifferent between this option and paying AD $10 million (of the $14 million) for the magnet rights. Note that the two reservation points overlap (at all points between $5 million and $10 million), and there is a positive bargaining zone. Note further that any agreement within the bargaining zone creates a joint surplus of $5 million. (Without the trade taking place, AD can earn $5 million and MD can earn $4 million, for a total of $9 million. By completing a trade, they have a total of $14 million to divide.) Thus, there is a range of distributive agreements that can be very profitable for both sides.

Note, however, that this analysis limits the negotiation to only one issue, namely the distribution of money, and one-issue negotiations are distributive by definition. If additional issues are found or added, there is the potential to increase the amount of total benefit available to the parties. Remember that one of the AD's benefits of not selling the product to MD is that they can obtain a competitive advantage by having a product improvement that is unavailable to their competitors. Before going into the negotiation, it might be very useful for AD to assess the value of adding restrictions to outside sales of the magnet by MD.

For example, AD could create the information table pictured in Table 6.1, which evaluates the value of various outcomes. The first two outcomes highlight the possible one-issue distributive results. Outcome 1 shows the $5 million dollar profit by keeping the product. Outcome 2 shows that if AD simply trans-

Table 6.1 Audio Division Negotiating Team

Outcome	Lifetime Expected Net Profit to AD
1. AD produces Z-25 and the product is sold only internally.	$5,000,000
2. MD produces and no limitations are put on their distribution efforts.	P
3. MD produces and is prohibited from selling to AD competitors for 6 months.	$2,000,000 + P
4. MD produces and is prohibited from selling to any El-Tek competitors for 6 months.	$2,100,000 + P
5. MD produces and is prohibited from selling to AD competitors for 12 months.	$2,500,000 + P
6. MD produces and is prohibited from selling to AD competitors for 12 months and from selling to other El-Tek competitors for 6 months.	$2,600,000 + P
7. MD produces and is prohibited from selling to any El-Tek competitors for 12 months.	$2,700,000 + P
8. MD produces and is prohibited from selling to AD competitors for 20 months.	$2,900,000 + P
9. MD produces and is prohibited from selling to AD competitors for 20 months and from selling to other El-Tek competitors for 6 months.	$3,000,000 + P
10. MD produces and is prohibited from selling to AD competitors for 20 months and from selling to other El-Tek competitors for 12 months.	$3,100,000 + P
11. MD produces and is prohibited from selling to any El-Tek competitors for 20 months.	$3,200,000 + P

fers the product to MD, AD's profit will be equal to the negotiated transfer price P. The remaining outcomes incorporate the sales restriction issue on two levels. These include restricting sales to AD's direct competitors and restricting sales to all El-Tek competitors in general. Each outcome is evaluated in monetary terms that include the expected net profit of the specified restrictions, in addition to the negotiated transfer price P. For example, outcome 3 includes the prohibition of sales to AD competitors only for 6 months and is expected to yield AD $2 million plus the transfer price. Compare this to outcome 6, wherein sales are restricted to AD direct competitors for 12 months and all El-Tek competitors for 6 months. This option is estimated to be worth $2.6 million plus the transfer price. In reviewing each of the outcomes, note that AD is more concerned with prohibiting sales to AD competitors than to El-Tek competitors. (Compare outcomes 5 and 6, wherein the marginal value of adding a 6-month restriction to all El-Tek competitors yields only an additional $100,000.) Note also that the value of this protection has diminishing returns due to obtaining product leadership in a relatively short period of time. (Compare outcomes 3 and 5, wherein the first 6 months of protection from AD direct competitors are worth $2 million, but the next 6 months add only $500,000 in value.)

Conversely, MD can also assess the costs of having their sales restricted in the same manner. These estimates are shown in Table 6.2; please take a moment to review it. Finally, Table 6.3 combines the assessments of AD and MD from Tables 6.1 and 6.2. This combination allows us to look at how three underlying issues—transfer price, AD competitor protection, and El-Tek competitor protection—collectively affect the joint surplus available to the parties. Let's look at this table in more detail.

First, note that all of the outcomes that include protection for all El-Tek competitors (outcomes 4, 6, 7, 9, 10, and 11) decrease the joint gain available from this product compared to similar outcomes that restrict to only AD com-

Table 6.2 Magnetic Division Negotiating Team

Outcome	Lifetime Expected Net Profit to AD
1. AD produces Z-25 and the product is sold only internally.	$4,000,000
2. MD produces and no limitations are put on their distribution efforts.	$14,000,000 − P
3. MD produces and is prohibited from selling to AD competitors for 6 months.	$13,100,000 − P
4. MD produces and is prohibited from selling to any El-Tek competitors for 6 months.	$10,400,000 − P
5. MD produces and is prohibited from selling to AD competitors for 12 months.	$12,200,000 − P
6. MD produces and is prohibited from selling to AD competitors for 12 months and from selling to other El-Tek competitors for 6 months.	$9,500,000 − P
7. MD produces and is prohibited from selling to any El-Tek competitors for 12 months.	$6,800,000 − P
8. MD produces and is prohibited from selling to AD competitors for 20 months.	$11,000,000 − P
9. MD produces and is prohibited from selling to AD competitors for 20 months and from selling to other El-Tek competitors for 6 months.	$8,300,000 − P
10. MD produces and is prohibited from selling to AD competitors for 20 months and from selling to other El-Tek competitors for 12 months.	$5,600,000 − P
11. MD produces and is prohibited from selling to any El-Tek competitors for 20 months.	$2,000,000 − P

Table 6.3 Joint Profit Resolutions (in millions)

Outcome	AD	MD	AD + MD
1. AD produces and sells only internally.	5.0	4.0	9.0
2. MD produces; AD limit equals 0 months and other limit equals 0 months.	P	14.0 − P	14.0
3. MD produces; AD limit equals 6 months and other limit equals 0 months.	2.0 + P	13.1 − P	15.1
4. MD produces; AD limit equals 6 months and other limit equals 6 months.	2.1 + P	10.4 − P	12.5
5. MD produces; AD limit equals 12 months and other limit equals 0 months.	2.5 + P	12.2 − P	14.7
6. MD produces; AD limit equals 12 months and other limit equals 6 months.	2.6 + P	9.5 − P	12.1
7. MD produces; AD limit equals 12 months and other limit equals 12 months	2.7 + P	6.8 − P	9.5
8. MD produces; AD limit equals 20 months and other limit equals 0 months.	2.9 + P	11.0 − P	13.9
9. MD produces; AD limit equals 20 months and other limit equals 6 months.	3.0 + P	8.3 − P	11.3
10. MD produces; AD limit equals 20 months and other limit equals 12 months.	3.1 + P	5.6 − P	8.7
11. MD produces; AD limit equals 20 months and other limit equals 20 months.	3.2 + P	2.0 − P	5.2

petitors (outcomes 3, 5, and 8). Thus, collectively the two parties are better off not creating restrictions regarding other El-Tek competitors. Further, the highest joint benefit is achieved when the magnet is transferred and MD is restricted from selling to AD's competitors for 6 months. While this reduces MD's profits (before paying AD) from $14 million to $13.1 million compared to outcome 2, AD's profit increases by $2 million—resulting in an additional $1.1 million of profit to divide. This profit is created by the fact that AD gains more from the 6-month restriction than MD loses. However, additional protection beyond 6 months decreases the joint profit, since additional protection (for example, outcome 5) costs MD more than it benefits AD.

A comparison of the distributive and integrative analyses of El-Tek is shown in Figure 6.2. This diagram plots AD's profit on the vertical axis and MD's profit on the horizontal axis. Lines A and B are the reservation prices that we discussed earlier. Point X is the no-agreement alternative of AD keeping the magnet. 45-degree lines can be drawn for the various outcomes (2 through 11) that show the possible agreements on the outcomes after P is negotiated. For example, the points on the outcome 2 line (C) yield profit of $14 million, while all the points on the outcome 3 line (D) yield profit of $15.1 million. (Of course, more lines can be drawn for all the possible settlements.)

It can be seen that it is in the best interest of both negotiators to reach an agreement on the most northeasterly line. As mentioned earlier, one of the key skills of negotiation is to determine the other party's reservation point and aim for a resolution that is marginally acceptable to the other party based on that value. Thus, AD prefers being as close to MD's reservation price as possible on this line, and MD prefers being as close to AD's reservation price as possible. The task facing the negotiators is to simultaneously attempt to create an integrative agreement, while doing as well as possible on the distributive dimension. Negotiators often make a mistake by focusing on one dimension or the other, rather than thinking about these dimensions of negotiation simultaneously.

When I have students simulate the El-Tek negotiation, a common question from someone who did very well on a less than fully integrative agreement (for example, someone playing the role of AD, who received a payment of $9.5

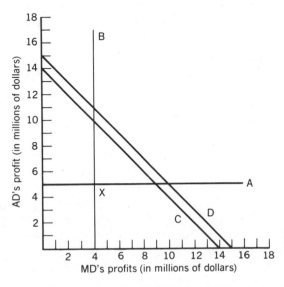

Figure 6.2 The El-Tek negotiation

million out of the $14 million on an outcome 2 agreement) is: "Why shouldn't I be happy with this agreement?" In fact, this agreement is typically one of the better outcomes for someone playing the role of AD. The answer is that although this is a fine agreement for AD, if MD took this agreement, MD could also have accepted an agreement that called for 6 months' protection and a payment of $8.3 million. This would have given MD $4.8 million (rather than $4.5 million) and would have given AD $10.3 million (rather than $9.5 million), and both parties would be better off!

An agreement is defined as pareto efficient when there is no other agreement that would render both parties better off or one party better off while keeping the second party at the same level. Anytime you have a pareto-inefficient agreement, there exists an alternative agreement to which the parties can move that would create greater joint benefit. In the El-Tek case, the set of outcome 3 agreements between the two parties' reservation prices represents the pareto-efficient frontier. As the foregoing example illustrates, there is also a distributive issue concerning how to share the additional joint benefit.

How to Get the Information
to Create Integrative Agreements

The previous section focused on the elements of an integrative analysis assuming full knowledge of information for both parties. However, negotiators typically have access to only their own information. How can negotiators create an integrative agreement when they do not have the information from the other side? We will now review five strategies for collecting that information. No one strategy is guaranteed to work in a specific situation. Collectively, however, these strategies increase the likelihood of reaching a pareto-efficient agreement.

Build Trust and Share Information   The easiest way to find the best integrative agreement in the El-Tek case is to combine information with your opponent. With this information, it becomes a simple arithmetic task to determine the outcome that maximizes joint benefit. Unfortunately, this is easier said than done. We often do not trust the other side in a negotiation, because we believe that giving away information could hurt us on the distributive dimension. However, consider this problem from El-Tek's overall perspective. For the president of El-Tek, an integrative approach is ideal because it guarantees that the divisions will not jeopardize corporate profitability by focusing on the distributive dimension. Even between organizations, firms often develop fully trusting relationships based on kinship, a close subculture, or years of working together. In these cases, the parties learn that they are better off in the long run by creating fully integrative agreements. The extra joint benefit of an integrative approach more than offsets the one-time gain that a party might achieve on a particular transaction through more distributive tactics.

One way to approach information sharing is to discuss a distribution rule in advance of sharing information. If AD fears that they will be at a competitive disadvantage if MD knows that they can earn only $5 million on their own, the parties could agree upon how to divide any surplus before sharing confidential information. For example, they might agree that AD gets 60 percent of any surplus, and MD gets 40 percent. With this understanding, they can then share information to create the optimal integrative agreement. To the extent that less than full trust exists for the information-sharing aspect of this process, the parties could also agree to an independent party's review of all the financial assessments (this could be done by the corporate controller).

Ask Questions   Full information sharing will not always be to your advantage. For example, you may have some information that *will* work against you if the other party obtains it. In addition, the other party is often unwilling to fully disclose confidential information. What do you do next? Ask lots of questions! Most people have a tendency to see negotiating primarily as an opportunity to influence the other party. As a result, most of us do more talking than listening. Even when the other side is talking, we concentrate on what we are going to say next rather than listening for new information. This persuasion process is the basis of most sales training and is effective when the other party is collecting information from you. In negotiations, however, the other party already knows its interests, but you need to understand them better in order to negotiate effectively.

One strategy to collect this information is to focus on question asking and active listening. "MD, how much would you lose if you didn't sell to our competitors?" "How much would a 6-month restriction cost you?" "How much would a 12-month restriction cost you?" They may not answer these questions. However, they are more likely to answer the questions if you ask them than if you do not. Before you start the negotiation, assess what information you need from the other side, then ask the questions necessary to collect this information.

Give Away Some Information   You do not have a trusting atmosphere, and they are not answering your questions in any useful way. What do you do next? Give away some information! Do not tell them your BATNA—this will only anchor what you will get out of the negotiation. Rather, tell them some information of comparatively minor importance. As AD, tell MD that restricting sales to your competitors is more important in the early months than in the later months. You have not given away any information that they can use unilaterally against you, and you may open up a dialogue. Behaviors in negotiation are often reciprocated (Lewicki and Litterer, 1985). When you scream at people, they tend to scream back. When you apologize to a negotiation opponent, they tend to reciprocate. And when you give them some information, they tend to return some information. This strategy can create the information sharing necessary to create mutually beneficial agreements.

Make Multiple Offers Simultaneously   Many negotiators try to put an offer on the table early to anchor the discussion. Unfortunately, this offer is often made before the negotiator knows enough to make a fully integrative offer. Because the effect of anchoring is so strong, you should actively collect information before putting an offer on the table. In some cases, you may still not have enough information by the time it is necessary to extend an offer. When this happens, do not present only one offer; present several. Most of us put one offer on the table, and when it is turned down, we know little more than we did before we made the offer. If we had presented several alternatives, we might have learned more.

Consider the following: As AD, you offer MD the transfer of the magnet for $9 million with no restrictions, or for $7 million with a 6-month restriction to AD competitors, or for $6.5 million with a 12-month restriction to AD competitors. MD refuses all of these proposals. Now you ask which of these proposals is closest to being acceptable. MD evaluates the proposals according to Table 6.2 and sees that the proposals provide a net profit of $5 million, $6.1 million, and $5.7 million, respectively. MD answers that, of these unacceptable proposals, the second one is least unreasonable. As AD, you now have more information to work with in forming a mutually beneficial agreement. Note that all three proposals by AD were equally valuable to AD, and AD did not give away anything that would not be given away by making only one offer. By making multiple offers, AD appears more flexible and collects valuable information.

Search for Post-settlement Settlements Raiffa (1985) suggests that after negotiators have found a mutually acceptable agreement, they should employ a third party to help them search for a pareto-superior agreement—one that is better for both parties. Under this scenario, each negotiator can reserve the right to veto any ñew settlement proposed by the third party and revert to the original agreement. With this insurance in hand, Raiffa contends that negotiators may be more willing to allow a third party to create a superior agreement. This new agreement is known as a post-settlement settlement (PSS).

Based upon Raiffa's insight, negotiators should look for a PSS as a last step in searching for a fully integrative agreement. This process does not necessarily require a third party. After an initial agreement is reached, there is often ample opportunity for contract modification. If you are not confident that you have achieved a pareto-efficient outcome, it may be in your best interest to propose to the other side a PSS process whereby both parties agree to be bound by the initial agreement if no better agreement is found. If a better agreement is found, however, the two parties will share the surplus. Thus, if AD and MD reached an agreement to transfer the magnet for $7 million with no limits, they could use a PSS process to share information to locate an agreement that would be worth $550,000 more to both sides (outcome 3—$5.55 million and 6-month AD protection). A PSS process offers a last attempt, with limited risk to either party, to ensure that a pareto-efficient agreement is found. A PSS process can be initiated by using any of the previously defined four strategies after an initial agreement is reached. As Raiffa (1985, p. 9) writes:

. . . we must recognize that a lot of disputes are settled by hardnosed, positional bargaining. Settled, yes. But efficiently settled? Often not . . . they quibble about sharing the pie and often fail to realize that perhaps the pie can be jointly enlarged . . . there may be another carefully crafted settlement that both (parties) might prefer to the settlement they actually achieved.

Summary These five strategies offer a variety of ideas for seeking out fully integrative alternatives. No one strategy will work in all situations. Collectively, however, they increase the potential joint benefit that parties will reach through negotiating. It is important to repeat that no integrative strategy eliminates the distributive aspect of negotiation, and any integrative advice is incomplete if it fails to deal explicitly with the distributive dimension. By having frameworks for thinking about negotiations on both integrative and distributive dimensions, negotiators should be able to improve their performance on both dimensions.

Building Off Differences to Create Integrative Agreements

The previous section focused on information-collection strategies. In many situations, however, after you collect information from the other side, it may still be difficult to identify tradeoffs for negotiation. Have you ever been in a situation where you have thought, "We seem to be talking at two different levels," or "I don't even feel that we're talking about the same thing." No agreement seems possible in these situations. Interestingly, it may be just these differences in perception that can eventually lead to finding an integrative solution. Lax and Sebenius (1986; Sebenius, 1989) have documented a number of ways in which other differences create opportunity. When there is a difference, there is usually a trade available. We saw in El-Tek that differences in weightings of competitive issues created the opportunity for tradeoffs. Other perceived differences that create trades include differences in assessments of the probability of future events, differences in risk preferences, and differences in time preferences.

Differences in Assessments of the Probability of Future Events MD had a set of assessments concerning the profitability of various outcomes ($14 million with no restrictions, $13.1 million with a 6-month AD restriction, and so on). Assume that AD had their own assessment of the profitability that MD would receive from the product and believed that MD would earn $40 million with a 6-month restriction and $40.9 million with no restrictions. On the surface, this difference in perceptions could create a barrier to agreement. AD might expect a payment of around $20 million, and MD would never pay that amount. If trust was lacking, there might be little that MD could do to convince AD of the accuracy of MD's forecast. Impasse would seem inevitable. Now consider the following agreement: 6 months' restriction, MD gets the first $9 million of profitability, and AD gets 80 percent of the profitability from the magnet over $9 million. This agreement allows the parties to bet on their beliefs about future events. If MD's forecast is correct, this agreement would be much better for them than a 50:50 split of the expected $15.1 million ($13.1 million + $2 million). If AD's forecast is correct, this agreement would be better for them than a 50:50 split of the expected $42 million ($40 million + $2 million). While they will not both be right, a trade is good for maximizing the real outcomes to the two parties, because $14 million and $40 million are both much higher outcomes than the $9 million that the two parties would get without an agreement. Thus, this "contingent contract" allows for a trade in which both parties believe that they will do very well.

Mark Twain noted that "it is difference of opinion that makes horse races" (Lax and Sebenius, 1986). Contingent contracts are bets that allow for agreement in situations in which perceived differences in future expectations prevent the parties from reaching a simpler agreement. Essentially, a contingent contract creates multiple issues out of a single issue. The negotiation is not limited to what MD pays AD, but determines what MD pays AD if X occurs, if Y occurs, if Z occurs, and so on, and the different weights that the parties place on these issues allow the trade to take place.

Differences in Risk Preferences   Now consider the situation in which both parties in El-Tek agree on MD's forecast of future events, but both also agree that these are only estimates. (In the format in which the case was presented, the numbers were described as fixed assessments.) Both agree that while MD is expected to earn $13.1 million with a 6-month restriction to AD competitors, the true outcome could be anywhere from $4.1 million to $22.1 million. Now let's add the assumption that AD is very concerned that they receive at least the $5 million that they could earn on their own and are unwilling to take any agreement that would risk ending up below this level. MD, on the other hand, is willing to take risks if they are rewarded for risk taking. Thus, AD is comparatively more risk averse than MD. AD might reject an offer that split the profitability of the magnet equally, since the extreme negative situation would result in a profit below their $5 million number. Again, a tradeoff is possible by giving AD more guaranteed money and MD more of the upside potential. For example, one possible agreement might read: AD gets 6 months' protection, the first $4 million of magnet profitability, and 15 percent of the profitability above $4 million. With this agreement, AD gets its guarantee, and MD gets a higher expected return for taking the higher risk. Rather than seeing one party's relative risk aversion as a problem, the parties use it as an opportunity to trade. In general, different risk-sharing strategies can be developed to allow for trades that might not otherwise occur.

Differences in Time Preferences   Now let us consider a situation in which MD is having a very poor year and would like immediate profitability to keep their current situation from being made public. In particular, MD is concerned that most of the fixed costs of manufacturing will be incurred on the front end. However, AD is more concerned with the overall profitability that they earn from the product. Assuming that the product will earn equal profitability across its two-year life, the transfer might be less attractive to MD if they were to split the profitability as the profit is earned. However, both sides might be happier with an agreement whereby MD gets 75 percent of the first-year profitability and 20 percent of the second-year profitability, while AD gets 25 percent of the first-year profitability and 80 percent of the second-year profitability. In this agreement, MD gets the immediate return that it desires, and AD gets a slightly higher return for waiting. Again, the parties are finding an issue to trade by focusing on the different time preferences.

When time-preference differences exist, future consequences can often be rearranged in a way that gives earlier return to the more impatient party. These differences in time preference might be due to individual differences, cultural differences, or the specific situations of the parties. Regardless, they should be seen as an opportunity, not as a barrier to agreement.

Summary The three topics in this section all focus on situations in which some perceived "troublesome" difference can be used as an opportunity to create benefit. Like the tradeoffs discussed earlier in the chapter, this benefit may be the ability to reach an agreement that would not otherwise occur, or may simply create an agreement that both parties prefer over the agreement that they would have reached if they hadn't rearranged the agreement to account for their differences. The key point is that differences can be used to create opportunities rather than barriers.

INTEGRATION AND CRITIQUE

This chapter has introduced a number of methods for increasing the potential for successful negotiations. First, the decision analytic approach was outlined, with its focus on information collection—namely, the importance of establishing reservation points, exploring the underlying interests of the parties, and weighting the relative importance of these interests. The distributive and integrative dimensions of negotiation were then introduced to distinguish between dividing versus expanding the "pie" in bargaining situations, and the concept of the bargaining zone was offered as a useful tool for conceptualizing agreement along specific dimensions. Next, five strategies were developed for creating more integrative agreements. These strategies include obtaining added resources, trading issues, providing nonspecific compensation, cost cutting, and bridging. In addition, five information-collection strategies were outlined for uncovering integrative potential in negotiation situations. These include building trust, asking questions, giving away some information, making multiple offers, and searching for post-settlement settlements. Finally, the concept of building off differences was introduced as an additional strategy for finding integrative opportunities. Together, these techniques provide a prescriptive framework for thinking rationally about two-party negotiations given the real-world parameters of a situation.

As we saw in the first five chapters, however, ours is not a fully rational world, particularly when it comes to our own decision making. A central lesson of this book is that you may have decision biases that limit your ability to follow rational advice, like the decision analytic approach. In this sense, the decision analytic approach is only a first step in helping you to become a better decision maker in multiparty contexts. This approach cries out for additional descriptive models that allow you as the focal negotiator to better anticipate your own likely behaviors and those of the other parties. If you as the focal negotiator, or the other side, do not act fully rationally, what systematic departures from rationality can be predicted? How can you better anticipate the actual behavior of the opponent, and how do you identify and overcome barriers that might prevent you from following decision analytic advice? The decision analytic approach tells us that we must consider the actual, not necessarily rational, decisions of the other side. A useful addition to the decision analytic approach would be to identify the specific deviations from rationality that can be anticipated in our own and in other parties' decision making. This is the focus of attention in Chapter 7.

SEVEN
NEGOTIATOR
COGNITION

The decision analytic approach to negotiation tells us that it is rational for two parties to strike an agreement whenever a positive bargaining zone exists. Why, then, do actors in such two-party negotiations frequently fail to settle? The decision analytic approach also asserts that our agreements should be fully integrative. Why, then, do most negotiation settlements result in outcomes that are not pareto-efficient?

This chapter explores the ways in which the competitive dynamics of negotiations place cognitive limitations on our abilities to be rational negotiators. Drawing from our earlier discussions of individual limits to rationality and additional research in negotiations, we will explore five key issues that affect our reasoning as negotiators (also referred to as *negotiator cognitions*): (1) the mythical fixed pie of negotiation, (2) the framing of negotiator judgment, (3) the nonrational escalation of conflict, (4) negotiator overconfidence, and (5) the tendency to ignore the cognitions of others. In the following chapter, each section clarifies how negotiator decision making often differs from a prescriptive analysis of negotiator behavior and discusses how we as negotiators can better respond to these deviations.

ISSUE 1: THE MYTHICAL FIXED PIE OF NEGOTIATIONS

As stated in Chapter 6, integrative agreements are nonobvious solutions to conflict that yield higher joint benefit than purely distributive agreements. However, negotiators often fail to reach the integrative solutions (recall the case of the sisters who fought over the orange). Why is this? Perhaps it is because of the **fixed pie assumption,** which represents a fundamental bias in human judgment. That is, negotiators have a systematic intuitive bias that distorts their behavior. When negotiating over an issue, they assume that their interests necessarily and *directly* conflict with the other party's interests.

The fundamental assumption of a fixed pie seems to be rooted in social norms that lead us to interpret most competitive situations as win–lose. This win–lose orientation is manifested in our society in athletic competition, admission to academic programs, corporate promotion systems, and so on. Individuals tend to generalize from these objective win–lose situations and create similar expectations for other situations that are not necessarily win–lose. Faced with a mixed-motive situation requiring both cooperation and competition, it is the competitive aspect that becomes salient, resulting in a win–lose orientation and a distributive approach to bargaining. This, in turn, results in the development of a strategy for obtaining the largest possible share of the perceived fixed pie. Such a focus inhibits the creative problem solving necessary for the development of integrative solutions.

In reality, most conflicts are not purely distributive problems, because most conflicts have more than one issue at stake, with the parties placing different values on the different issues. Once this condition exists, the conflict is objectively no longer a fixed pie. Consider a Friday evening on which you and your spouse are going to dinner and a movie. Unfortunately, you prefer different restaurants and different movies. It is easy to adopt a distributive attitude toward each event to be negotiated. In contrast, if you do not assume a fixed pie, you may find out that you care more about the restaurant selection and your spouse cares more about the movie choice. Similarly, purchasing goods is often treated as a distributive problem. Often, however, a retailer is suddenly willing to reduce the purchase price if payment is made in cash (no receipt, and so on), while you care only about price.

The tendency of negotiators to initially approach bargaining with a mythical fixed pie perception has been documented by Bazerman, Magliozzi, and Neale (1985). Their simulation allowed individuals, acting as buyers and sellers, to complete transactions on a three-issue, integrative bargaining problem. The goal was to complete as many transactions with as many opponents as possible in a fixed amount of time, while maximizing total individual profit. The profit available to sellers and buyers for various levels of the three issues on a per transaction basis is shown in Tables 7.1a and 7.1b. Note that buyers achieve their highest profit levels and sellers their lowest profits at the A levels of delivery, discount, and financing; whereas sellers achieve their highest profits and buyers their lowest profits at the I levels. A negotiated transaction consisted of the two parties agreeing to one of the nine levels for each of the three issues. As can be observed, a simple compromise solution of E-E-E results in a $4,000 profit to each side. However, if the parties are able to reach the fully integrative solution of A-E-I (by trading issues), then each receives a profit of $5,200.

The mythical fixed pie bias argues that negotiators will approach this competitive context with a fixed pie assumption and only relax this assumption when provided with evidence to the contrary. This hypothesis was supported by the results. Figure 7.1 plots the average of buyer and seller profit of all agreements (sample size equals 942 transactions) reached in each five-minute segment of the market (aggregated across six runs of the market simulation). The diagonal line in this figure shows the joint profits to the two parties if they

Table 7.1 Buyer and Seller Schedules for Positively and Negatively Framed Negotiations

Table 7.1a Seller Net Profit Schedule

	Delivery Time		Discount Terms		Financing Terms
A	$ 000	A	$ 000	A	$ 000
B	200	B	300	B	500
C	400	C	600	C	1,000
D	600	D	900	D	1,500
E	800	E	1,200	E	2,000
F	1,000	F	1,500	F	2,500
G	1,200	G	1,800	G	3,000
H	1,400	H	2,100	H	3,500
I	1,600	I	2,400	I	4,000

Table 7.1b Buyer Net Profit Schedule

	Delivery Time		Discount Terms		Financing Terms
A	$4,000	A	$2,400	A	$1,600
B	3,500	B	2,100	B	1,400
C	3,000	C	1,800	C	1,200
D	2,500	D	1,500	D	1,000
E	2,000	E	1,200	E	800
F	1,500	F	900	F	600
G	1,000	G	600	G	400
H	500	H	300	H	200
I	000	I	000	I	000

Table 7.1c Seller Expense Schedule
(Gross Profit = $8,000)

	Delivery Time		Discount Terms		Financing Terms
A	$-1,600	A	$-2,400	A	$-4,000
B	-1,400	B	-2,100	B	-3,500
C	-1,200	C	-1,800	C	-3,000
D	-1,000	D	-1,500	D	-2,500
E	-800	E	-1,200	E	-2,000
F	-600	F	-900	F	-1,500
G	-400	G	-600	G	-1,000
H	-200	H	-300	H	-500
I	000	I	000	I	000

Table 7.1d Buyer Expense Schedule
(Gross Profit = $8,000)

	Delivery Time		Discount Terms		Financing Terms
A	$ 000	A	$ 000	A	$ 000
B	-500	B	-300	B	-200
C	-1,000	C	-600	C	-400
D	-1,500	D	-900	D	-600
E	-2,000	E	-1,200	E	-800
F	-2,500	F	-1,500	F	-1,000
G	-3,000	G	-1,800	G	-1,200
H	-3,500	H	-2,100	H	-1,400
I	-4,000	I	-2,400	I	-1,600

Source: Bazerman, Magliozzi, and Neale (1985).

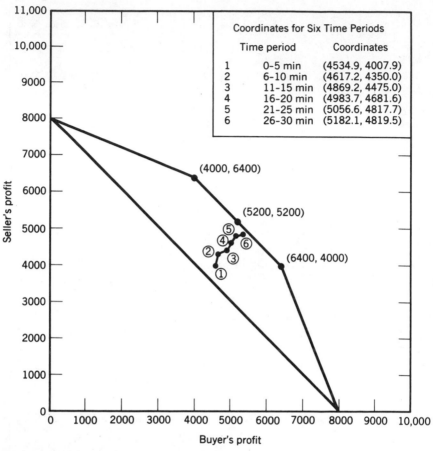

Figure 7.1 Average profit for buyers and sellers of transactions completed in each five-minute segment of the market (aggregated across markets).

make simple compromises (for example, E-E-E). The curved line shows the pareto-efficient frontier available to the negotiators. (Recall from Chapter 6 that the pareto-efficient frontier is defined as the set of agreements for which there is no point that would simultaneously improve the outcomes to either or both parties.) This figure shows that negotiators start the free-market simulation by obtaining agreements that would be predicted by a mythical fixed pie hypothesis (that is, the transactions approach the distributive point of $4,000, $4,000). As the negotiators gain experience, however, the myth is disproved, and far greater integrative behavior is observed (the transactions approach the fully integrative point of $5,200, $5,200).

The pervasiveness of the fixed pie perception, as well as the importance of integrative bargaining, can be seen in the housing market. When interest rates rose dramatically to between 12 percent and 17 percent in 1979, 1980, and 1981, the housing market came to a halt. Sellers continued to expect the value of their property to increase. However, buyers could not afford the monthly payments on houses they aspired to own, due to the drastically higher interest rates. Viewing the problem as a distributive one, buyers could not afford the prices that sellers were demanding. This fixed pie assumption (which was prevalent throughout the industry) led to the conclusion that transactions would not occur until seller reservation points decreased, buyer reservation points increased, interest rates came down, or all three. However, once the industry began to view real estate transactions integratively, some relief was provided. Specifically, sellers cared a great deal about price—partly to justify their past investment. Buyers cared about finding some way to afford a house they aspired to own—perhaps their first house. The integrative solutions were the wide variety of creative financing developments (such as seller financing) of the early 1980s, which allowed sellers an artificially high price in exchange for favorable financing assistance to the buyer. Creative financing integrated the interests of buyers and sellers, rescuing an entire industry from our common fixed pie assumptions.

The mythical fixed pie is also partially responsible for the decline in the U.S. manufacturing sector over the last 20 years. Since management and unions were accustomed to viewing their negotiations as fixed-sum, they never stopped to realize the real loss that might accrue if they failed to reach more integrative agreements. After enough companies went under and enough employees lost their jobs, the two sides realized that worker participation, employee ownership, and flexible work rules were strategies that could make both sides better off. Unfortunately, a crisis from which we may never recover was necessary to get management and union leaders to break their fixed pie assumptions.

The foregoing arguments suggest that while fixed pies do exist, most resolutions depend on finding favorable tradeoffs between negotiators—tradeoffs which necessitate eliminating our intuitive fixed pie assumptions. Chapter 5 argues that individuals are often limited in finding creative solutions by the false assumptions that they make. The fixed pie perception is a fundamentally false assumption that hinders finding creative, integrative solutions. A fundamental task in training negotiators lies in identifying and eliminating this false assumption and institutionalizing the creative process of integrative bargaining.

ISSUE 2: THE FRAMING OF NEGOTIATOR JUDGMENT

Consider the following two scenarios:

You are a wholesaler of refrigerators. Corporate policy does not allow any flexibility in pricing. However, flexibility does exist in terms of expenses that you can incur (shipping, financing terms, and so on), which have a direct effect on the profitability of the transaction. These expenses can all be expensed in dollar-value terms. You are negotiating a $10,000 sale. The buyer wants you to pay $2,000 in expenses. You want to pay less expenses. When you negotiate the transaction, do you try to mini-mize your expenses (reduce these losses from $2,000) or maximize net price (or price less expenses—that is, do you increase the net price from $8,000)?

You bought your house in 1983 for $60,000. You currently have the house on the market for $109,900, with a real target of $100,000 (your estimation of the true market value). An offer comes in for $90,000. Does this offer represent a $30,000 gain in comparison with the original purchase price, or a $10,000 loss in comparison with your current target?

The answer to the question posed in each scenario is "both." Each is an "Is the cup half full or half empty?" situation. From a rational perspective, and based on our intuition, the difference in the two points of view is irrelevant. However, as described in Chapter 3, Kahneman and Tversky (1979, 1982; Tversky and Kahneman, 1981) have demonstrated that important differences exist in the ways in which individuals respond to questions framed in terms of losses versus gains. This difference is critical to describing negotiator behavior.

To exemplify the importance of "framing" to negotiation, consider the follow-ing labor–management situation: The union claims they need a raise to $12 an hour and that anything less represents a loss given current inflation. Manage-ment argues that they cannot pay more than $10 an hour and that anything more imposes an unacceptable expense. What if each side had the choice of settling for $11 an hour (a certain settlement) or going to binding arbitration (a risky settlement)? Since each side is viewing the conflict in terms of what they have to lose, following Tversky and Kahneman's (1981) findings, each side is predicted to be risk seeking and unwilling to take the certain settlement. Changing the frame of the situation to a positive one, however, results in a very different predicted outcome. If the union views anything above $10 an hour as a gain, and management views anything under $12 an hour as a gain, then risk aversion will dominate, and a negotiated settlement will be likely. Using an example conceptually similar to the foregoing scenario, Neale and Bazerman (1985) found that negotiators with positive frames are significantly more con-cessionary and successful than their negatively framed counterparts.

In the study by Bazerman, Magliozzi, and Neale (1985) described earlier, it was found that the frame of buyers and sellers systematically affected their negotiation behavior. Negotiators were led to view transactions in terms of either (1) net profit (gains) or (2) expenses (losses) away from the gross profit of the transactions. The net profit (gain) payoff tables were shown in Tables 7.1 a and 7.1b. To create a negatively framed, or "losses," condition, these tables were converted into "expenses" that the subject would incur—that would be taken away from the $8,000 gross profit received for each completed transac-tion. This transformation is shown in Tables 7.1c and 7.1d. Since net profit is defined to be equal to gross profit minus expenses, Table 7.1a and 7.1b are objectively equivalent to Tables 7.1c and 7.1d. For example, the seller's profit for A-E-I is $5,200, the sum of 0 + $1,200 + $4,000 (Table 7.1a). In Table 7.1c, this same transaction would result in expenses of $2,800, the sum of $1,600 +

$1,200 + 0. When $2,800 is subtracted from the $8,000 gross profit, the same net $5,200 is received. While both frames of the schedule yield the same objective profit result, positively (gain) framed negotiators experienced the risk aversion necessary to have an incentive to compromise. This incentive to compromise led negotiators with a positive frame to (1) complete a larger number of transactions and (2) obtain greater overall profitability than negotiators with a negative frame.

What determines whether a negotiator will have a positive or negative frame? The answer lies in the selection of a perceptual anchor. Consider the anchors available to a union negotiator in negotiating a wage: (1) last year's wage; (2) management's initial offer, (3) the union's estimate of management's reservation point, (4) the union's reservation point, or (5) your bargaining position, which has been publicly announced to your constituency. As the anchor moves from 1 to 5, what is a modest *gain* in comparison to last year's wage is a *loss* in comparison to the publicly specified goals, and the union negotiator moves from a positive frame to a negative frame. For example, for workers who are currently making $10 an hour and demanding an increase of $2 an hour, a proposed increase of $1 an hour can be viewed as a $1 an hour gain in comparison to last year's wage (anchor 1) or a loss of $1 an hour in comparison to the goals of the union's constituency (anchor 5). In order to avoid the adverse effects of framing, negotiators should always be aware of their frames and examine alternative frames.

A curious, consistent, and robust finding is that buyers tend to outperform sellers in symmetric negotiation experiments (cf. Bazerman et al., 1985; Neale, Huber, and Northcraft, 1987). Given the artificial context of the experiment and the symmetry of the design, there is no logical reason that buyers would do better than sellers. However, Neale and colleagues (1987) found that sellers think about the transaction in terms of gaining resources (how much do I gain by selling the commodity?), whereas buyers view transaction in terms of loss (how much do I have to give up?). As a result, buyers tend to be risk seeking and sellers tend to be risk averse. When a risk-averse party meets with a risk-seeking party, the risk-seeking party is more willing to risk the agreement by holding out longer, and the risk-averse party must make the additional concession to close the agreement. The critical issue is that there are naturally occurring frames in life. One that has been identified is the differing frames that are created by the buying and selling roles.

It is easy to see that the frames of negotiators can result in the difference between an important agreement and impasse. Both sides in negotiations typically talk in terms of a certain wage or price that they must get—setting a high reference point against which gains and losses are measured. If this occurs, any compromise below (or above) that reference point represents a loss. This perceived "loss" leads negotiators to adopt a negative frame to all compromise proposals, exhibit risk-seeking attitudes, and be less likely to reach settlement.

In addition, framing has important implications for the tactics that negotiators use. The framing effect suggests that in order to induce concessionary behavior in an opponent, a negotiator should always create anchors that lead the opposition to a positive frame and negotiate in terms of what the other side has to gain. In addition, the negotiator should make it clear to the opposition that the opponent is in a risky situation where a sure gain is possible.

Finally, the impact of framing has important implications for mediators. To the extent that the goal is compromise, a mediator should strive to have both parties view the negotiation in a positive frame. This is tricky, however, since the anchor that will lead to a positive frame for one negotiator is likely to lead to a negative frame for the other negotiator. This suggests that when mediators meet with each party separately, they need to present different anchors to create risk aversion in each party. Again, if mediators are to affect the frame, they also want to emphasize the realistic risk of the situation, thus creating uncertainty and leading both sides to prefer a sure settlement.

ISSUE 3: THE NONRATIONAL ESCALATION OF CONFLICT

Consider the following situation:

> It is 1981. PATCO (the Professional Air Traffic Controllers Organization) decides to strike to obtain a set of concessions from the U.S. government. It is willing to "invest" in a temporary loss of pay during the strike in order to obtain concessions. No government concessions result or appear to be forthcoming. PATCO is faced with the option of backing off and returning to work under the former arrangement or increasing their commitment to the strike to try to force the concessions it desires.

In this example, PATCO has committed resources to a course of action. PATCO is then faced with escalating that commitment or backing out of the conflict. This example illustrates the concept of escalation (from Chapter 4) in a competitive situation. The escalation literature predicts that PATCO is far more likely to persist in its course of action than a rational analysis would have dictated—which, in fact, it did.

It is easy to see the process of the nonrational escalation of commitment unfold in a wide variety of actual situations. The negotiation process commonly leads both sides to initially make extreme demands. The escalation literature predicts that if negotiators become committed to these initial public statements, they will nonrationally adopt a nonconcessionary stance. To the extent that negotiators believe that they "have too much invested to quit," inappropriate stubbornness is likely. Further, if both sides incur losses as a result of a lack of agreement (as is the case in a strike), their commitment to their positions is likely to increase, and their willingness to change to a different course of action (that is, compromise) is likely to decrease. For example, it could be argued that in the Malvinas/Falklands conflict, once Argentina had suffered the initial loss of life, it had the information necessary to rationally pursue a negotiated settlement. The escalation literature, in contrast, accurately predicts that the loss of life (a significant commitment to a course of action) would lead Argentina to a further escalation of its commitment not to compromise on the return of the Malvinas to Britain. More recently, the decision of the "hard-liners" in China to fire on the students in the spring of 1989 can be explained in terms of the nonrational escalation of commitment. Virtually all analysts agree that this decision was irrational from any political analysis. However, the "hard-liners" had made public commitments to stop the student protests. When nothing else worked, they escalated their commitment, killed many people, and weakened their political standing within the international community.

One important result from the escalation literature is that the public announcement of one's position increases one's tendency to escalate nonrationally (Staw, 1981). Once the general public (or one's constituency) is aware of the commitment, one is far less likely to retreat from his/her previously announced position. This suggests that escalation can be reduced if negotiators and third parties avoid the formation of firmly set public positions. However, implementation of this recommendation is contradictory to everything known about how negotiators (such as labor leaders, political leaders, representatives of management) behave when they represent constituencies. A firmly set public position is typically perceived as necessary to build constituency support and allegiance. Thus it may be that what is best for the constituency is not necessarily what the constituency rewards.

An understanding of escalation can also be very helpful to a negotiator in anticipating the behavior of an opponent. When will the other party really hold out, and when will it give in? The escalation literature predicts that the other side will hold out when they have "too much invested" in their position to quit. This suggests that there are systematic clues to indicate when you can threaten an opponent and win versus when such threats are likely to simply escalate commitment to prior positions. Strategically, this suggests that a negotiator should avoid inducing any statements or behaviors from an opponent that will create the perception of having too much invested to quit.

ISSUE 4: NEGOTIATOR OVERCONFIDENCE

Consider the following scenario:

> You are an advisor to a major-league baseball player. In baseball, a system exists for resolving compensation conflicts that calls for a player and a team owner who do not agree to submit final offers to an arbitrator. Using final-offer arbitration, the arbitrator must accept one position or the other, not a compromise. Thus, the challenge for each side is to come just a little closer to the arbitrator's perception of the appropriate compensation package than the opposition. In this case, your best intuitive estimate of the final offer that the team owner will submit is a package worth $200,000 per year. You believe than an appropriate wage is $400,000 per year but estimate the arbitrator's opinion to be $300,000 per year. What final offer do you propose?

This scenario sets up a common cognitive trap for negotiators. As we learned in Chapter 2, individuals are systematically overconfident that their judgments are correct. Thus, they are likely to be overconfident in estimating the position of a neutral third party and in estimating the likelihood that the third party will accept their position. In the baseball example, if the arbitrator's true assessment of the appropriate wage is $250,000, and you believe it to be $300,000, you are likely to submit an inappropriately high offer and overestimate the likelihood that the offer will be accepted. Consequently, the overconfidence bias is likely to lead the advisor to believe that less compromise is necessary than a more objective analysis would suggest.

Farber (1981) discusses the problem of negotiator overconfidence in terms of negotiators' divergent expectations. That is, each side is optimistic that the neutral third party will adjudicate in its favor. Consider the situation in which (1) the union is demanding $8.75 an hour; (2) management is offering $8.25 an hour; and (3) the "appropriate" wage is $8.50 an hour. Farber suggests that the union will typically expect the neutral third party to adjudicate at a wage somewhat over $8.50, while management will expect a wage somewhat under $8.50. Given these divergent expectation, neither side is willing to compromise at $8.50. Both sides will incur the costs of impasse and aggregately do no better through the use of a third party. In the baseball scenario, if one side had a more objective assessment of the opponent's offer and the position of the arbitrator, it could use this information strategically to its advantage in final-offer arbitration.

Research demonstrates that negotiators tend to be overconfident that their positions will prevail if they do not "give in." Neale and Bazerman (1983; Bazerman and Neale, 1982) show that negotiators in final-offer arbitration consistently overestimate the probability that their final offer will be accepted. In laboratory studies in which there was only a 50 percent chance of all final offers being accepted, the average subject estimated that there was a much higher probability that his or her offer would be accepted. In terms of Walton and McKersie's bargaining zone, overconfidence may inhibit a variety of settlements, despite the existence of a positive bargaining zone. If we consider a final offer as a judgment as to how much compromise is necessary to win the arbitration, it is easy to argue that when negotiators are overconfident that a particular position will be accepted, their reservation point becomes more extreme, and their incentive to compromise is reduced. If a more accurate assessment is made, the negotiator is likely to be more uncertain and uncomfortable about the probability of success and is more likely to accept a compromise. Based on the biasing impact of this overconfidence, Neale and Bazerman (1985) found "appropriately" confident negotiators to exhibit more concessionary behavior and to be more successful than overly confident negotiators.

Training negotiators to recognize the cognitive patterns of overconfidence should include the realization that overconfidence is most likely to occur when a party's knowledge is limited. As we learned in Chapter 2, most of us follow the intuitive cognitive rule "When in doubt, be overconfident." This suggests that negotiators should seek objective assessments of worth from a *neutral* party, realizing that this neutral assessment is likely to be systematically closer to the other party's position than the negotiator might have intuitively predicted.

ISSUE 5: IGNORING THE COGNITIONS OF OTHERS

Imagine that you are in a foreign country. You meet a merchant who is selling a very attractive gem. Although you have purchased a few gems in your life, you are far from an expert. After some discussion, you make the merchant an offer that you believe, but that you are not certain, is on the low side. He quickly accepts, and the transaction is completed. How do you feel? Most people would feel uneasy with the purchase after the quick acceptance. This feeling is known as the "winner's curse." Yet why would you voluntarily make an offer that you would not want accepted? Now consider the problem in Exercise 7.1.

Exercise 7.1 **Acquiring a Company**

In the following exercise you will represent Company A (the acquirer), which is currently considering acquiring Company T (the target) by means of a tender offer. You plan to tender in cash for 100% of Company T's shares but are unsure how high a price to offer. The main complication is this: the value of Company T depends directly on the outcome of a major oil exploration project it is currently undertaking. Indeed, the very viability of Company T depends on the exploration outcome. If the project fails, the company under current management will be worth nothing—$0/share. But if the project succeeds, the value of the company under current management could be as high as $100/share. All share values between $0 and $100 are considered equally likely. By all estimates, the company will be worth considerably more in the hands of Company A than under current management. In fact, whatever the ultimate value under current management, *the company will be worth fifty percent more under the management of A than under Company T.* If the project fails, the company is worth $0/share under either management. If the exploration project generates a $50/share value under current management, the value under Company A is $75/share. Similarly, a $100/share value under Company T implies a $150/share value under Company A, and so on.

The board of directors of Company A has asked you to determine the price they should offer for Company T's shares. This offer must be made *now, before* the outcome of the drilling project is known. From all indications, Company T would be happy to be acquired by Company A, *provided it is at a profitable price.* Moreover, Company T wishes to avoid, at all cost, the potential of a takeover bid by any other firm. You expect Company T to delay a decision on your bid until the results of the project are in, then accept or reject your offer before the news of the drilling results reaches the press. Thus, *you (Company A) will not know the results of the exploration project when submitting your price offer, but Company T will know the results when deciding whether or not to accept your offer.* In addition, Company T is expected to accept any offer by Com-

pany A that is greater than the (per share) value of the company under current manage-ment.

As the representative of Company A, you are deliberating over price offers in the range of $0/share (this is tantamount to making no offer at all) to $150/share. What price offer per share would you tender for Company T's stock?

My Tender Price is: $____per share.

Source: from Samuelson and Bazerman (1985).

The "Acquiring a Company" exercise is conceptually similar to the gem-merchant problem. In the "Acquiring a Company" exercise, one firm (the ac-quirer) is considering making an offer to buy out another firm (the target). However, the acquirer is uncertain about the ultimate value of the target firm. It knows only that its value under current management is between $0 and $100, with all values equally likely. Since the firm is expected to be worth 50 percent more under the acquirer's management than under the current ownership, it appears to make sense for a transaction to take place. While the acquirer does not know the actual value of the firm, the target knows its current worth exactly. What price should the acquirer offer for the target?

The problem is analytically quite simple (as will be demonstrated shortly), yet intuitively quite perplexing. The responses of 123 MBA students from Boston University are shown in Figure 7.2. The table shows the dominant response was between $50 and $75. How is this $50-to-$75 decision reached? One common, but wrong, explanation is that "on average, the firm will be worth $50 to the target and $75 to the acquirer; consequently, a transaction in this range will, on average, be profitable to both parties." Now consider the logical

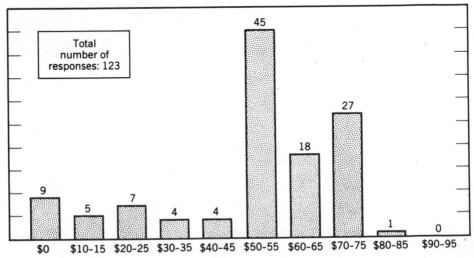

Figure 7.2 The distribution of price offers.

process that a rational response would generate in deciding whether to make an offer of $60 per share:

> If I offer $60 per share, the offer will be accepted 60 percent of the time—whenever the firm is worth between $0 and $60 to the target. Since all values are equally likely, between $0 and $60, the firm will, on average, be worth $30 per share to the target when the target accepts a $60 per share offer, and will be worth $45 per share to the acquirer, resulting in a loss of $15 per share ($45 to $60). Consequently, a $60 per share offer is unwise.

It is easy to see that the same kind of reasoning applies to *any* positive offer. On the average, the acquirer obtains a company worth 25 percent less than the price it pays when its offer is accepted. If the acquirer offers $X and the target accepts, the current value of the company is worth anywhere between $0 and $X. As the problem is formulated, any value in that range is equally likely, and the expected value of the offer is therefore equal to $X/2. Since the company is worth 50 percent more to the acquirer, the acquirer's expected value is 1.5($X/2) = 0.75($X)—only 75 percent of its offer price. Thus, for any value of $X, the best the acquirer can do is not to make an offer ($0 per share). The paradox of the situation is that even though in all circumstances the firm is worth more to the acquirer than to the target, any offer above $0 leads to a negative expected return to the acquirer. *The source of this paradox lies in the high likelihood that the target will accept the acquirer's offer when the firm is least valuable to the acquirer—that is, when it is a "lemon"* (Akerlof, 1970).

The answer to this problem is so counterintuitive that only 9 of 123 subjects correctly offered $0 per share. Recent replications with Massachusetts Institute of Technology master's students in management have produced similar results. Finally, even subjects who were paid according to their performance exhibit the same pattern of responses as depicted in Figure 7.2 (Bazerman and Carroll, 1987).

Most individuals have the analytical ability to follow the logic that the optimal offer is $0 per share. Yet without assistance, most individuals make a positive offer. Thus, individuals systematically exclude information from their decision-making processes that they have the ability to include. They fail to realize that their expected return is *conditional* on an acceptance by the other party, and that an acceptance is most likely to occur when it is least desirable to the negotiator making the offer.

The famous comedian Groucho Marx understood the tendency to ignore the decisions of others. He said that he didn't want to be a member of any club that would have him as a member. Why? Their acceptance of his application told him something about their standards, and if they were so low as to accept him, he didn't want to be a member of that club! The key feature of the "winner's curse" in the bargaining context is that one side often has much better information than the other side, the party with the better information is usually the seller. Although we are all familiar with the slogan "buyer beware," our intuition seems to have difficulty putting this idea into practice when asymmetric information exists. Most people realize that when they buy a commodity they know little about, their uncertainty increases. The evidence presented here indicates that against an informed opponent, our expected return from such a transaction decreases dramatically. Practically, the evidence suggests that people under-value the importance of getting accurate information when making important transactions. They undervalue a mechanic's unbiased evaluation of a used car, a professional inspector's assessment of a house, or an independent jeweler's assessment of a coveted gem. Thus, the knowledgeable gem merchant will accept your offer selectively, taking the offer when the gem is probably worth less than your estimate. To protect yourself, you need to develop or borrow professional expertise to balance the inequity of information. While the experi-mental evidence presented was highly artificial, the negative effects of the winner's curse should be considered by any negotiator dealing with a better-informed opponent.

Neale and Bazerman (1983) found that individuals who had a greater ten-dency to think about the perspective of others were more successful in labora-tory negotiations. This focus on the perspective of the other party allowed them to better predict the opponent's goals, expectations, and reservation points. While taking the perspective of the other party is important, most individuals lack sufficient perspective-taking ability (Bazerman and Neale, 1983; Davis, 1981; Bernstein and Davis, 1982). Overall, *negotiators tend to act as if their opponent was a fairly inactive party to the negotiation and systematically ig-nore valuable information that is available.* Bazerman and Neale (1982) sug-gest that training mechanisms should be developed to increase the perspec-tive-taking ability of negotiators. This is consistent with the literature on negotiator role reversal, which suggests that having each bargainer verbalize the viewpoint of the other increases the likelihood of a negotiated resolution (see Pruitt, 1981). Thus, increasing the tendency of negotiators to take their opponents' perspective should be the mediator's central focus.

This tendency to ignore the perspective of others can be seen in the escala-tion bias described in Chapter 4. Why do bidders get involved in Shubik's dollar-auction exercise? Because they see the potential for profit early in the auction and then fail to take the perspective of what the auction will look like to other bidders. *The central message of this section is obvious: Consider the decisions of the other party before you commit to a course of action as a negotiator.* This piece of advice is counterintuitive; most individuals falsely act as if the opponent is a passive party to the negotiation.

INTEGRATION

From Chapter 6, we learned how to think rationally when approaching two-party decision-making contexts. In this chapter, we explore why it is not always easy for us, or for our opponents, to act rationally in these situations. Drawing upon the biases in individual decision making introduced in Chapters 2 through 5, we see that we experience similar biases in two party decision-making contexts. First, we too readily assume a fixed pie mentality in negotiations. Second, our ability to assess possible settlement options is impacted by the framing of those options. Framing dramatically affects not only how we view decisions as the focal negotiator, but also whether or not a settlement is likely to be reached by the parties or not. Third, we find that it is important to recognize our own, as well as our opponents', tendencies to nonrationally escalate commitment, especially after public statements have been made. Fourth, our tendency toward overconfidence inappropriately impacts on our ability to assess the reasonableness of our positions. Finally, and probably most important, we tend to ignore the cognitions of others when assessing negotiation situations. All of these biases can lead to foolish behaviors and unwise settlements in two-party decision making. Yet, like the behaviors outlined in earlier chapters, we are often not aware of these biases. To become more successful negotiators in multiparty decision-making contexts, we need to understand the analytical concepts introduced in Chapter 6, while becoming more aware of the cognitive barriers that inhibit us and our opponents in applying these concepts. In the next chapter, the material from these chapters is extended to more complex multiparty situations.

EIGHT
DECISION MAKING WITH MORE THAN TWO PARTIES

In Chapters 6 and 7 we examined multiparty decision making in the context of two-party, competitive negotiations. But what happens when more than two parties are involved and the parties have a cooperative, as well as competitive, orientation? This is usually the case in work groups and project teams within business and not-for-profit organizations. What about situations in which many parties must make coordinated decisions but there is little opportunity for communication? This is the case when multiple firms within an industry make simultaneous investment and strategic decisions, representing a mixture of motives from competition to peaceful coexistence.

The factors determining the dynamics of these multiparty situations are far more complex than individual or two-party contexts. A simple examination of numbers makes this point very clearly. In any multiparty situation, two elements of study must be taken into account: the cognitions of each player and the interpersonal relationships between the players. In two-party contexts, there are two sets of cognitions and one dyadic interaction to consider. In three-party contexts, the network grows to three sets of cognitions and three possible dyadic interactions. By the time we reach five-party situations, there are five sets of cognitions and ten possible dyadic interactions, not to mention the subsystems of three- and four-person coalitions. As the number of parties grows, the network of cognitions and relationships becomes increasingly complex. In addition to the network complexity, other factors, like communication, influence multiparty decision-making groups in a variety of ways.

Because of this complexity, it would be impossible within the context of this book to provide a comprehensive overview of decision making in situations beyond two-party negotiations. The shear volume of issues requires that we limit our coverage in this chapter. In this chapter we will bring to your attention only a select number of issues that are particularly pertinent to better understanding multiparty decision making. In the first section, we will review the dynamics of competitive bidding between more than two parties when there is little communication involved. In the second section we will explore the issue of assisted decision making within multiparty contexts—that is, when an outside party must be brought in to assist the parties in reaching a final decision. In the third section we will look at decision making within a group context. The fourth section will highlight the issues of subgroup coalitions and their effect on group decision making. Finally, the fifth section will examine multiparty situations in the form of social dilemmas. As you can see, this chapter covers a broad spectrum. Throughout, the salient features that will be examined include increasing the number of parties and communication.

In reviewing this material, it is important to keep in mind that all of the issues that we have covered in Chapters 1 through 7 are relevant to these situations. As a starting point in any multiparty situation, you must always consider the individual cognitions of the players and the competitive interpersonal dynamics between each of the players.

COMPETITIVE BIDDING

In business, organizations frequently bid against competitors to obtain important resource inputs, like qualified job applicants and reasonably priced raw materials. In addition, many firms, like defense contractors and architects, rely on competitive bidding as a basic source of revenue. Often, in these situations, there are several parties involved whose identities may or may not be known to the focal organization. There is frequently little opportunity for communication between competing parties. Given competitive bidding's centrality to the conduct of business, it would seem that "winning" in these situations is the desired objective. Consider the following scenarios:

> Your consulting firm is trying to acquire a young, highly regarded MBA student from a prestigious university. Many other organizations are also interested in this apparently talented individul. In fact, your firm seems to be competing against these other firms for her services. Finally, she accepts your offer. Will she prove to be as productive as you believe? Will it be worth the costs of hiring her?

> As the owner of a small movie theatre, you must bid against a number of other theatres for the rights to exhibit first-run films. A new film is scheduled to be released in six months that is expected to be the hottest property since *Batman*. Like your fellow theatre owners, you must bid for the rights to show the movie, sight unseen. You submit your bid and it is high enough to win the right to show the movie in your theatre. You "beat" a large number of nearby competitors. Is it time to celebrate?

> Your conglomerate is considering a new acquisition. Many other firms are also "bidding" for this firm. The target firm has suggested that they will gladly be acquired by the highest bidder. The actual value of the target firm is highly uncertain; even the target firm does not know what they are "worth." With at least a half dozen firms pursuing the target, your bid is the highest. Your offer is accepted and you obtain the acquisition. Have you been successful?

You are the owner of a baseball team. A hitter with an erratic performance (the "inconsistent slammer") has declared his free agency. In the free-agent draft, 11 teams (including yours) drafted the player and appear interesting in negotiating for his services. After negotiating with each team, the player accepts your offer, explaining that "your team offered the best package." Is the player going to be worth the money you have offered to pay him?

In each of the foregoing scenarios, a naive analysis would suggest that you should be glad to have won the competitive situation. However, research evidence (cf. Bazerman and Samuelson, 1983) argues that in many of these scenarios you are likely to have become the most recent victim of the "winner's curse" in competitive bidding. The winner's curse in competitive bidding is conceptually related to the winner's curse in negotiation, introduced in Chapter 7. In the two-party negotiation setting, the winner's curse occurred due to the negotiator's failure to consider the perspective of the other negotiator, usually the seller. In the current setting, the winner's curse occurs due to the failure of the winning bidder to consider the implications of having bid higher than that of many of the other bidders—all of whom are at the same information disadvantage relative to the seller.

Bazerman and Samuelson (1983) argue that a possible reason that you were the highest bidder is that you significantly overestimated the actual value of the commodity being sold. Figure 8.1 provides a graphic depiction of what may have occurred. Curve E shows the distribution of bidder estimates for the true value of the commodity, and curve B depicts the distribution of bids. The depiction assumes (1) that the mean of the distribution is equal to the true value of the commodity—that is, no aggregate under- or overestimation is expected—and (2) that bidders discount their estimates a fixed amount in making bids—which explains the leftward shift of the estimate distribution. The figure suggests that a winning bid—that is, one from the right tail of the distribution—is likely to exceed the actual value of the commodity. The highest bidder is likely to have been one of the highest estimators, and unless they had reason to believe that they had better information than the other bidders, overpayment can be expected. With this framework in mind, Bazerman and Samuelson predicted and found in their research that *the winning bidder in auctions of highly uncertain commodities with a large number of bidders commonly pays more than the commodity is worth.*

Why does the winning bidder fall prey to the winner's curse? The answer lies in the failure of bidders to draw a key inference: If a particular bidding group assumes that their bid will win the auction, this information should tell the bidder that they are likely to have overestimated the value of the commodity in comparison to other bidders. Based on this reasoning, bidders on highly uncertain commodities should adjust downward their estimates of the true value of the commodity and lower their bids accordingly. Thus, if they do win, they are less likely to have overbid, or at least not by the same margin.

The importance of the winner's curse in competitive bidding can be seen in the context of corporate takeovers. Corporate takeovers in the 1980s have provided ample evidence that acquiring companies often compete against

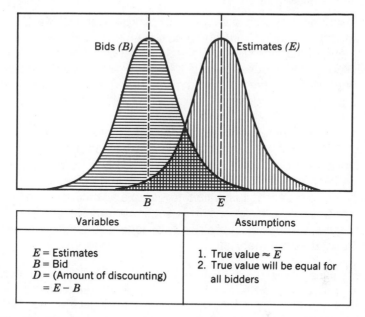

Variables	Assumptions

E = Estimates
B = Bid
D = (Amount of discounting)
   = $E - B$
	1. True value ≈ $\overline{E}$
	2. True value will be equal for
	   all bidders

Figure 8.1   Graphic illustration of the winner's curse. (*Source:* M. H. Bazerman and W. F. Samuelson, "I Won the Auction but Don't Want the Prize." *Journal of Conflict Resolution,* Vol. 27, pp. 618–634. Copyright © 1983 by Sage Publications, Inc. Reprinted by permission of Sage Publications Inc.)

each other and pay too much for what they get. As many as one third of all acquisitions prove to be failures, and an additional one third fail to live up to expectations (*Wall Street Journal,* 1981). In addition, any financial synergy that is created by mergers usually goes to the target, not the acquirer. On average, the financial benefit goes exclusively to the shareholders of the acquired company. Bazerman and Samuelson's analysis suggests that potential acquirers should temper their optimism by recognizing that the winning bidder is likely to acquire a company that is worth far less than the winning bidder's estimate of the expected value. More specifically, Bazerman and Samuelson point out that competitive decision makers should be particularly concerned about the winner's curse when there are a large number of bidders and the uncertainty around the true value of the commodity is high.

This section shows that judgmental deficiencies are an important concern in multiparty competitive-bidding contexts, a key activity encountered in organizations. As a member of a decision-making group within an organization, you should be aware that it is important to incorporate the perceptions of competitors on an individual, as well as organizational, level when making important decisions.

ASSISTED DECISION MAKING

In Chapter 6, I asserted that, because many managerial decisions are made in conjunction with other organizational actors who have preferences different from our own, negotiation is a central part of organizational life. Directly linked to this view is the assertion that acting as an outside party in resolving disputes is a major part of managerial life. When subordinates disagree, the decision is often "kicked up" to a superior. This can occur in two-party or several-party disputes; regardless of the number involved, the manager is required to assist the group in reaching a decision. This role is typically referred to as that of a "third" party.

The theme of manager as "third" party is central to a growing body of literature (cf. Bazerman and Lewicki, 1983; Lewicki, Sheppard, and Bazerman, 1986; Sheppard, 1983). As a manager, you are likely to be in situations in which you are assisting as a third party, as well as ones in which you are assisted by a third party. In both cases, it is critical to be able to think systematically about how third parties make decisions. This section examines this process.

To focus the discussion, consider two generic examples of the choices facing third parties in organizations:

> You are a manager with two divisions reporting to you. You have a limited budget that must be divided between the two divisions. You have asked the two division managers to reach an agreement on the proportion of the budget that each division needs and should receive. Not surprisingly, the needs of the two managers exceed the amount of funds that you have to disperse.

> Again, you have reporting responsibilities for two divisions. This time they are in dispute about the price at which division A should sell goods to division B. Division A argues that the market price is fair, while division B argues for the variable cost to division A. The organization prefers to have transactions occur within the firm whenever possible.

In responding to these situations, a critical question concerns the procedure that a third party uses to intervene (Kochan, 1980; Thibaut and Walker, 1975). You can make the decision unilaterally; this method is frequently referred to as **arbitration.** You can facilitate the process so as to help the parties reach their own mutually agreeable resolution; this behavior is referred to as **mediation.** In addition, you can generate a number of intermediate intervention styles. An interesting perspective on this issue is offered by Sheppard (1983, 1984; Lewicki and Sheppard, 1985). This research shows that the styles that managers most frequently exercise are not the ones that have been most frequently identified by researchers. Managers often behave like "inquisitorial judges," who collected information on a dispute from the parties and then render a decision. Alternatively, they behave as "conflict deflectors" (also dubbed "kick in the pants"), who tell the conflicting parties to resolve the dispute themselves or they will resolve it for them! It is interesting to note that most managers have a stated preference for mediation that is not matched by actual behavior.

Past work on third-party intervention has focused on alternative forms of intervention while ignoring an equally important aspect of the third-party process—the judicial decision-making processes of the third party. Often, the third party must make a decision between conflicting parties. What norms or biases govern these decisions? In an organization, a rational model would suggest that the conflict should be resolved in the manner that maximizes the outcomes to the total organization. This perspective will be illustrated in a moment under the "global perspective" norm of reaching decisions in organizations. However, we will also consider four other norms that offer alternative considerations. These include need, equity, equality, and anchoring. Each of the five builds on different criteria for what constitutes a just decision.

Global Perspective The most clearly articulated goal for resolving disputes comes from the profit-maximization goals inherent in a free-market economy. That is, the manager should resolve the dispute such that the settlement maximizes the profit of the larger entity—the organization. This approach assumes that the interests of the disputants are only indirect. That is, the interests of the parties matter only to the extent that they affect the global welfare of the organization—for example, if one party is particularly valuable and threatens to quit if an unacceptable resolution is chosen. This norm is consistent with the philosophical bases of capitalism and the rational-actor decision model. However, it is inconsistent with a number of other philosophical principles and behaviors that are known to affect managers. These inconsistencies are discussed next in the context of the other four norms.

Need A common way of distributing scarce resources is based on need. Which patient needs the operation first? Who needs the only family car most? The same logic applies within organizations; for example, which division would benefit most from an allocation of additional resources? If need is defined based on being necessary to further the organization's profitability, then the criterion of need collapses to the same decision criterion as the global perspective. However, need may also refer to the needs of organizational members. For example, need may refer to which employees have the greatest family need for a pay increase. In this case, the criterion of need may be in direct conflict with a global perspective.

Equity A third principle that third parties might follow is the equity norm. This norm suggests that disputes should be resolved in a way that recognizes the legitimate rights of the disputants. What budget has each party earned? What salary is deserved by each of the multiple subordinates that you must reward? The equity principle assumes that some concept of fairness can be determined for a particular context. The equity principle is consistent with the equity theory of motivation. This theory suggests that employees are motivated to receive a just return for their efforts in proportion to the efforts and rewards of other parties to whom they compare themselves (Adams, 1963, 1965). In the salary case, the implications of this point are obvious. In a budget scenario, equity might be operationalized in terms of a division's demonstrated capacity to efficiently use resources, past performance, and so on. Implicit in the equity principle is the idea that individuals and groups should receive resources in direct proportion to some notion of earned rights or inputs into the organization.

Recent work by Kahneman, Knetsch, and Thaler (1986) suggests that most individuals favor an equitable-decision rule and will frequently forego an optimal, value-maximizing decision in favor of an equitable decision.

Equality   In contrast to the arguments in favor of a global perspective or equity, Rawls's (1971) equalitarian theory of justice argues that resources should be distributed equally to all individuals or groups, except in cases where an unequal distribution works to everyone's advantage. This notion of equality suggests that most disputes should be resolved such that disputants receive equal shares of the disputed resources. While the socialistic implications of this norm are not consistent with capitalistic principles, Starke and Notz (1981), among others, argue that the tendency to compromise, which is operationally a decision to follow the equality norm, is common among third parties.

Anchoring   While the positions just identified can be defended based on philosophical and economic models of third-party decision making, Kahneman and Tversky's concept of anchoring and adjustment from Chapter 2 asserts that humans have a systematic tendency to make judgments by selecting an anchor and making only minor adjustments from that anchor. Thus, the anchoring-and-adjustment heuristic suggests that third parties are likely to select the most commonly available anchor—that is, the existing distribution of disputed resources—and make only incremental adjustments from that position. For example, budget disputes will be resolved such that this year's budget is not very different from last year's; salary increases will be made so that the new salary structure reflects last year's salary structure; and so on. Given this viewpoint, a global-perspective, equity, or equality decision-making norm will be adopted only to the extent that minor adjustments from the status quo can create these conditions.

Integration   Comparing alternative norms of arbitration was the focus of a recent study by Bazerman (1985). The study examined the norms used by experienced arbitrators in the labor–management context. (Since the outside party in this study was not part of a more global organization, the global perspective norm was not evaluated.) The arbitration literature has historically focused on whether arbitrators follow an equity norm or equality norm. However, Bazerman found that the most common practice of arbitrators was to use the anchoring norm. Arbitrators made only minor adjustments to last year's contract, thus maintaining an approximation of the agreements that were accepted in the past.

This finding suggests that managerial behavior in third-party contexts might be inappropriately prone to using past norms to guide future decisions. For example, are budgets decided starting with a "clean slate," or are they simply adjustments from last year's budget? Both a global-perspective norm and an equity norm would recommend a "clean slate" approach to budget formation, since heuristically, adjustments to an existing position are known to be insufficient. However, most budget-setting practices are better described by the anchoring norm. Similarly, Chapter 2 gave the situation of pay raises being determined by a fixed adjustment to last year's salary as an example of the anchoring-and-adjustment bias. If we think of the performance-appraisal system as the organization's method of distributing limited resources (that is, income) through an arbitration system (that is, the employees are not asked to try to resolve the dispute themselves), this system also fits under the anchoring norm of third-party decision making. While the empirical evidence for this argument has only just begun to emerge, the logic behind the anchoring norm as a predominant decision-making behavior of third parties in organizations is compelling. Many managers, when confronted with this argument, feel a need to rethink the way in which they deal with the distribution of scarce resources.

The key message of this section is that assisting in multiparty decision making as a third party is an important role of the manager. As a manager, you have a third-party style, which includes implicit decision-making strategies for resolving disputes, that you may not be fully aware of and may want to adjust. In particular, you may be inappropriately influenced by anchoring in resolving disputes. Further, when on the receiving end of a third-party resolution, you may want to manage the situation in advance to correct for possible adverse effects from anchoring by the third party.

GROUP DECISION MAKING

As mentioned earlier, work groups and project teams are a predominant decision-making form within organizations. In these situations, the presumed motive is one of cooperation in facilitating the best possible outcome for the organization. In general, it has been found that work group performance varies erratically, and many groups fail to achieve their apparent potential (Steiner, 1972). Thus, maximizing group effectiveness is a common goal across organizations.

Despite many years of research by social psychologists and organizational researchers, it has been difficult to obtain conclusive predictors of group effectiveness. We do know, however, that a number of factors feed into performance. Some of these include the nature of the task being accomplished and the way in which that task fits into the larger organization, the distribution of individual abilities and the way in which the group is structured around these abilities, the availability of necessary resources to accomplish the task, and the supportiveness of the surrounding organization in facilitating the group's efforts.

Since these conditions vary widely across organizations and cannot usually be controlled in any particular situation, the manager must make do with the resources at hand; the most relevant question to judgment and decision making is, What are the biases and judgmental deficiencies to which groups of individuals are generically prone? This is the question that this section seeks to address.

The following paragraphs do *not* offer a comprehensive discussion of group decision making, since this is readily available elsewhere (see, for example, Brandstatter, Davis, and Stocker-Kreichgauer, 1982; Guzzo, 1982; Steiner, 1972). Rather, this section highlights some important findings about group decision making in the context of the judgment-bias perspective developed in Chapters 1 through 7. The topics in this section include "risky shift," "groupthink," the impact of decision heuristics within groups, and group negotiations.

"Risky Shift"

One of the most interesting and widely researched findings in the group decision-making literature is Stoner's (1961) discovery that, on the whole, groups are more risk seeking than individual member's risk preferences would predict. According to this phenomenon, known as the "risky shift," individuals joined together in groups tend, on average, to produce riskier decisions in uncertain situations than do individuals working independently. Using Stoner's methodology (a 12-item Choice Dilemma Questionnaire, or CDQ), this effect has been tested across a wide variety of experimental settings and subjects and has been found to be remarkably stable.

Interestingly, while groups generally tend to take more risks, the shift for various items on the CDQ differs substantially both in direction and magnitude. Some items consistently produce risky shifts; some items produce no significant shift; and two items regularly generate cautious shifts (that is, the groups are less risky than individuals). In addition, newly constructed and tested trials that are similar in form to the CDQ have been found to consistently generate cautious shifts (Cartwright, 1973). Added questions concerning the risky-shift paradigm are raised by contradictory research in "real-life" situations (with investors, juries, and consumers) and in laboratory research that does not employ the CDQ. Sometimes a risky shift occurs; sometimes a cautious shift occurs; and sometimes no shift occurs. Thus, a critical question emerges: When does a risky shift versus cautious shift occur?

Moscovici and Zavalloni (1969) and Doise (1969) have developed a coherent and empirically validated explanation of the inconsistent effects of the risky shift phenomenon. They argue that the behavior of groups can be better characterized in terms of a "group polarization" effect. That is, group discussions tend to magnify or enhance the predominant view within the group. For example, if the individuals are initially in favor of a moderately high degree of risk, then the group discussion will further enhance the favorability of the risk. These researchers have found consistent support for this hypothesis. For example, they reevaluated the CDQ and found that group responses are more risk seeking on items on which individuals are already fairly risk seeking and more risk averse on items on which individuals are fairly risk averse.

The group-polarization argument helps us to understand how individual opinions affect and are affected by group discussion. However, an alternative explanation of the risky shift is provided by the framing effect from Chapter 3. This explanation stems from Vinoker's (1971) initial assertion that individuals *and* groups will choose that option that maximizes their expected utility. As we noted in Chapter 3, in maximizing utility, individuals tend to be risk averse in positively framed situations and risk seeking in negatively framed situations. Incorporating this concept into multiparty decision-making situations, one might hypothesize that group participation by various members encourages the verbalization of uncertain decisions in multiple frames, thus diluting the impact of any one specific frame (Bazerman, 1984). This hypothesis implies that groups will move away from the classical utility curve toward an expected-value, or risk-neutral, decision strategy. Examining Figure 3.1, we would expect that (1) judgments made by individuals will tend to follow the classical utility curve, and (2) group decisions will tend to adjust toward the risk-neutral line. *Consequently, this analysis predicts a risky shift on positively framed items and a cautious shift on negatively framed items.* Preliminary empirical evidence supports this position and contradicts the polarization argument (Neale et al., 1986). Further examination of the CDQ items finds that they tend to be positively framed, which would predict the risky shift. Would we currently be examining the cautious-shift paradigm, which Stoner expected, had he initially conducted his experiment with negatively framed items?

From this section, we have learned that group decision making in uncertain situations often leads to different results in terms of risk than individual decision making. Sometimes the decisions are riskier; sometimes they are more cautious. When acting as members of decision-making groups, we must be aware of this "shift" phenomenon and try to recognize when it might occur. As managers evaluating the decisions of others, we may also want to be attuned to the potential effects of opinion polarization and framing on group outcomes.

"Groupthink"

Perhaps the most well-known effect in the group decision-making literature is the "groupthink" effect. Janis (1972) coined this term to refer to the tendency of some groups who work together over a period of time to produce poorly reasoned decision. When social pressures and conflict avoidance overtake the desire to rigorously question alternatives, contradicting opinions are suppressed in favor of concurrence seeking. Eventually, the growing cohesiveness within the group leads to a shared illusion of invulnerability. Janis (1972, p. ■) writes:

> In my earlier research with ordinary citizens I had been impressed by the effects—both unfavorable and favorable—of the social pressures that develop in cohesive groups . . . Members tend to evolve informal objectives to preserve friendly intragroup relations, and this becomes part of the hidden agenda at their meetings . . . ordinary citizens become more concerned with retaining the approval of fellow members of their work group than with coming up with good solutions to the tasks at hand.

Janis used this argument to explain a number of historical failures, including the Bay of Pigs. Kennedy's Bay of Pigs invasion ranks as one of the poorest decisions ever made by the U.S. government. American intelligence officers with little background or experience in military matters attempted to secretly place a small brigade of Cuban exiles on a beachhead in Cuba with the objective of overthrowing the Castro government. The result was a fiasco.

Janis explains the Bay of Pigs, and many other poor decisions, by arguing that, in cohesive groups, the desire for concurrence leads to specific symptoms that inhibit the expression of critical ideas. These symptoms include an illusion of invulnerability, collective rationalization, belief in the inherent morality of the group, stereotypes of out-groups, direct pressure on dissenters, individual self-censorship, illusion of unanimity, and self-appointed mindguards. These symptoms are then argued to lead to a number of deficiencies in the decision-making process. These deficiencies include incomplete survey of alternatives, incomplete survey of objectives, failure to examine risks of preferred choice, failure to reappraise initially rejected alternatives, poor information search, selective bias in processing information at hand, and failure to work out contingency plans (Janis and Mann, 1977).

Janis is arguing that groupthink interferes with rational decision making; thus, groupthink can be viewed as a heuristic that limits effective decision making within highly cohesive groups. Specifically, individuals within these groups assume that unquestioning concurrence will result in good, or at least adequate, decisions; and any improvement sought by the expression of critical doubts is not worth the conflict that would result. The results of the groupthink hypothesis are compatible with the discussion of overconfidence in Chapter 2. In both cases, the decision-making body overestimates the infallibility of its judgment.

The Impact of Decision Heuristics within Groups

One approach to studying group decision making would be to examine the impact of the individual decision heuristics within groups. Unfortunately, very few studies have been conducted that explore the biases associated with these heuristics at the group level. However, a few exceptions exist and are highlighted here.

Argote, Seabright, and Dyer (1986) have investigated the use of the representativeness heuristic in both individual and group behavior. Their results indicate that groups exhibit the representativeness heuristic in the same directional pattern as individuals do. Further, they find that the magnitude of the biasing effect is even greater in groups than in individuals. Thus, biases like insensitivity to base rates, insensitivity to sample size, misconceptions of chance, regression to the mean, and the conjunction fallacy may affect group decision making to an even greater degree than they affect individual decision making.

Sniezek and Henry (1989) investigated the effect of group decision making on accuracy and confidence in assessing unknown situations. They found, in general, that groups are more accurate than individuals in their judgments regarding uncertain events. This is particularly true in groups in which there is a broad variance in individual judgments and a relatively high level of disagreement. However, groups are still just as susceptible to unreasonably high levels of confidence in their judgments. Some 98 percent of the subjects believed that their group judgments were in the top half of all group judgments with respect to accuracy. This finding suggests that overconfidence occurs in groups as well as in individuals.

Bazerman, Giuliano, and Appleman (1984) found groups, on average, to nonrationally escalate commitment to a previously selected course of action to a degree equal to that of individuals. The difference, however, is that there is much more variance in the behavior of separate groups. Many more groups than individuals do not escalate commitment, but groups that do, tend to do so to a greater degree than individuals. It seems that the added inputs of multiple group members increase the likelihood of recognizing the irrationality of escalating commitment to previous unsuccessful actions. If this realization does not occur, however, the group dynamic reinforces support for the initial decision and increases the level of rationalization to escalate commitment.

Group Negotiations

So far, the literature on group decision making that we have reviewed has assumed that the group has a cooperative orientation and that all members of the group share the same goal. In reality, most group decision-making situations within organizations are neither purely cooperative nor purely competitive, but involve aspects of both (Bazerman, Mannix, and Thompson, 1988). Each party needs the cooperation of other parties, yet the parties are often competing for fixed resources. Within this context, group decision making can often be most accurately understood as a negotiation in which three or more persons, representing their own interests, make decisions to resolve conflicting preferences. Thus, one useful way of thinking about group decision making is as a mixed-motive negotiation. Consider the following situation:

> Three vice-presidents meet to discuss the development of a new product within their corporation. Their company has a decentralized philosophy that discourages higher-level management from intervening in decisions across divisions; each division is designed to act as its own small company. The three divisions managed by these vice-presidents developed the product together. When development takes place across divisions, the vice-presidents of the divisions must make several decisions before the product can be sold externally. If agreements cannot be reached, and the product remains unsold, each vice-president will still benefit from internal uses of the product in their division. If the product is sold externally, the primary concern of these vice-presidents is the amount of profit each division will receive from the sale. The vice-presidents are concerned about profit allocation because salaries and promotions are determined by the profitability of the division. In addition to the profit-

allocation problem, the vice-presidents must negotiate production, marketing, and other issues. Each vice-president has different priorities across the issues relevant to the product's development, as well as different product-related information. The resolution of these additional issues has implications for the total amount of resources that the vice-presidents have to divide.

After resolving a number of issues, the company receives an offer from an external firm to buy the product for $10 million. They must now decide whether to accept the offer and, if they do, how to divide the proceeds.

Will members behave competitively in this group decision-making task? Or will they participate in a problem-solving search for a decision that is in the best interest of the entire organization? An opportunity for problem solving exists because all three members are interested in maximizing the profitability of the company. However, competition also exists because each vice-president has a different area of responsibility and different priorities. Thus, elements of both competition and cooperation are present in this scenario.

The benefit that each division receives through the internal use of the product and from external sales determines the value of the product to each vice-president. Imagine that the benefits from keeping the product are $2 million to division A, $3 million to division B, and $4 million to division C. These values provide the reservation points for each division. To accept an outside offer, each negotiator has to obtain an outcome at least as great as his reservation point. Thus, these values define the viable bargaining space, representing possible settlements. If no agreements exist within this space—for example, if the only external offer is for $8 million—then no agreement for an outside sale exists that is mutually beneficial to all parties.

In many ways, this problem resembles the El-Tek negotiation described in Chapter 6. The three vice-presidents must work together to find a way to obtain the integrative benefit of $10 million that is available through the outside offer (compared to the $9 million available through internal use). There is also a distributive aspect to the problem of how to divide the extra $1 million. In moving from a two-party to multiparty negotiation context, however, there are many reasons to expect that the negotiation will be more difficult. These reasons include increased information-processing demands, the necessity for decision rules, and more complex interpersonal processes.

Information Processing Demands   Group negotiations are cognitively more complex than dyadic processes. The group context requires an understanding of multiple opponents and partners, each with his own interests, goals, and so on. As we saw in Chapter 6, the negotiation literature emphasizes the importance of a full cognitive understanding of the other party (Raiffa, 1982). This complexity is multiplied when more parties exist. Increased information load can lead to systematic errors in negotiator judgment (Thompson, Mannix, and Bazerman, 1988).

Accurate assessment of the other negotiators' reservation points is critical for successful group negotiations. As the number of parties increase, the task of assessing the other parties' reservation points is more difficult. Negotiators may not have the time and resources necessary to obtain information. Negotiators may falsely assume that the other parties' reservation points are more similar than they really are; negotiators may use their assessment of one party's reservation point as an anchor for their judgment of the other party.

Decision Rules   We have discussed group negotiation as if acceptance by all parties is essential if a binding agreement is to be reached. This assumption is necessary in two-party negotiations. In group negotiations, however, a unanimous rule for decision making is just one of many alternatives (Mannix, Thompson, and Bazerman, 1989). For example, majority rule is another common rule for reaching decisions in groups. Individuals in group negotiations must select and implement a decision rule to determine how individual preferences will be combined to yield a group decision. Negotiators have to decide on the criteria that will constitute a choice or decision. The decision rule, and the ensuing coalition dynamics, are likely to have a profound effect on the nature of the distribution of outcomes. Decision rules also affect the problem solving necessary for reaching integrative agreements in the multiparty context (Thompson, Mannix, and Bazerman, 1988). Voting, the most commonly accepted decision rule, encourages coalitional behavior. Parties focus more on how to get enough votes for their perspective, rather than on sharing information to make a wise decision (Bazerman, Mannix, and Thompson, 1988). If the vice-presidents have a majority-rule decision procedure, two of the three vice-presidents can override the third member and form an agreement that is to their benefit but that does not benefit the third member *or* the overall organization. Further implications of such coalitional behavior are discussed in the next section.

Complex Interpersonal Processes   Interpersonal dynamics are more complex as the number of parties expands. Social-psychological research suggests that in larger groups, individuals tend to conform more and look to the group to determine appropriate behavioral norms—the rules of conduct established by the members of the group to maintain behavioral consistency (Asch, 1951; Shaw, 1981). This phenomenon is very similar to groupthink. As the group size increases, uncertainty increases, and apprehensiveness about others' interpersonal evaluations of our behavior increases. We tend to look more to the group to decide how to behave, and we are less likely to dissent, thus limiting the behaviors available for identifying creative, integrative agreements.

Norms also govern perceptions of fairness in the group. Fisher and Ury (1981) advocate the use of objective standards as a guideline to what is fair. However, there is a great diversity in definitions of appropriate standards of resource distribution, as we saw in the section on assisted decision making. These include global perspective, equity, equality, need, and anchoring. As group negotiators, we need to be aware of various norms of distribution. Acting in accordance with an equity norm, when the other group members hold an equality norm, may lead to inefficient outcomes and harm the social relationships among parties. We must consider the fairness of their proposals in order to be effective in group decision-making contexts.

Summary   The critical observation of this section is that group decision making is often a mixed-motive task. As group decision makers, we often fail to think about this decision-making context in a systematic way. The beginning of this section described the ways in which the nature of group decision making is susceptible to judgmental errors. As a manager, you need to be aware that many judgmental biases also occur in groups. From the group negotiation perspective, we also see that the conflicting interests of group members can increase the difficulty of making a rational decision. Actions that are best for the individual may or may not be best for the group. The complexity of group decision situations adds opportunity for error on levels beyond pure judgment—in processing information, determining appropriate decision rules, and interpreting interpersonal processes.

COALITIONS

The book *Greed and Glory on Wall Street: The Fall of the House of Lehman* (Auletta, 1986) provides a fascinating description of the disintegration of a firm that had been a major force on Wall Street for over 100 years. The decline begins with a power struggle between two coalitions, the "traders" and the "bankers," over the distribution of profits and the allocation of ownership shares (Mannix, 1989). The coalition of traders, with their short-term focus on distributing profits, is able to gain enough power to obtain and redistribute a large percentage of the firm's equity. This results in an unwise pattern of decisions that help the traders in the short-run, but deplete the firm's resources and destroy the long-term viability of the organization (Mannix, 1989). The result is the need to sell the firm under the threat of bankruptcy.

Mannix (1989) views coalition behavior as a type of defection, where some organization members obtain short-term gains, while individuals, groups, and the overall organization are hurt in the long run. Optimally, a "rational" organization would have all members focusing on the same organizational objective. In reality, members frequently focus on their own interests and those of their particular coalitions, detracting from efforts that benefit the overall organization. To the extent that more and more effort goes to the formation of coalitions, as was the case at Lehman, the interests of the overall organization are threatened. In a fascinating study of coalitional behavior in groups, Mannix found that the conditions that encourage coalitional behavior do, in fact, detract from the long-term survival and growth of the organization.

Many organizational writers do not agree with this fairly negative depiction of coalitions. Rather, they argue that coalitions are a fact of life and should be analyzed as a necessary entity in organizations. While this is descriptively accurate, it is necessary to realize that coalitional behavior does imply that some individuals are working for some objective other than what is best for the organization.

Consider the following situation (adapted from Raiffa, 1982):

Organizations A, B, and C are three independent companies. Each has designated a representative to send to a three-way negotiation. The representatives are empowered to commit their organizations. The three organizations have been told that if they work together, there are benefits to be gained. Indeed, the benefits are explicitly defined.

If A, B, and C can agree to work together, they can share benefits totaling 121 points (or think in terms of thousands of dollars, if you like). How they divide the benefit is up to them. However, an agreement requires that all parties agree to the same allocation of benefits. If only two of the parties agree to work together, there are lesser amounts of benefit points available, as follows:

A alone gets	0
B alone gets	0
C alone gets	0
Just A and B together get	118
Just A and C together get	84
Just B and C together get	50
A, B, and C together get	121

Again, any pair that decides to work together must provide an explicit allocation of how they will divide the benefit. Only one agreement is possible. That is, either a two- or three-way agreement can emerge with a specified allocation of benefit points.

What should happen in this situation? (Think about this question before reading further.)

One possibility is that B will rush out to work with A and propose a two-way agreement of 50 for B and 68 for A. They can then jointly offer 3 to C, if C wants to be part of a three-way coalition. While this is viable, A may decide that she is better off going to C, offering 8, while keeping 76 for herself. A can then go to B and offer B the 37 that can be gained by moving to a three-way agreement. C is happy to hear about this option of getting 8, but thinks that perhaps B would be willing to give C 10 on a two-way agreement and leave A out. B decides that it may now be wise to offer A a new agreement that gives 76 to A and 42 to B. This cycle of better offers can go on forever. There will always be a better offer available to one party by connecting to the previously excluded party. And if a three-way agreement is tentatively created, two of the parties will be able to do better by forming a two-way agreement and excluding the third party.

From this brief example, a number of important characteristics of coalitions can be observed. First, what is best for a coalition—the parties in a two-way agreement—is not necessarily best for the total group. Second, a large number of possible coalitions might form, and the sequence of the communication flow is often critical to determining which coalitions form. For example, who talks to whom first establishes a pertinent reference point. Similarly, past histories between parties can influence whether parties will gravitate toward a similar coalition. Third, coalitions are inherently unstable. Coalitions often form based on temporary alliances, and when the opportunity set of a member changes, the coalition is threatened. We see this pattern of instability in a number of parliamentary democracies throughout the world.

Alternative coalitional behavior can occur without any party's seeing their actions as "political." While the manager wants what is "best for the organization" (like the politician who wants what is "best for the country"), the various managers have differing ideas on what is best for the organization. Not surprisingly, their different views on what is best for the organization are often correlated with what is best for them. This scenario suggests that managers often form alliances that can later be used to influence organization decisions and actions (Cyert and March, 1963; Pennings and Goodman, 1977; Pfeffer and Salancik, 1978).

Careful analysis requires that organizational actors think systematically about coalition formation and stability. However, because of biases in judgment, managerial choices frequently fall short of rationality in this process. In the subsections that follow, the judgmental aspects of coalition formation and the decision to maintain an existing coalition are analyzed.

Coalition Formation   Game theorists and social psychologists make predictions on which coalitions will form based on rationalistic criteria (Murnighan, 1978). For example, the coalitions that form are those that most directly increase the resources of coalition members. While such models have demonstrated predictive validity, we argue that the actual behavior of potential coalition members is better described by focusing on the bounds of rationality that affect coalition formation. Specifically, the concepts of availability, overconfidence, and the tendency to ignore the cognitions of others can be applied to the topic of coalition formation to predict how actual coalitions form.

The availability heuristic suggests that the perceived probability of an event (such as the forming of a specific coalition) is influenced by the degree to which that event is easily available in memory. Consequently, previous successful coalitions will tend to reemerge. While this behavior often leads to efficient methods of coalition formation, there is also the danger that alternative combinations will be overlooked because of the exclusive focus on readily available coalitions. This tendency is exemplified in the forming of corporate boards of directors, coalitions empowered to make many of the most important decisions within organizations. Research has shown that directors are chosen in ways that lead to the formation of an elite group within American society (a megacoalition) that networks through overlapping board memberships (Bazerman and Schoorman, 1983; Schoorman, Bazerman, and Atkin, 1981). Many researchers argue that these interlocks are created by the elite group as a coordinating force across companies that subversively counters antitrust legislation limitations. An alternative interpretation is that existing boards are not so consciously chosen. Instead, members simply rely on available information

COALITIONS **159**

when recommending additional board members; they choose individuals with whom they have enjoyed working or who have impressed them in the past. Consequently, the same names come up over and over. (The representativeness heuristic could also be used to explain the same behavior to the extent that these individuals are representative of the type of individual whom the focal organization seeks to attract.)

Overconfidence can also impact coalition formation. Chapter 2 demonstrated that individuals have inappropriate confidence in their fallible judgment, and Chapter 7 provided evidence that this effect can be generalized to negotiators in their assessment of their likely success in negotiations. This section now offers the prediction that individuals are likely to be overconfident in their ability to form a powerful new coalition. For example, when William Agee of the Bendix Corporation was building a coalition among stockholders for the takeover of Martin Marietta, he was overconfident in his ability to form that coalition and complete the takeover. In the end, Agee agreed to sell Bendix to Allied, a "white knight," to save Bendix from the hostile attack by Martin Marietta. It can be further argued that Agee was forced into this situation because he failed to consider the cognitions of others at an early stage in the development of his coalition plan.

Coalition Stability   Turning to the area of coalition stability, a variety of rational models exist to predict behavior (Murnighan, 1978, 1986; Murnighan and Brass, 1990). For example, coalitions will be stable to the extent that there is a structural organizational link that enhances their viability. Again, the behavioral decision theory literature makes predictions that respond to these rationalistic arguments. Specifically, the framing, escalation, anchoring, and mythical fixed-pie effects all provide guidance in predicting long-term coalitional stability.

Consider a situation in which an existing coalition is in power. As our example showed, there are often alternative coalitions that can be formed that increase the power of particular coalition members. Accordingly, agreement by coalition members to maintain an existing coalition can be viewed as risk-averse behavior, while exploring alternative coalitions can be viewed as risk-seeking behavior. With this view of coalition stability, the framing effect in Chapter 3 predicts that coalition stability will be higher when coalition members have a positive, as opposed to negative, frame. As we showed earlier, the same objective situation can often be perceived in either frame.

The escalation literature asserts that individuals tend to make decisions in ways that escalate commitment to previously chosen courses of action. This perspective predicts that individuals will often maintain an existing coalition beyond the point when it is rational to pursue alternative coalitions. This point is further emphasized by our tendency to anchor our new decisions (the formation of a new coalition) by a previously existing anchor (the existing coalition).

Finally, our discussion of the notion of a mythical fixed pie (Chapter 7) may also be relevant to explaining the maintenance of existing coalitions. Consider the situation in which a dominant coalition exists, and it is in this coalition's best interests to add new members. This view requires that existing members recognize that the additions will increase the resources available to the total coalition. The mythical fixed-pie argument would predict, however, that existing coalition members will have a tendency to fail to recognize the full potential of expanding the pie. Instead, they will focus on the costs, both actual and perceived, of adding new members.

Summary   This section has asserted that coalitions have a dramatic impact on how decisions are made within groups and within organizations. Critical to the effect of coalitions is an understanding of how coalitions form and remain stable over time. This section's focus of the role of judgment in coalition formation and stability offer new explanations of coalition behavior, which may be more useful to the managerial audience than traditional rational analyses. The suggestions offered here, if empirically valid, provide specific guidance to organizational actors in thinking about coalition behavior. For example, the central role of the availability heuristic in affecting how coalitions form should lead you, as a manager, to think more carefully about how you ally yourself within organizational contexts. Similarly, the impact of framing, escalation, and anchoring on coalitional stability suggest that we may tend to stay in coalitions beyond their useful life. The views offered here allow you not only to critique your own behavior, but also to better understand the behavior of other organizational actors.

SOCIAL DILEMMAS

In his seminal article "The Tragedy of the Commons," Hardin (1968) introduced a dilemma confronting a group of herdsmen. In this parable, the herdsmen graze their cattle in a common pasture. Each herdsman knows that it is to his advantage to increase the size of his herd, because each additional animal represents personal profit to him. However, the cost of grazing, measured by the damage done to the pasture, is shared by all of the herdsmen. If the total number of animals gets too large, the pasture will be overloaded and will eventually be destroyed. Thus the herdsmen have a collective interest in establishing individual cattle allotments which limit the total number of cattle grazing in the pasture to a utilization rate that matches the rate of pasture replenishment. At the same time, it is in each herdsman's interest to marginally expand his grazing cattle beyond his allotment. Hardin argues that most herdsmen will respond to the short-term incentive and increase the size of their herds—leading to the ultimate destruction of the commons. What would you do?

Since the publication of this work, many people have drawn an analogy between the commons dilemma and the broader resource scarcity and pollution issues that we face as a society. Similarly, an analogy can be drawn to competing investment decisions among competitors in the marketplace, as the example in this section will show. In these situations, each party (the individual or the firm) makes a tradeoff between cooperation and noncooperation. Within these options, each party also chooses its level of adherence to or infraction against the shared resource. Intrigued by the dynamics of this choice, social science researchers have attempted to simulate the commons dilemma in a variety of situations. Laboratory experiments, field studies, and computer simulations have supported Hardin's view of the *tragedy* of the commons—namely, the early depletion of the shared resource.

In the classic social dilemma, parties communicate only through their actions, not verbally; for example, the herdsmen indicate their level of cooperation by the number of cattle they choose to graze. The following scenario from a two-party business context provides a useful forum for examining the dynamics of choice within social dilemma situations that can apply to any multiparty context. Consider the following:

> You are a product manager in charge of the marketing of a liquid dishwasher detergent. These are only two significant competitors in the market for liquid dishwasher detergent: your company and your major competitor. You are faced with the decision of whether or not to put on an advertising campaign that provides consumers with adverse information about your competitor's product. This adverse advertising might detail the destructive impact that the liquid dishwasher detergent has on the dishwasher's motor, its potential to leave spots on the dishes, and so on.
>
> Unfortunately, the other company is simultaneously thinking about whether or not to advertise the negative aspects of your product. Thus, the future profitability of your product depends not only on the decision you make, but also on the decision the other company makes. Specifically, if neither firm puts on a adverse advertising campaign, each firm will make $1 million for the sales period. If one firm puts on a derogatory advertising campaign but the competing firm does not, the firm that advertises will obtain a profit of $2 million, and the competitor will lose $2 million (as a result of a change in market share). If both firms advertise adverse information about the other firm, then total sales of liquid dishwasher detergent will fall and both firms will lose $1 million. No discussion with the other firm is possible. Do you advertise or not?

These relevant outcomes are summarized in the following table:

	A Don't Advertise	A Advertise
B Don't Advertise	A: $1 million profit B: $1 million profit	A: $2 million profit B: ($2 million loss)
B Advertise	A: ($2 million loss) B: $2 million profit	A: ($1 million loss) B: ($1 million loss)

A simple analysis of this decision makes the choice quite easy. If your competitor does not advertise, you will get $1 million if you do not advertise and $2 million if you do advertise. If your competitor does advertise, you will *lose* $2 million if you do not advertise and $1 million if you do advertise. In either case, no matter what the other company does, you are better off advertising. Thus, each party in this dilemma has a "dominating" strategy to advertise (Dawes, 1988); however, if both parties advertise, they both do worse than they would have done if neither had advertised. It would be fairly easy to negotiate a no-advertising agreement if the parties were allowed to talk and reach a binding agreement. However, this option is often not available in business contexts (as a result, for example, of antitrust laws).

This problem is similar to the classic problem concerning two prisoners (adapted from Rapaport and Chammah, 1965):

> Imagine that two accomplices in a crime have been apprehended by the police and are being interrogated separately. The police are confident that even if neither prisoner confesses or squeals on the other, they can convict both prisoners on minor charges and put them in prison for two years. However, the police really want at least one conviction on a higher charge, so they have offered each prisoner a deal. If either prisoner gives evidence that would lead to the conviction of his/her accomplice on higher charges, charges will be dropped and he/she will go free while his/her accomplice gets a ten-year sentence. If both squeal, then they will each get six-year sentences. Thus, for each prisoner, if his/her partner squeals, he/she could end up with the ten-year sentence while his/her partner goes free. What should the prisoners do? What would you do?

Just like the advertising problem, the two prisoners are confronted with a situation in which they are both better off staying silent (or not advertising) than both squealing (deciding to advertise). However, individually, each party is better off squealing (advertising), regardless of what the other party does.

As these examples and the commons dilemma show, a social dilemma evolves whenever each party in a competitive environment has a dominating strategy, yet it is everyone's best interests to collectively not choose this dominating option (Dawes, 1988). Neither the two-party case nor the multiparty case has an easy solution for creating cooperation. It is rational to compete! One of the confining aspects of the two-party examples as previously defined is that the choices are presented as one-shot decisions. In contrast, the commons dilemma and most managerial decisions are ongoing, with repeated decisions concerning whether or not to cooperate. In the most fundamental form of the multiple-round dilemma, the players communicate with one another through the sequences of their own behavior. Players can indicate cooperative or competitive orientations through their on-going choices. As we know, there is some incentive for both parties to cooperate in the long run, particularly if the situation is on-going. Thus, the existence of multiple rounds creates a context in which parties must consider the ramifications of their actions for the future; how can they build a successful long-term competitive strategy?

Axelrod (1984) has studied the prisoner's dilemma game in a multiperiod format to examine how, and whether, cooperation can emerge in on-going social dilemma situations. To test this problem, he invited experts to submit programs for a Computer Prisoner's Dilemma Tournament. Each entry outlined a strategy that designated each round's choice based on the history of past interactions. He then ran the 14 entries and a random strategy against each of the other strategies in a round-robin tournament.

The winner of the tournament was the simplest of all the programs submitted, Tit for Tat. Tit for Tat's strategy starts with cooperation and thereafter reciprocates with what the other player does on the previous move. Thus, on the first round, the prisoner is silent. On the next round, he does whatever his partner did on the first; in other words, he is silent if his partner was silent, or he squeals if his partner squealed, and so on. Axelrod then published the results of the tournament and solicited entries for a second round. This time he received 62 entries, including many attempts to improve on Tit for Tat. But Tit for Tat won again! Why? Because it develops far more cooperative relationships than any other strategy and wins the overall tournament by facilitating many mutually high scores. Thus it creates an "integrative agreement" with as many opponents as possible.

Based upon his results, Axelrod offers the following advice for players in ongoing dilemma situations:

1. **Don't be envious.** People tend to use as a standard of comparison their own success relative to the other players. This standard leads to envy, and in the social dilemma, envy is self-destructive. A better standard of comparison is how well you are doing relative to how well someone else could be doing in your shoes. Given the strategy of the other players, are you doing as well as possible?

   Tit for Tat won the tournament because it did well when played against a wide variety of other strategies. On average, it did better than any of the other strategies in the tournament; yet, Tit for Tat never once scored better in a game than the other player! In fact, it can't. Tit for Tat achieves either the same score as the other player, or a little less.

   The moral here is that there is no point in being envious of the success of the other player, since in an iterated Prisoner's Dilemma of long duration, the other's success is virtually a prerequisite for doing well yourself. Remember the object of the game: to score as well as possible over a series of interactions with another player who is also trying to score well. Note that this says nothing about scoring better than your opponent on any particular round.

2. **Don't be the first to defect.** Avoid unnecessary conflict by cooperating as long as the other player does. Axelrod calls this being *nice*. A couple of important qualifications are necessary here. First, when the future of the interaction is not important enough relative to immediate gains from defection, then simply waiting for the other to defect is not a good idea. If the other player is not likely to be seen again, defecting right away is more profitable than being nice. Second, if everyone else is using a strategy of always defecting, then a single individual can do no better than to use this same strategy.

3. **Reciprocate both cooperation and defection.** The Tit for Tat strategy represents a balance between retaliating and forgiving. Extracting more than one defection for each defection of the other risks escalation. On the other hand, extracting less than one-for-one retribution risks exploitation. The precise level of forgiveness that is optimal depends on the environment. In

particular, if the main danger is unending mutual recriminations, then a generous level of forgiveness is appropriate. But, if the main danger is from strategies that are good at exploiting easy-going rules, then an excess of forgiveness is costly.

4. **Don't be too clever.** Your strategy must be clear if you want the other player to respond to your pattern of action. Keeping your intentions hidden is useful in a zero-sum situation, where any inefficiency in the other player's behavior will be to your benefit. But in a non-zero-sum situation, it does not always pay to be so clever. In the iterated Prisoner's Dilemma, you benefit from the other player's cooperation. The trick is to encourage that cooperation. A good way to do that is to make it clear that you will reciprocate. Words can help here, but as everyone knows, actions speak louder than words. That is why the easily understood actions of Tit for Tat are so effective.

Summary In sum, what accounts for Tit for Tat's success is its combination of being nice, retaliatory, forgiving, and clear. Its niceness prevents it from getting into unnecessary trouble. Its retaliation discourages the other side from persisting whenever defection is tried. Its forgiveness helps restore mutual cooperation. And its clarity makes it intelligible to the other player, thereby eliciting long-term cooperation.

The foundation of this cooperation is not really trust, but the durability of the relationship. There is a difference between my trusting you as a person versus your having a tangible incentive to maintain our relationship. Thus, whether the players trust each other or not is less important in the long run than whether the conditions are ripe for them to build a stable pattern of cooperation with each other.

While Axelrod's advice was built around a two-party problem, the logic of the advice applies when more than two parties are involved in the dilemma. Price wars (whether between airlines, oil-producing nations, or breakfast cereal manufacturers), promotional strategies, advertising wars, and military competition can all be fruitfully addressed using Axelrod's insights. It is easy to see similar, yet more complicated, dynamics with more than two parties. Since more people are involved, the harm of a defection is spread out across more people, and any one actor is less affected by a specific defection. In addition, as the number of people in the social dilemma is increased, the anonymity of a defection is also increased (for example, you are unlikely to be labeled a defector for not contributing to public television [Dawes, 1988]). As a result, the general level of defection can be expected to be higher as the number of individuals involved in the dilemma increases.

Despite the logic for defection in many social dilemma contexts, much cooperation is observed. Why? Dawes (1988) argues that many people will cooperate because they believe that it is the right thing do to. In addition, Dawes has found that the opportunity to communicate has a substantial effect on cooperation, when the communication deals with the dilemma facing the participants. The failure of the frequent flyer programs discussed in Chapter 4 was exacerbated by the lack of communication and the lack of creativity in finding substitutes for direct communication. It is obvious that there are no simple answers to most competitive problems. However, far too often we adopt a very simple strategy that escalates conflict when we do not stop and consider our opponent's response. Axelrod offers some unique advice that is worth considering the next time before you "defect."

CONCLUSION

This chapter has covered a broad spectrum of issues concerning the nature of decision making when more than two parties are involved. As noted in the introduction, multiparty decision contexts are inherently more complex than individual or two-party situations. This is due, in part, to the richness of the interpersonal networks and the number of individual cognitions that are involved.

In the first section on competitive bidding, we learned that the "winner's curse" effect is a potential pitfall in numerous business contexts. It originates when we fail to adequately account for the cognitions of our competitors. In the second section, on assisted decision making, we saw that the role of the third party is critical to managerial life. An important component of that role is an understanding of the multiple criteria upon which third parties can base their decisions. These criteria include the global perspective, need, equity, equality, and anchoring. In particular, third parties seem prone to anchored decisions. In the third section on group decision making, we observed that groups are as susceptible as individuals to biased judgments. If was further remarked that even in cooperative intraorganizational contexts, most group decision-making situations are in reality mixed-motive, combining cooperation and competition. The fourth section highlighted the role of coalitions in multiparty contexts and used our knowledge of judgment from earlier chapters to better explain coalitional behavior. Finally, the fifth section on social dilemmas offered further insight into mixed-motive situations in an interorganizational context. From Axelrod's fascinating experiment, we learned that is best to be nice, retaliatory, forgiving, and clear in these situations.

Together, the information presented in this chapter offers a vast number of issues to consider in evaluating multiparty decision making. Unfortunately, there are no easy formulas for fully understanding these contexts. I only hope that from the array of information presented here, you have been able to pick up some key lessons. Perhaps the most important observation is that the descriptive understanding of individual and two-party judgment that you have developed in Chapters 1 through 7 can be translated to multiparty judgment. As in individual contexts, you need to become more aware of your unconscious responses in multiparty contexts by thinking carefully and creatively when approaching new decision situations.

NINE
IMPROVING DECISION MAKING

The capacity of the human mind for formulating and solving complex problems is very small compared with the size of the problems whose solution is required for objectively rational behavior in the real world . . .

Herbert A. Simon

This quote articulates a central thrust of this book. While most of us make judgments that are good enough to get us by in everyday life and in the corporate world, the contention of this book is that there is plenty of room to improve our judgment. Humans are not "bad" decision makers, but we do fall short of objectively rational behavior. In addition, there are specific ways in which our minds fail to achieve rationality. As we have seen throughout the book, this is true in individual, as well as multiparty, decision-making contexts. The only remaining question is what we can do to correct these deficiencies. This concluding chapter outlines a variety of strategies to address this question.

In responding to the need to take corrective action, this chapter considers prescriptive responses to the limitations to rationality that have been described. In many areas of inquiry in the social sciences, descriptive and prescriptive work are not well connected. However, the area of decision making is a notable exception. A primary reason for this exception is that so much of the descriptive work is done against a prescriptive background. That is, descriptive researchers often describe decision making in comparison to a rational prescription. For example, the tendency to escalate was defined as a systematic bias in comparison to the decision of a rational model. This means that prescriptive work can be seen as a set of techniques to correct previously identified deficiencies.

This chapter presents four alternative and complementary strategies for making better decisions than those that we can expect without adjusting our intuition. These four strategies are (1) acquiring expertise, (2) debiasing judgment, (3) using linear models, and (4) adjusting intuitive prediction. Each improvement strategy will be briefly reviewed, with references that provide direction for pursuing these judgment improvement strategies in more detail.

STRATEGY 1: ACQUIRING EXPERIENCE AND EXPERTISE

Many of the biases that have been examined in this book have been tested on student samples, with subjects who were not being rewarded for accurate performance and who were making decisions in task domains with which they were unfamiliar. Thus, one optimistic possibility is that experts or experienced decision makers making important decisions might be far less affected by biases. Does this book blow these mistakes out of proportion? This is certainly an important question, since knowing the impact of obtaining experience and expertise might be a key to more effective decision making (Neale and North-craft, 1989). The impact of experience and expertise is the focus of this section.

It has been argued that individuals in the real world will correct their judgments by learning from feedback about past decisions. This view is represented by Kagel and Levin (1986, p. 917) in their analysis of the winner's curse in competitive bidding discussed in Chapter 8:

> Given sufficient experience and feedback regarding the outcomes of their decisions, we have no doubt that our experimental subjects, as well as most bidders in "real world" settings, would eventually learn to avoid the winner's curse in any particular set of circumstances. The winner's curse is a disequilibrium phenomenon that will correct itself given sufficient time and the right kind of information feedback.

In fact, Kagel and Levin (1986) do show a reduction in the winner's curse in the auction context as *the market,* not necessarily specific players, learns over time. Some of this learning is through the disappearance of the most aggressive bidders from the market. Additional learning occurs by observing the consistent losses being suffered by "winners" in the auction.

There can be little disagreement that we do learn many things through our life experiences. However, the case of judgmental distortions is less clear. Tversky and Kahneman (1986) have argued that basic judgmental biases are unlikely to be corrected in the real world. Responsive learning requires accurate and immediate feedback, which is rarely available because:

> (i) outcomes are commonly delayed and not easily attributable to a particular action; (ii) variability in the environment degrades the reliability of feedback . . . ; (iii) there is often no information about what the outcome would have been if another decision had been taken; and (iv) most important decisions are unique and therefore provide little opportunity for learning (see Einhorn and Hogarth, 1978) . . . any claim that a particular error will be eliminated by experience must be supported by demonstrating that the conditions for effective learning are satisfied (pp. s274–s275).

In an examination of learning to avoid the winner's curse in the "Acquiring a Company" problem described in Chapter 7, Ball, Bazerman, and Carroll (1990) used a repeated trial version to test the ability of individuals to learn to incorporate the decisions of others into their own decision making. Subjects were playing for real money; they played twenty times; full feedback was provided immediately after each trial based on a random determination of the value of the firm; and subjects could observe changes in their asset balance (which virtually always went down). Thus, the ideal conditions existed for learning when compared to the limitations cited by Tversky and Kahneman. The only limitation that was not eliminated, namely variability of the environment (*ii* above), is part of the winner's curse phenomenon. Thus, Ball, Bazerman, and Carroll (1990) addressed whether or not the ability to consider the cognitions of the other party in a bilateral negotiation problem can be learned in a highly favorable environment.

Remembering that $0 is the correct answer and that $50 to $75 is the answer typically obtained when decision makers ignore the cognitions of others, examine the mean bids across the twenty trials in Figure 9.1. There is no obvious trend toward learning the correct response across the twenty trials. In fact, only 5 of 72 subjects from a leading MBA program learned. Our general conclusion is that a variety of the biases that affect negotiators are not fully eliminated simply by experience or feedback.

This evidence paints a very pessimistic picture of the idea that experience will, in fact, cure the decision biases identified in this book. Thus, there is need to investigate alternative ideas for developing more rational decision-making skills. Neale and Northcraft (1989) propose that biased decision-making outcomes may be eliminated or ameliorated through the development of expertise. We often think of experience and expertise as closely related. However, Neale and Northcraft view experience simply as repeated feedback, while expertise requires that the decision makers have a conceptual understanding of what constitutes a rational decision-making process and that they recognize the biases that limit the rationality of this decision-making process. Thus, to develop expertise, decision makers need to acquire a better idea of how to make rational decisions and how to avoid biases. Neale and Northcraft refer to expertise as developing a "strategic conceptualization."

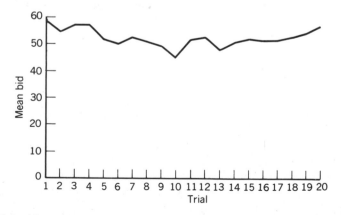

Figure 9.1 Mean offers across 20 trials of the "Acquiring A Company" problem.

We can see the relevance of Neale and Northcraft's experience/expertise distinction by considering the question of whether or not experience decision makers have much to gain by studying decision making. In my own executive teaching work, this is a very important question. What do we have to offer to a very experienced decision maker? First, Northcraft and Neale's (1987) study of anchoring and adjustment in real estate agents suggests that experienced decision makers can be very biased. In addition, while most "effective decision makers" are effective in a very specific domain, experience without expertise can be quite dangerous when they are transferred to a different context or when the environment changes. Evidence from Chapter 2 suggests that as the amount of ignorance increases, individuals become *more* overconfident in their fallible judgment. Consider the recent history of labor–management relations in the United States (briefly discussed in Chapter 7). In the 1960s, we had very experienced negotiators on both sides. When the environment changed and the United States became less competitive, however, the experience of labor and management led them to use old decision-making strategies in a new, more competitive environment. This led to a disastrous period of layoffs for organized labor and declines in U.S. manufacturing. These negotiators had lots of experience, but lacked expertise—that is, the strategic conceptualization of how to successfully adapt to a internationally oriented environment.

Dawes (1988) highlights the drawbacks of learning from experience when he notes that Benjamin Franklin's famous quote "experience is a dear teacher" is often misinterpreted to mean "experience is the best teacher." Dawes asserts that what Franklin really meant was that "experience is an expensive teacher," because he goes on to observe, "yet fools will learn in no other [school]." Dawes writes,

> Learning from an experience of failure . . . is indeed "dear," and it can even be fatal . . . moreover, experiences of success may have negative as well as positive results when people mindlessly learn from them. . . . people who are extraordinarily successful—or lucky—in general may conclude from their "experience" that they are invulnerable and consequently court disaster by failing to monitor their behavior and its implications . . .

This view of experience reiterates the comparative value of expertise and the development of a "strategic conceptualization." Developing expertise, as defined by Neale and Northcraft, specifically avoids the danger of "mindless" learning. It requires constant monitoring and awareness of our decision-making processes. It does not simply rely upon the feedback of uncertain, uncontrollable, and often delayed results.

The final benefit of developing a strategic conceptualization concerns transferability. If you ask many experienced decision makers how they do what they do, they will often tell you that it is an art that comes from years of observation and experience. But what they are really saying is that they do not explicitly know how they do what they do. This obviously reduces their ability to pass on their knowledge to others—a key task of management. Thus, a final drawback of experience without expertise is that it limits the ability to transfer knowledge to future generations.

A key element of developing a strategic conceptualization is learning to avoid the many biases in individual and group contexts that have been discussed throughout this book. The awareness that has been created in Chapters 1 through 8 is a first step toward developing your strategic conceptualization of decision making. However, awareness is not the complete answer to becoming a better decision maker. Debiasing is the topic of the next section of this chapter.

STRATEGY 2: DEBIASING JUDGMENT

Debiasing refers to a procedure for reducing or eliminating biases from the cognitive strategies of the decision maker. Fischhoff (1982) has provided the most extensive discussion of procedures for debiasing judgment. He proposes four strategies that reflect increasing pessimism about the ease of perfecting decision making: (1) warning about the possibility of bias; (2) describing the direction of the bias; (3) providing a dose of feedback; (4) offering an extended program of training with feedback, coaching, and whatever else it takes to improve judgment. Research on the hindsight bias (Fischhoff, 1977) from Chapter 2 has shown that even when biases are explicitly described to subjects and subjects are asked to avoid the bias, the bias remains. However, research on the overconfidence bias has found that intensive, personalized feedback is moderately effective in improving judgment (Bazerman and Neale, 1983; Lichtenstein and Fischhoff, 1980). Overall, debiasing is a difficult process that must be guided by a psychological framework for *changing.*

Fischhoff's research is quite instructive for developing a model to improve intuition. His work suggests that debiasing is quite difficult. In addition, it suggests that feedback on an individual's own decisions is an important ingredient to successful judgment improvement. Based on Lewin's framework in Chapter 1, Fischhoff's debiasing research, and my own judgment-training programs with MBA and executive students, this section makes specific suggestions for debiasing judgment.

Unfreezing   In Chapter 1, Lewin told us that many behaviors at the individual, group, and organizational levels are ingrained, part of the individual's and organization's standard repertoire, and thus quite difficult to change. He suggested that individuals find protection in the status quo. Translated into decision terms, individuals are often risk averse and prefer the certain outcomes of known behavior to the uncertain outcomes of innovative behavior. Lewin goes on to note that, in order for change to occur and last over time, an explicit unfreezing process needs to take place. The importance of Lewin's unfreezing concept is central to changing the decision-making processes of individuals. This is true for at least three reasons. First, individuals have used their current intuitive strategy for many years. To want to change would be to admit that there was something wrong with past strategies. This is likely to be psychologically disturbing. Thus, individuals may be motivated to avoid the emotionally disturbing information provided by the knowledge of judgmental deficiencies.

Second, individuals who are successful (it is assumed that this includes most MBA students, managers selected for executive education programs, and readers of this book) have generally received positive reinforcement for many of their past decisions. According to the basics of reinforcement theory, individuals tend to continue behaviors that are positively rewarded. For example, many successful executives rose to the top using intuitive strategies. This increases individuals' resistances to any information indicates that their judgment is systematically deficient in some demonstrable manner.

Third, balance theory (Heider, 1958) suggests that individuals typically keep their cognitions in some consistent order. For successful managers, the cognition that "there is something fundamentally wrong with my decision-making processes" is inconsistent with their cognition about their success. The cognition "I am currently an excellent decision maker" is much more in balance, and according to balance theory, that cognition is more likely to dominate.

Overall, a pattern emerges of an intelligent manager who has multiple reasons for believing in the quality of his decision-making processes and resisting any changes in intuitive strategies. In contrast, this book provides substantial evidence that there is significant room for improvement in the intuitive strategies of many bright, successful managers. Thus, we conclude that improving intuition is an important activity for successful managers, but that cognitive resistance to change is a predictable pattern.

To combat this resistance, this book used a quiz-and-feedback format that was designed to unfreeze your thinking processes. Most readers make a substantial number of mistakes on these items and respond by wanting to know where they went wrong and how they could have known to do better. This process unfreezes the notion that your decision-making processes have no need for improvement and that the book has little to offer. You are no longer frozen to past decision processes but want to know what can be changed to create improvement. In other cases (such as the dollar auction), vivid examples were given that had the potential to unfreeze your thinking by leading you to identify with individuals who fell victim to judgmental deficiencies. Thus, this book sought to create change in judgment by exposing you to concrete evidence that led you to question your current judgment strategies. A pure text format or lecture is unlikely to have achieved this objective.

Change   The next stage consists of the change itself. The individual is now unfrozen from past behaviors and is willing to consider alternatives. However, change is far from guaranteed. The resisting forces are likely to remain, and the individual is likely to continually reassess the desirability of change. In terms of changing decision-making processes, there are three critical pieces of the change process itself: (1) clarification of the existence of specific judgmental deficiencies, (2) explanation of the roots of these deficiencies, and (3) reassurance that these deficiencies should not be taken as a threat to the individual's self-esteem.

The first piece consists of abstracting from the concrete example that was used for unfreezing to identify the more general bias that exists. In addition, for the bias to have face validity to the individual, an explanation of why the bias exists is necessary. This often consists of clarifying the heuristic or phenomenon that underlies the bias. Finally, this information may be threatening enough to increase the individual's resistance that was partially overcome in the unfreezing stage. Thus, reassurance is necessary. Specifically, it is critical that the individual understand that virtually everyone has biases, that they do not imply that one is a poor decision maker, only that room for improvement exists.

Refreezing Once the change takes place, it is still easy for the individual to revert back to past practices. The old biases still exist and can be easily used. The new procedures are foreign and must develop their place as intuitive strategies. This takes place with practice over time. The individual needs to knowingly use the new knowledge in multiple applications. Slowly, the new strategies will become second nature and will take the place of old practices as intuitive strategies. However, frequent application and repeat training are necessary if the change is to last and become institutionalized as part of the individual's intuitive strategies.

You have now been through the first two stages of this change process: unfreezing and change. Now, for refreezing to occur, you must continue to examine your decisions for bias. Even after you have finished this book, you need to pay attention to your decision-making processes; you need to schedule routine check-ups to evaluate your recent important decisions—those made both individually and as a negotiator or work group member; and you need to remain aware of the limits of your decision-making processes.

STRATEGY 3: USING LINEAR MODELS BASED ON EXPERT JUDGMENT

The judgment-improvement strategy in the previous section responded directly to the biases discussed in this book. Since the presentation of this book is based on a debiasing approach to judgment improvement, this approach is the central strategy to judgment improvement. However, there are a number of reasons for examining alternative approaches. First, we will never be entirely debiased. Second, even if we could always make the "rational" choice, the amount of time that it would take to perfect our decision making may not be worth the effort. In addition, we are often faced with the problem of creating a decision-making environment under which *others*, who may not be debiased, will be making decisions. Under these conditions, there are strategies that respond to the limitations of human judgment by creating alternative mechanisms to debiasing intuition in *specific* contexts.

One alternative mechanism for debiasing consists of using an expert's knowledge to build a linear model that simulates judgment in making future decisions. This strategy attacks the traditional view of expert decision making as being a mysterious phenomenon, unamenable to the precise description that a model implies (Bowman, 1963; Slovic, 1982). This traditional view of expert decision making can be seen in a letter that I received from a well-known arbitrator when I asked the arbitrator to make a number of decisions as part of a study on the decision-making processes of arbitrators, discussed in Chapter 8 (Bazerman, 1985, p. 563):

> . . . You are on an illusory quest! Other arbitrators may respond to your questionnaire; but in the end you will have nothing but trumpery and a collation of responses which will leave you still asking how arbitrators decide cases. Telling you how I would decide in the scenarios provided would really tell you nothing of any value in respect of what moves arbitrators to decide as they do. As well ask a youth why he is infatuated with that particular girl when her sterling virtues are not that apparent. As well ask my grandmother how and why she picked a particular "mushmelon" from a stall of "mushmelons." Judgment, taste, experience, and a lot of other things too numerous to mention are factors in the decisions.

In contrast, I believe that in repeatable decision-making situations, experts can be replaced by models based on their judgments, and these models can make better predictions than the experts! This section examines a strategy that allows for capturing the arbitrator's decision-making model (or his grandmother's choice of a mushmelon).

The statistical technique that is typically used is regression analysis. (Our purpose is not to examine the technical properties of such procedures, but to describe the essence of using a linear model to capture an expert's decision-making processes. Slovic and Lichtenstein [1971] review the technical use regression analysis to capture decision processes.) This approach necessitates that an expert make decisions on a large number of cases, each of which is defined by the same set of factors. A regression equation is then developed for that expert which describes his idiosyncratic model for making decisions. This procedure, referred to as **policy capturing,** has previously been used to investigate performance appraisal (Anderson, 1977; Naylor and Wherry, 1965; Zedeck and Kafry, 1977), promotion policy (Stumpf and London, 1981), and job choice (Zedeck, 1977), among many other managerial and nonmanagerial applications.

One compelling example of the use of linear models is provided by Dawes's (1971) work on graduate admissions decisions. He modeled the average judgment of a four-person committee. The predictors in the model were (1) a score from the Graduate Record Examination, (2) overall undergraduate grade point average, and (3) quality of the undergraduate school. Dawes used the model to predict the average rating of 384 applicants. He found that the model could be used to reject 55 percent of the applicant pool without ever rejecting an applicant that the selection committee had in fact accepted. In addition, the weights used to predict the committee's behavior were better than the committee itself in predicting future faculty ratings of the accepted and matriculated applicants! Dawes estimated in 1971 that the use of a linear model as a screening device by the nation's graduate schools (not to mention the larger domains of undergraduate admissions, corporate recruiting, and so on) could result in an annual savings of about $18 million worth of professional time.

Researchers have found that linear policy-capturing models produce superior predictions across an impressive array of domains. In addition, research has found that more complex models produce only marginal improvements above a simple linear framework. Why do linear models work so well? Dawes (1979) argues the underlying reason is that people are much better at selecting and coding information (such as what variables to put in the model) than they are integrating the information (using the data to make a prediction). Einhorn (1972) illustrates this point in a study of physicians who coded biopsies of patients with Hodgkin's disease and then made an overall rating of severity. The individual ratings had no predictive power of the survival time of the patients—all of whom died. The variables that the physicians selected to code did, however, predict survival time when optimal weights were determined with a multiple regression model. The point is that the doctors knew what information to consider, but they did not know how to integrate this information consistently into valid predictions.

In addition to the difficulty we have in integrating information, we are also unreliable. Given the same data, we will not always make the same decision. Our decisions are affected by mood, subjective interpretations, random fluctuations, and the like. In contrast, a linear model will always make the same decisions with the same inputs. Thus, the model captures the underlying policy that the expert uses without the random error that the expert adds in making decisions. Further, the expert is likely to be affected by a number of the biases that inappropriately impact specific cases. In contrast, the model includes only the actual data that is empirically known to have predictive power, not the salience or representativeness of that or any other available data. This point was brought home to me in the graduate school application of Mark Sonet (name has been changed). Sonet was a graduate student in the department of one of my early faculty positions. He was extremely bright, had a history of excellent board scores, had good grades, and had been in a number of graduate programs before, but never seemed to make much progress toward completing his doctorate. I was looking over some recent admissions decisions and noticed an applicant who had excellent grades, had excellent board scores, had previous graduate school background, seemed to have found his real interests, and was rejected. It seemed apparent to me that the applicant was well above the standards of the department and would have been easily accepted by a Dawes-type admissions procedure. When I asked why the applicant was rejected, I was told that he looked too much like Mark Sonet!

A number of similar examples can be easily identified in financial decisions, corporate personnel decisions, bank loan decisions, and routine purchasing decisions. The common aspect of these domains is that each requires the decision maker to make multiple routine decisions based on the same set of variables. These characteristics lend themselves well to the linear policy-capturing methodology, and ample evidence suggests that the linear models of the experts will outperform the experts. In addition, the linear policy-capturing procedure allows the organization to see what factors are important in the decision of its experts. Thus, the feedback and training potential of linear models, independent of their superior predictive powers, make them a valuable managerial tool.

While the evidence suggests the ample power of the policy-capturing methodology, its use is not that well diffused. Why? Resistance. Early in the development of the methodology, technical arguments on the predictive ability of linear models emerged (Dawes, 1979). These arguments have generally been addressed, and the literature provides strong support of the models. But this does not stop individuals from failing to believe in the predictive ability of the models. Stronger resistance comes in the form of ethical concerns and the general resistance to change.

The ethical concerns are well illustrated by this woman's statement, cited in Dawes (1979, p. 580)

When I was at the Los Angeles Renaissance Fair last summer, I overheard a young woman complain that it was "horribly unfair" that she had been rejected by the Psychology department at the University of California, Santa Barbara, on the basis of mere numbers, without even an interview. "How could they possibly tell what I'm like?" The answer is they can't. Nor could they with an interview . . .

Dawes goes on to argue that for decision makers to believe that they can predict better based on a half-hour interview than on the information contained in a transcript covering 3½ years of work and the carefully devised aptitude assessment of graduate board exams demonstrates unethical conceit on the part of the decision maker.

The other main factor against the use of linear models is that they have not been used in the past. Change is threatening. "What will my role be if I don't make the decisions?" "What do bank loan officers or college admissions officers do if they don't make decisions?" These concerns are common and express the fear that people are not central to the use of linear models. But people are important. People make the initial decisions, which are the ingredients to the model, and determine the variables to put into the model. People determine when the model needs to be updated. People monitor the performance of the model. Nevertheless, Lewin tells us that resistance to change can be expected. The use of linear decision models is clearly no exception to this expectation.

The foregoing models deal with weights that are determined by modeling the decisions of experts. Sometimes these data do not exist, but alternative procedures do exist. These include having experts provide the weights, using equal weighting procedures, and determining optimal weights according to the desired outcome as determined by a regression equation. Each of these has desirable properties over human intuition in repetitive decisions in which the same variables are used for prediction. A full discussion of these procedures is beyond the scope of this book. The reader is referred to Slovic and Lichtenstein (1971), Dawes and Corrigan (1974), and Dawes (1979).

Finally, a number of other procedures exist, that, like the policy-capturing methodology, try to model what experts do. These alternative procedures deal with the wider domain of general decision making and problem solving. Examples include recent developments in artificial intelligence and expert systems. These paradigms seek to provide knowledge representations and inference mechanisms to the computer in ways that allow for capturing and improving on what experts know about human problem-solving processes (Hayes-Roth, Waterman, and Lenat, 1983). Again, examination of these other modeling procedures is beyond the scope of the book, but identifying their existence is relevant to understanding the role of models in replacing human intuition in specific decision contexts.

STRATEGY 4: ADJUSTING INTUITIVE PREDICTIONS

The nature of managerial work requires reviewing the tentative decisions of others, transforming recommendations into decisions, and adjusting previously made decisions. This decision task is fundamentally different from the one implied by the rational decision model specified in Chapter 1. Clearly, as a managerial decision maker, you want to include the content of others' decisions and recommendations. Often, an initial decision is made with more information than you care to reevaluate. However, you are aware that these decisions are influenced by a set of biases. How can you systematically adjust the decisions of others to account for biases in order to make better final decisions? Consider the following managerial situation:

> You are the director of marketing for a retail chain that has 40 stores in 14 cities. Sales in these stores average between $2,000,000 and $4,000,000, with mean sales of $3,000,000. Twenty-five of those stores have opened in the last three years. Plans for the future include opening 30 new sites in the next four years. Because of this growth, you have a site location analyst assigned to predict the sales in each potential site. Unfortunately, predicting sales in new markets is very difficult, and even the best analyst faces a great deal of uncertainty. You are partially evaluated on the accuracy of the forecasts coming out of your department. The site location analyst has just handed you her latest forecast. It forecasts sales of $3,800,000 for a new potential site. The facts verify that the demography of this area should place this location as one of top producers in the chain. What is your reaction to the forecast?

At a naive level, there is reason to have confidence in the forecast. The analyst knows more of the details than you do about the data that underlies the prediction. In addition, your overview also predicts that the store will do well in comparison to existing stores. This evaluation is based on matching the representativeness of this site to other existing sites. However, one basic idea of statistical prediction, which is often counterintuitive, is the concept of regression to the mean bias, described in Chapter 2. There we saw that the extremeness of our predictions should be moderated toward the mean by the degree of uncertainty in the prediction (Kahneman and Tversky, 1982).

Assume that the site location analyst was excellent. In fact, there was a perfect (1.0) correlation between her predictions and actual sales. In that case, it would be appropriate to use the $3,800,000 prediction. However, also consider the case in which there is a correlation of 0 between her predictions (which are based on the demographic data) and actual sales. Then her forecast is meaningless. The only pertinent information is that the average store has sales of $3,000,000, and this figure becomes your best estimate. Most likely this is a case of intermediate predictability, the most common state. The forecast should then fall between sales of the mean store and the site location manager's estimate—becoming progressively closer to the analyst's estimate as her proven ability to predict sales accurately increases (Kahneman and Tversky, 1982). This analysis suggests that, as the director, you will want to reduce the forecast to somewhere between $3,000,000 and $3,800,000, depending upon your assessment of the correlation between the analyst's forecasts and actual sales. Essentially, you should use your broadened understanding of human judgment from this book to determine a systematic adjustment to the analyst's initial decision.

The foregoing analysis provides a rough guide to the adjustment of the analyst's forecast. Kahneman and Tversky (1982) have formalized this process into a five-step procedure. These steps are outlined here using the site location problem as an example. In reviewing each step, you should be thinking about how to convert the systematic training suggested in the five-step process into an intuitive, natural response. In this way, you, as a manager, can recognize the existence and direction of a wide range of biases across a wide range of decisions and make similar adjustments without undergoing a formal procedure each time.

1. **Select a comparison group.** This first step consists of selecting the set of past observations to which the current decision or forecast is to be compared. In the site location problem, comparing the new store to the population of all company stores is an obvious group. However, alternatives exist. The existence of multiple comparison groups is common. For example, it might be decided that only the stores that have opened in the last three years are appropriate for comparison. This option might be chosen if the recent stores are quite different from the established stores and are closer in description to the future store. A more inclusive group allows for a larger base for comparison, but its heterogeneity may reduce its comparability to the targeted forecast.

2. **Assess the distribution of the comparison group.** The next step involves assessing the characteristics of the past observations to which the current

decision is being compared. If the comparison group consists of all stores, we know the range and mean from the data presented. If we limit the group to recent stores, these data would need to be recalculated. In addition, we might want to get additional data about the shape of the distribution around the mean.

3. **Incorporate intuitive estimation.** This step calls for identifying the decision or forecast of the expert. In this case, it is the site location analyst's. Her estimate of $3,800,000 provides the intuitive estimate that needs to be adjusted. The next two steps attempt to improve this forecast.

4. **Assess the predictability of the analyst's forecast.** This is the most difficult step in the corrective procedure. It consists of determining the correlation between the decision or forecast and the comparison group data. It may be possible to assess this correlation by comparing past estimates to actual sales. In the absence of these data, you must determine some subjective procedure for this assessment. Kahneman and Tversky (1982) discuss this procedure in more detail. For our purposes, the key point is that the analyst's estimate assumes a correlation of 1.0 between her prediction and actual sales. In virtually all cases, we can produce a less biased estimate than the implicit assumption of a 1.0 correlation implies.

5. **Adjust the intuitive estimate.** This step calculates the adjustment that reduces the bias error of the initial decision or forecast. For example, this procedure should produce an estimate of $3,800,000 when the correlation in step 4 is 1.0, an estimate of $3,000,000 when the correlation is 0, and estimates proportionally in between when the correlation is in between. This adjustment can be formalized as follows:

$$\text{Adjusted estimate} =$$
$$\text{Group Mean} + \text{Correlation (Initial estimate} - \text{Group Mean)}$$

In our example, it is easy to see that this leads to a prediction of $3,400,000 when the correlation is 0.5; $3,600,000 when the correlation is 0.75; and so on. The person making the adjustment should fully understand the logic of the procedure and then evaluate its relevance to the decision at hand. In arguing for this adjustment, it should be remembered that we are again likely to face a problem of resistance to change.

These five steps provide a clearly delineated process for debiasing an individual's forecasting intuition by adjusting for the regression-to-the-mean bias. The formal procedure will typically improve the forecast. More important, a manager who understands the process can use this understanding to intuitively assess the degree to which an initial estimate should be regressed to the mean.

It is in this informal sense that we have a model for adjusting a wide range of biased decisions in both individual and multiparty contexts. Broadly, it involves three phases. First, we need to accurately perceive and analyze the context within which the decision is being made. Next, we need to distinguish the potential bias(es) surrounding the decision and its decision makers. Finally, we need to identify and make the appropriate logical adjustment(s) for that decision. As we can see from the example, this judgment-improvement technique can be used to evaluate and adjust our own, as well as others', intuitive judgments in a variety of situations.

CONCLUSION

In this final chapter, we have introduced four strategies for improving the deficiencies in our decision making. The first two, acquiring expertise and debiasing, seek to create broad change in our intuitive responses to decision-making situations. In general, they strive to heighten our awareness of our cognitive limitations and our susceptibility to bias. The second two strategies, using linear models and adjusting intuitive judgments, provide techniques for improving specific decisions in specific contexts. They offer concrete methods for testing and adjusting actual decisions. Together, these four strategies provide tools for "changing" and "refreezing" your intuitive decision-making processes over the months to come.

An optimistic, but naive, view of this book would expect that its readers would immediately improve their decision making. I say naive because it is premature to expect the change process intended by this book to be fully integrated at this point. If unfreezing did not take place, the book failed. If you were not provided with sufficient information for the change, the book failed. However, the responsibility for the refreezing and use of the decision-improvement strategies suggested in this last chapter lies with you. Refreezing requires a period when you are constantly reviewing your decision-making processes for the errors identified in this book. Refreezing also requires that you are vigilant in your search for biases in the more complex world of decisions that you face. Creating lasting internal improvement in decision making is a complex task that occurs gradually over time through persistent monitoring. It is far easier to identify a bias while reading a book about decision making than it is to identify a bias when you are in the middle of an organizational crisis. Raiffa (1984) has found that his students are most likely to use appropriate decision-making strategies in an exam where he is the teacher. However, these same students will often fail to generalize the relevance of these strategies to similar problems in other courses taught by other instructors. Thus, making adjustments to your decision-making processes requires constant attention.

In addition to improving your own decisions, the ideas in this book should be very useful for informing you about the decisions of others. We are often faced with situations in which we are suspicious of another party's decision making. However, we lack a way to articulate what is wrong with their logic. We think that they are wrong, but we do not know why. The information in this book provides some systematic clues for understanding and explaining the biases of others. You can practice spotting others' biases by examining tonight's newspaper or watching a sporting event on television. Reporters, sportscasters, and other public-information providers constantly make statements that exemplify the biased decision-making processes outlined in this book.

Overall, I hope that this book has raised your awareness of the importance of the decision-making *process,* not just the *results.* I am frightened by the number of managers who reward results, rather than good decisions. As we have seen, many decisions are made under uncertainty or for the wrong reasons. Thus, many good decisions turn out badly, and many bad decisions turn out well. To the extent that a manager rewards results, and not the decision-making process itself, the manager is likely to be rewarding behaviors that may not be functional in the future.

Davis (1971) argues that "interesting" writing leads readers to question issues that they never thought about before. Thus, it may be more important to identify new issues than to provide new answers to old questions. I hope that this book has made you aware of aspects of your decision-making process that create new questions and problems. I hope that this book has been "interesting."

REFERENCES

Adams, J. L. (1986). *Conceptual blockbusting.* Reading, MA.: Addison Wesley.

Adams, J. S. (1963). Toward an understanding of inequity. *Journal of Abnormal and Social Psychology* **67,** 422–436.

Adams, J. S. (1965). Inequity in social exchange. In L. Berkowitz (Ed.), *Advances in experimental social psychology,* Vol. 2. New York: Academic Press.

Akerlof, G. (1970). The market for lemons. *Quarterly Journal of Economics,* **89,** 488–500.

Alba, J. W., and Marmorstein, H. (1987). The effects of frequency knowledge on consumer decision making. *Journal of Consumer Research* **14,** 14–25.

Alpert, M., and Raiffa, H. (1969). *A progress report on the training of probability assessors.* Later published in D. Kahneman, P. Slovic, and A. Tversky (Eds.), *Judgment under uncertainty: Heuristics and biases.* Cambridge: Cambridge University Press, 1982.

Anderson, B. L. (1977). Differences in teachers' judgmental policies for varying numbers of verbal and numerical uses. *Organizational Behavior and Human Performance* **19,** 68–88.

Argote, L., Seabright, M. A., and Dyer, L. (1986). Individual versus group: Use of base-rate and individuating information. *Organizational Behavior and Human Decision Processes* **38,** 65–75.

Arkes, H. R., and Blumer, C. (1985). The psychology of sunk costs. *Organizational Behavior and Human Performance* **35,** 124–140.

Aronson, E. (1968). *The social animal.* San Francisco: Freeman.

Asch, S. E. (1951). Effects of group pressure on the modification and distortion of judgment. In H. Guetzkow (Ed.), *Groups, leadership, and men.* Pittsburgh: Carnegie Press.

Auletta, K. (1986). *Greed and glory on Wall Street: The fall of the house of Lehman.* New York: Warner Books.

Axelrod, R. (1984). *The evolution of cooperation.* New York: Basic Books.

Ball, S. B., Bazerman, M. H., and Carroll, J. S. An evaluation of learning in the bilateral winner's curse, *Organizational Behavior and Human Decision Processes,* in press.

Bar-Hillel, M. (1973). On the subjective probability of compound events. *Organizational Behavior and Human Performance* **9,** 396–406.

Bartlett, S. (1978). Protocol analysis in creative problem-solving. *Journal of Creative Behavior* **12,** 181–191.

Bazerman, M. H. (1982). Impact of personal control on performances: Is added control always beneficial? *Journal of Applied Psychology* **67,** 472–479.

Bazerman, M. H. (1983). Negotiator judgment: A critical look at the rationality assumption. *American Behavioral Scientist* **27,** 211–228.

Bazerman, M. H. (1984). The relevance of Kahneman and Tversky's concept of framing to organization behavior. *Journal of Management* **10,** 333–343.

Bazerman, M. H. (1985). Norms of distributive justice in interest arbitration. *Industrial and Labor Relations Review* **38,** 558–570.

Bazerman, M. H., Beekun, R. I., and Schoorman, F. D. (1982). Performance evaluation in a dynamic context: The impact of a prior commitment to the ratee. *Journal of Applied Psychology* **67,** 873–876.

Bazerman, M. H., and Brett, J. M. (1988). El-Tek: A two party negotiation simulation. Dispute Resolution Research Center, Northwestern University.

Bazerman, M. H., and Carroll, J. S. (1987). Negotiator Cognition. In L. L. Cummings and B. M. Staw (Eds.) *Research in organizational behavior,* Vol. 9, pp. 247–288. Greenwich, Conn.: JAI Press.

Bazerman, M. H., Giuliano, T., and Appelman, A. (1984). Escalation in individual and group decision making. *Organizational Behavior and Human Performance* **33,** 141–152.

Bazerman, M. H., and Lewicki, R. J. (1983). *Negotiating in organizations.* Beverly Hills: Sage.

Bazerman, M. H., Magliozzi, T., and Neale, M. A. (1985). The acquisition of an integrative response in a competitive market. *Organizational Behavior and Human Performance* **34,** 294–313.

Bazerman, M. H., Mannix, E., and Thompson, L. (1988). Groups as mixed-motive negotiations. In E. J. Lawler and B. Markovsky (Eds.), *Advances in group processes: Theory and research,* Vol. 5, Greenwich, Conn.: JAI Press.

Bazerman, M. H., and Neale, M. A. (1982). Improving negotiation effectiveness under final offer arbitration: The role of selection and training. *Journal of Applied Psychology* **67,** 543–548.

Bazerman, M. H., and Neale, M. A. (1983). Heuristics in negotiation: Limitations to dispute resolution effectiveness. In M. H. Bazerman and R. J. Lewicki (Eds.), *Negotiating in organizations.* Beverly Hills: Sage.

Bazerman, M. H., and Samuelson, W. F. (1983). I won the auction but don't want the prize. *Journal of Conflict Resolution* **27,** 618–634.

Bazerman, M. H., and Schoorman, F. D. (1983). A limited rationality model of interlocking directorates: An individual, organizational, and societal decision. *Academy of Management Review* **8,** 206–217.

Bazerman, M. H., Schoorman, F. D., and Goodman, P. S. (1980). A cognitive evaluation of escalation processes in managerial decision-making. Paper presented to 40th Annual Meeting of the Academy of Management, Detroit.

Bernstein, W. M., and Davis, M. H. (1982). Perspective taking, self-consciousness, and accuracy in person perception. *Basic and Applied Social Psychology* **3,** 1–19.

Bowman, E. H. (1963). Consistency and optimality in managerial decision making. *Management Science* **9,** 310–321.

Brandstatter, H., Davis, J. H., and Stocker-Kreichgauer, G. (1982). *Group decision making.* London: Academic Press.

Brockner, J., Nathanson, S., Friend, A., Harbeck, J., Samuelson, C., Houser, R., Bazerman, M. H., and Rubin, J. Z. (1984). The role of modeling processes in the "Knee Deep in the Big Muddy" phenomenon. *Organizational Behavior and Human Performance* **33,** 77–99.

Brockner, J., and Rubin, J. Z. (1985). *Entrapment in escalating conflicts.* New York: Springer-Verlag.

Brockner, J., Rubin, J. Z., Fine, J., Hamilton, T., Thomas, B., and Turetsky, B. (1982). Factors affecting entrapment in escalating conflicts: The importance of timing. *Journal of Research in Personality* **16,** 247–266.

Brockner, J., Rubin, J. Z., and Lang, E. (1981). Face-saving and entrapment. *Journal of Experimental Social Psychology* **17,** 68–79.

Brockner, J., Shaw, M. C., and Rubin, J. Z. (1979). Factors affecting withdrawal from an escalating conflict: Quitting before it's too late. *Journal of Experimental Social Psychology* **15,** 492–503.

Caldwell, D. F., and O'Reilly, C. A. (1982). Responses to failures: The effects of choices and responsibility on impression management. *Academy of Management Journal* **25,** 121–136.

Cambridge, R. M., and Shreckengost, R. C. (1980). Are you sure? The subjective probability assessment test. Unpublished manuscript. Langley, Va.: Office of Training, Central Intelligence Agency.

Campbell, D. T. (1969). Reforms as experiments. *American Psychologist* **24,** 409–429.

Cartwright, D. (1973). Determinants of scientific progress. *American Psychologist* **28,** 222–231.

Case, J. H. (1979). *Economics and the competitive process.* New York: New York University Press.

Chapman, L. J., and Chapman, J. P. (1967). Genesis of popular but erroneous diagnostic observations. *Journal of Abnormal Psychology* **72,** 193–204.

Cox, A. D., and Summers, J. O. (1987). Heuristics and biases in the intuitive projection of retail sales. *Journal of Marketing Research* **24,** 290–297.

Curran, J. J. (1987). Why investors make the wrong choices. *Fortune,* 1987 Investor's Guide.

Cyert, Richard M., and March, J. G. (1963). *A behavioral theory of the firm.* Englewood Cliffs, N.J.: Prentice-Hall.

Davis, M. S. (1971). That's interesting! *Philosophy of Social Science,* 309–344.

Davis, M. (1981). A multidimensional approach to individual differences in empathy. *JSAS Catalogue of Selected Documents in Psychology* **10,** 85.

Dawes, R. M. (1971). A case study of graduate admissions: Applications of three principles of human decision making. *American Psychologist* **26,** 180–188.

Dawes, R. M. (1979). The robust beauty of improper linear models in decision making. *American Psychologist* **34,** 571–582.

Dawes, R. M. (1988). *Rational choice in an uncertain world.* New York: Harcourt Brace Jovanovich.

Dawes, R. M., and Corrigan, B. (1974). Linear models in decision-making. *Psychological Bulletin* **81,** 95–106.

DeBono, E. (1971). *Lateral thinking.* New York: Harper.

Doise, W. (1969). Intergroup relations and polarization in individual and collective judgments. *Journal of Personality and Social Psychology* **12,** 136–143.

Einhorn, H. J. (1972). Expert measurement and mechanical combination. *Organizational Behavior and Human Performance* **7,** 86–106.

Einhorn, H. J., and Hogarth, R. M. (1978). Confidence in judgment: Persistence in the illusion of validity. *Psychological Review* **85,** 395–416.

Einhorn, H. J., and Hogarth, R. M. (1981). Behavioral decision theory: Processes of judgment and choice. *Annual Review of Psychology* **32,** 53–88.

Farber, H. S. (1981). Splitting-the-difference in interest arbitration. *Industrial and Labor Relations Review* **35,** 70–77.

Feldman, J. M. (1981). Beyond attribution theory: Cognitive processes in performance appraisal. *Journal of Applied Psychology* **66,** 127–148.

Festinger, L. (1957). *A theory of cognitive dissonance.* Evanston, Ill: Row, Peterson.

Fischhoff, B. (1975a). Hindsight ≠ foresight: The effect of outcome knowledge on judgment under uncertainty. *Journal of Experimental Psychology: Human Perception and Performance* **1,** 288–299.

Fischhoff, B. (1975b). Hindsight: Thinking backward. *Psychology Today* **8,** 71–76.

Fischhoff, B. (1977). Cognitive liabilities and product liability. *Journal of Products Liability* **1,** 207–220.

Fischhoff, B. (1980). For those condemned to study the past: Reflections on historical judgment. In R. A. Shweder and D. W. Fiske (Eds.), *New directions for methodology of behavior science: Fallible judgment in behavioral research.* San Francisco: Jossey-Bass.

Fischhoff, B., and Beyth, R. (1975). "I knew it would happen": Remembered probabilities of once-future things. *Organizational Behavior and Human Performance* **13,** 1–16.

Fischhoff, B., Lichtenstein, S., Slovic, P., Derby, S., and Keeney, R. (1981). *Acceptable risk.* New York: Cambridge University Press.

Fischhoff, B., Slovic, P., and Lichtenstein, S. (1977). Knowing with certainty: The appropriateness of extreme confidence. *Journal of Experimental Psychology: Human Perception and Performance* **3,** 552–564.

Fischhoff, B., Slovic, P., and Lichtenstein, S. (1981). Lay foibles and expert fables in judgments about risk. In T. O'Riordan and R. K. Turner (Eds.), *Progress in resource management and environmental planning,* Vol. 3, Chichester: Wiley.

Fisher, R., and Ury, W. (1981). *Getting to yes.* Boston: Houghton Mifflin.

Follett, M. P. (1940). Constructive conflict. In H. C. Metcalf and L. Urwick (Eds.), *Dynamic administration: The collected papers of Mary Parker Follett.* New York: Harper.

Friedman, M. (1957). *A theory of consumption function.* Princeton, N.J.: Princeton University Press.

Getzel, J. W. (1975). Problem-finding and the inventiveness of solutions. *Journal of Creative Behavior* **9,** 12–18.

Gilovich, T., Vallone, R., and Tversky, A. (1985). The hot hand in basketball: On the misperception of random sequences. *Cognitive Psychology* **17,** 295–314.

Guzzo, R. A. (1982). *Improving group decision making in organizations.* New York: Academic Press.

Hardin, G. (1968). The tragedy of the commons. *Science,* **162,** 1243–1248.

Hayes-Roth, F., Waterman, D. A., and Lenat, D. B. (1983). *Building expert systems.* Reading, Mass.: Addison-Wesley.

Hazard, T. H., and Peterson, C. R. (1973). *Odds versus probabilities for categorical events* (Technical report, 73-2), McLean, Va.: Decisions and Designs, Inc.

Heider, F. (1958). *The psychology of interpersonal relations*. New York: Wiley.

Hershey, J. C., and Schoemaker, P. J. H. (1980). Prospect theory's reflection hypothesis: A critical examination. *Organization Behavior and Human Performance* **3,** 395–418.

Huber, P. (1980). *Managerial decision making*. Glenview, Ill.: Scott, Foresman.

Hughes, E. J. (1978). The presidency versus Jimmy Carter. *Fortune,* December 4, p. 58.

Janis, I. L. (1972). *Victims of groupthink*. Boston: Houghton Miflin.

Janis, I. L., and Mann, L. (1977). *Decision making*. New York: Free Press.

Joyce, E. J., and Biddle, G. C. (1981). Anchoring and adjustment in probabilistic inference in auditing. *Journal of Accounting Research* **19,** 120–145.

Kagel, J. H., and Levin, D. (1986). The winner's curse and public information in common value auctions. *American Economic Review* **76,** 894–920.

Kahneman, D., Knetsch, J. L., and Thaler, R. (1986). Fairness as a constraint on profit seeking: Entitlements in the market. *American Economic Review* **76,** 728–741.

Kahneman, D., and Tversky, A. (1972). Subjective probability: A judgment of representativeness. *Cognitive Psychology* **3,** 430–454.

Kahneman, D., and Tversky, A. (1973). On the psychology of prediction. *Psychological Review* **80,** 237–251.

Kahneman, D., and Tversky, A. (1979). Prospect theory: An analysis of decision under risk. *Econometrica* **47,** 263–291.

Kahneman, D., and Tversky, A. (1982). Psychology of preferences. *Scientific American,* pp. 161–173.

Kochan, T. (1980). Collective bargaining and organizational behavior research. In B. Staw and L. Cummings (Eds.), *Research in Organizational Behavior,* Vol. 2. Greenwich, Conn.: J.A.I. Press.

Koriat, A., Lichtenstein, S., and Fischhoff, B. (1980). Reasons for confidence. *Journal of Experimental Psychology: Human Learning and Memory* **6,** 107–118.

Kuhn, T. S. (1970). *The structure of scientific revolutions,* 2nd ed. Chicago: University of Chicago Press.

Langer, E. J. (1975). The Illusion of control. *Journal of Personality and Social Psychology* **32,** 311–328.

Lax, D. A., and Sebenius, J. K. (1985). *The manager as negotiator*. New York: Free Press.

Lewicki, R. J. (1980). *Bad loan psychology: Entrapment in financial lending*. Academy of Management Annual Meeting.

Lewicki, R. J., and Litterer, J. A. (1985). *Negotiations*. Homewood, Ill.: Irwin.

Lewicki, R. J., and Sheppard, B. H. (1985). Choosing how to intervene: Factors affecting the use of process and outcome control in third-party dispute resolution. *Journal of Occupational Behavior* **6,** 49–64.

Lewicki, R. J., Sheppard, B. H., and Bazerman, M. H. (Eds.) (1986). *Research on negotiation in organizations,* Vol. 1. Greenwich, Conn.: JAI Press.

Lewin, K. (1947). Group decision and social change. In T. M. Newcomb and E. L. Hartley (Eds.), *Readings in social psychology*. New York: Holt, Rinehart and Winston.

Lichtenstein, S., and Fischhoff, B. (1977). Do those who know more also know more about how much they know? The calibration of probability judgments. *Organizational Behavior and Human Performance* **20,** 159–183.

Lichtenstein, S., and Fischhoff, B. (1980). Training for calibration. *Organizational Behavior and Human Performance* **26,** 149–171.

Lichtenstein, S., Fischhoff, B., and Phillips, L. D. (1982). Calibration of probabilities: State of the art to 1980. In D. Kahneman, P. Slovic, and A. Tversky (Eds.), *Judgment under uncertainty: Heuristics and biases.* New York: Cambridge University Press.

Loewenstein, G. (1987). Anticipation and the valuation of delayed consumption. *Economic Journal* **97,** 666 684.

Loewenstein, G. (1989). Anomalies in intertemporal choice: Evidence and an interpretation. Russell Sage Foundation working paper.

Loewenstein, G., and Thaler, R. H. (in press). Intertemporal choice: *Journal of Economic Perspectives.*

MacCrimmon, K. R., and Wehrung, D. A. (1986). *Taking risks.* New York: Free Press.

Mannix, E. A. (1989). *Coalitions in :' organizational context: A social dilemmas perspective,* unpublished dissertation, University of Chicago.

Mannix, E. A., Thompson, L., and Bazerman, M. H. (1989). Negotiations in small groups. *Journal of Applied Psychology* **74,** 508–517.

March, J. G., and Simon, H. A. (1958). *Organizations.* New York: Wiley.

Miller, P. M., and Fagley, N. S. (1988). The effects of framing, problem variations, and providing rationale on choice (working paper).

Mintzberg, H. (1975). *The nature of managerial work.* New York: Harper & Row.

Mintzberg, H. (1983). *Power in and around organizations.* Englewood Cliffs, N.J.: Prentice-Hall.

Moscovici, S., and Zavalloni, M. (1969). The group as a polarism of attitudes. *Journal of Personality and Social Psychology* **12,** 125–135.

Murnighan, J. K. (1978). Models of coalition behavior: Game theoretic, social psychological, and political perspectives. *Psychological Bulletin* **85,** 1130–1153.

Murnighan, J. K. (1986). Organizational coalitions: Structural contingencies and the formation process. In R. J. Lewicki, B. H. Sheppard, and M. H. Bazerman (Eds.), *Research on negotiation in organizations,* Vol. 1. Greenwich, Conn.: JAI Press.

Murnighan, J. K., and Brass, D. J. (1990). Intraorganizational coalitions. In M. Bazerman, R. Lewicki, and B. H. Sheppard (Eds.), *Handbook of negotiation research: Research on negotiations in organizations,* Vol. 3. Greenwich, Conn.: JAI Press.

Nathanson, B., Brockner, J., Brenner, D., Samuelson, C., Countryman, M., Lloyd, M., and Rubin, J. Z. (1982). Toward the reduction of entrapment. *Journal of Applied Social Psychology* **12,** 193–208.

Naylor, J. C., and Wherry, R. J. (1965). The use of simulated stimuli and the "JAN" technique to capture and cluster the policies of raters. *Educational and Psychological Measurement* **25,** 896–986.

Neale, M. A., and Bazerman, M. H. (1983). The effect of perspective taking ability under alternate forms of arbitration on the negotiation process. *Industrial and Labor Relations Review* **36,** 378–388.

Neale, M. A., and Bazerman, M. H. (1985). Perspectives for understanding negotiation: Viewing negotiation as a judgmental process. *Journal of Conflict Resolution* **29,** 33–55.

Neale, M. A., Bazerman, M. H., Northcraft, B. G., and Alperson, C. A. (1986). "Choice shift" effects in group decisions: A decision bias perspective. *International Journal of Small Group Research* **2,** 33–42.

Neale, M. A., Huber, V., and Northcraft, G. B. (1987). The framing of negotiations: Contextual versus task frames. *Organizational Behavior and Human Decision Processes* **38,** 305–317.

Neale, M. A., and Northcraft, G. B. (1989). Experience, expertise, and decision bias in negotiation: The role of strategic conceptualization. In B. Sheppard, M. Bazerman, and R. Lewicki (Eds.), *Research on negotiations in organizations,* Vol. 2. Greenwich, Conn.: JAI Press.

Nickerson, R. S., and McGoldrick, C. C. (1965). Confidence ratings and level of performance on a judgmental task. *Perceptual and Motor Skills* **20,** 311–316.

Nisbett, R. E., and Ross, L. (1980). *Human inference: Strategies and shortcomings of social judgment.* Englewood Cliffs, N.J.: Prentice-Hall.

Northcraft, G. B., and Neale, M. A. (1986). Opportunity costs and the framing of resource allocation decisions. *Organizational Behavior and Human Decision Processes* **37,** 28–38.

Northcraft, G. B., and Neale, M. A. (1987). Experts, amateurs and real estate: An anchoring-and-adjustment perspective on property pricing decisions. *Organizational Behavior and Human Decision Processes* **39,** 84–97.

Northcraft, G. B., and Wolf, G. (1984). Dollars, sense, and sunk costs: A life cycle model of resource allocation decisions. *Academy of Management Review* **9,** 225–234.

Pennings, J., and Goodman, P. S. (1977). Towards a workable framework. In P. S. Goodman, J. M. Pennings, et al. *New perspectives on organizational effectiveness.* San Francisco: Jossey-Bass.

Perrow, C. (1984). *Normal accidents.* New York: Basic Books.

Peters, T. J., and Waterman, R. H. (1982). *In search of excellence.* New York: Harper & Row.

Pfeffer, J., and Salancik, G. R. (1978). *The external control of organizations.* New York: Harper & Row.

Pitz, G. F. (1974). Subjective probability distributions for imperfectly known quantities. In L. W. Gregg (Ed.), *Knowledge and cognition,* pp. 29–41. New York: Wiley.

Pruitt, D. G. (1981). *Negotiation behavior.* New York: Academic Press.

Pruitt, D. G. (1983). Integrative agreements: Nature and antecedents. In M. H. Bazerman and R. J. Lewicki (Eds.), *Negotiating in organizations,* pp. 35–50. Beverly Hills: Sage.

Pruitt, D. G., and Rubin, J. Z. (1985). *Social conflict: Escalation, impasse, and resolution.* Reading, Mass.: Addison-Wesley.

Raiffa, H. (1982). *The art and science of negotiation.* Cambridge, Mass.: Harvard University Press.

Raiffa, H. (1984). Invited address to the Judgment and Decision Making Society (November), San Antonio.

Raiffa, H. (1985). Post-settlement settlements. *Negotiation Journal* 1:9–12.

Rapaport, A., and Chammah, A. M. (1965). *Prisoner's dilemma.* Ann Arbor: University of Michigan Press.

Rawls, J. (1971). *A theory of justice.* Cambridge, Mass.: Harvard University Press.

Ross, J., and Staw, B. M. (1986). Expo 86: An escalation prototype. *Administrative Science Quarterly* **31,** 274–297.

Rubin, J. Z. (1980). Experimental research on third party intervention in conflict: Toward some generalizations. *Psychological Bulletin* **87,** 379–391.

Rubin, J. Z. (1983). Negotiation: An introduction to some issues and themes. *American Behavioral Scientist* **27,** 135–147.

Rubin, J. Z., and Brockner, J. (1975). Factors affecting entrapment in waiting situations: The Rosencrantz and Guildenstern effect. *Journal of Personality and Social Psychology* **31,** 1054–1063.

Rubin, J. Z., Brockner, J., Small-Weil, S., and Nathanson, S. (1980). Factors affecting entry into psychological traps. *Journal of Conflict Resolution* **24,** 405–426.

Samuelson, W. F., and Bazerman, M. H. (1985). Negotiating under the winner's curse. In V. Smith (Ed.), *Research in experimental economics,* Vol. 3. Greenwich, Conn.: JAI Press.

Schelling, T. C. (1984). *Choice and consequence.* Cambridge, Ma.: Harvard University Press.

Schoemaker, P. J. H., and Kunreuther, H. (1979). An experimental study of insurance decisions. *The Journal of Risk and Insurance* **46,** 603–618.

Schoorman, F. D. (1988). Escalation bias in performance appraisals: An unintended consequence of supervisor participation in hiring decisions. *Journal of Applied Psychology* **73,** 58–62.

Schoorman, F. D., Bazerman, M. H., and Atkin, R. S. (1981). Interlocking directorates: A strategy for the management of environment uncertainty. *Academy of Management Review* **6,** 243–251.

Sebenius, J. K. (1989). International negotiations: Problems and new approaches. Working paper.

Shaw, M. E. (1981). *Group dynamics: The psychology of small group behavior.* New York: McGraw-Hill.

Sheppard, B. H. (1983). Managers as inquisitors: Some lessons from the law. In M. H. Bazerman and R. J. Lewicki (Eds.), *Negotiating in organizations.* Beverly Hills, Calif.: Sage.

Sheppard, B. H. (1984). Third party intervention: A procedural framework. In B. M. Staw and L. L. Cummings (Eds.), *Research in organizational behavior,* Vol. 6. Greenwich, Conn.: JAI Press.

Shubik, M. (1971). The dollar auction game: A paradox in noncooperative behavior and escalation. *Journal of Conflict Resolution* **15,** 109–111.

Simon, H. A. (1957). *Models of man.* New York: Wiley.

Slovic, P. (1972). Information processing, situation specificity, and the generality of risk-taking behavior. *Journal of Personality and Social Psychology* **22,** 128–134.

Slovic, P. (1982). Toward understanding and improving decisions. In W. C. Howell and E. A. Fleishman (Eds.), *Human performance and productivity,* Vol. 2, *Information processing and decision making.* Hillsdale, N.J.: Erlbaum.

Slovic, P., and Fischhoff, B. (1977). On the psychology of experimental surprises. *Journal of Experimental Psychology: Human Perception and Performance* **3,** 544–551.

Slovic, P., Fischhoff, B., and Lichtenstein, S. (1978). Accident probabilities and seat belt usage: A psychological perspective. *Accident Analysis and Prevention* **10,** 281–285.

Slovic, P., Fischhoff, B., and Lichtenstein, S. (1982). Response mode, framing, and information processing effects in risk assessment. In R. M. Hogarth (Ed.), *New directions for methodology of social and behavioral science: The framing of questions and the consistency of response.* San Francisco: Jossey-Bass.

Slovic, P., and Lichtenstein, S. (1971). Comparison of Bayesian and regression approaches in the study of information processing in judgment. *Organizational Behavior and Human Performance* **6,** 649–744.

Slovic, P., Lichtenstein, S., and Fischhoff, B. (1979). Images of disaster: Perception and acceptance of risks from nuclear power. In G. Goodman and W. Rowe (Eds.), *Energy risk management.* London: Academic Press.

Slovic, P., Lichtenstein, S., and Fischhoff, B. (1982). Characterizing perceived risk. In R. W. Kataes and C. Hohenemser (Eds.), *Technological hazard management.* Cambridge, Mass.: Oelgeschlager, Gunn & Hain.

Sniezek, J. A., and Henry, R. A. (1989). Accuracy and confidences in group judgment. *Organizational Behavior and Human Decision Processes* **43,** 1–28.

Starke, F. A., and Notz, W. W. (1981). Pre- and post-intervention effects of conventional vs. final offer arbitration. *Academy of Management Journal* **24,** 832–850.

Staw, B. M. (1976). Knee-deep in the big muddy: A study of escalating commitment to a chosen course of action. *Organizational Behavior and Human Performance* **16,** 27–44.

Staw, B. M. (1980). Rationality and justification in organizational life. In B. M. Staw and L. L. Cummings (Eds.), *Research in organizational behavior,* Vol. 2. Greenwich, Conn.: JAI Press.

Staw, B. M. (1981). The escalation of commitment to a course of action. *Academy of Management Review* **6,** 577–587.

Staw, B. M., and Ross, J. (1978). Commitment to a policy decision: A multi-theoretical perspective. *Administrative Science Quarterly* **23,** 40–64.

Staw, B. M., and Ross, J. (1980). Commitment in an experimenting society: An experiment on the attribution of leadership from administrative scenarios. *Journal of Applied Psychology* **65,** 249–260.

Staw, B. M., and Ross, J. (1987). Knowing when to pull the plug. *Harvard Business Review* **65,** 68–74.

Steiner, I. D. (1972). *Group process and productivity.* New York: Academic Press.

Stoner, J. A. F. (1961). *A comparison of individual and group decisions involving risk.* Unpublished master's thesis, Massachusetts Institute of Technology, School of Industrial Management.

Strickland, L. (1958). Surveillance and trust. *Journal of Personality* **26,** 200–215.

Stumpf, S. A., and London, M. (1981). Capturing rater policies in evaluating candidates for promotion. *Academy of Management Journal* **24,** 752–766.

Swalm, R. O. (1966). Utility theory: Insights into risk taking. *Harvard Business Review* **44,** 123–136.

Teger, A. I. (1980). *Too much invested to quit: The psychology of the escalation of conflict.* New York: Pergamon Press.

Thaler, R. (1980). Toward a positive theory of consumer choice. *Journal of Economic Behavior and Organization* **1,** 39–80.

Thaler, R. (1985). Using mental accounting in a theory of purchasing behavior. *Marketing Science,* **4,** 12–13.

Thaler, R., and Shefrin, H. M. (1981). An economic theory of self control. *Journal of Political Economy* **89,** 392–406.

Thibaut, J. W., and Walker, L. (1975). *Procedural justice: A psychological perspective.* Hillsdale, N.J.: Erlbaum.

Thompson, L., Mannix, E. A., and Bazerman, M. H. (1988). Group negotiation: Effects of decision rule, agenda, and aspiration. *Journal of Personality and Social Psychology* **54,** 86–95.

Tversky, A., and Kahneman, D. (1971). The belief in the "law of numbers." *Psychological Bulletin* **76,** 105–110.

Tversky, A., and Kahneman, D. (1973). Availability: A heuristic for judging frequency and probability. *Cognitive Psychology* **5,** 207–232.

Tversky, A., and Kahneman, D. (1974). Judgment under uncertainty: Heuristics and biases. *Science* **185,** 1124–1131.

Tversky, A., and Kahneman, D. (1981). The framing of decisions and the psychology of choice. *Science* **211,** 453–463.

Tversky, A., and Kahneman, D. (1983). Extensional versus intuitive reasoning: The conjunction fallacy in probability judgement. *Psychological Review* **90,** 293–315.

Tversky, A., and Kahneman, D. (1986). Rational choice and the framing of decisions. *Journal of Business* **59,** 251–294.

Tyler, T., and Hastie, R. (1990). The social consequences of cognitive illusions. In M. H. Bazerman, R. J. Lewicki, and B. H. Sheppard (Eds.), *Handbook of negotiation research.* Greenwich, Conn.: JAI Press.

Vinoker, A. (1971). Review and theoretical analysis of the effects of group processes upon individual and group decisions involving risk. *Psychological Bulletin* **75,** 234–250.

Wall Street Journal (1981). To win a bidding war doesn't insure success of merged companies. September, p. 1.

Wallas, G. (1926). *The art of thought.* New York: Harcourt.

Walton, R. E., and McKersie, R. B. (1965). *A behavioral theory of labor negotiations: An analysis of a social interaction system.* New York: McGraw-Hill.

Wason, P. C. (1960). On the failure to eliminate hypotheses in a conceptual task. *Quarterly Journal of Experimental Psychology* **12,** 129–140.

Wason, P. C. (1968a). Reason about a rule. *Quarterly Journal of Experimental Psychology* **20,** 273–283.

Wason, P. C. (1968b). On the failure to eliminate hypothesis . . . a second look. In P. C. Wason and P. N. Johnson-Laird (Eds.), *Thinking and reasoning.* Harmandsworth: Penguin.

Winklegren, W. A. (1974). *How to solve problems.* San Francisco: Freeman.

Wood, G. (1978). The knew-it-all-along effect. *Journal of Experimental Psychology: Human Perception and Performance* **4,** 345–353.

Yates, J. F., and Carlson, B. W. (1986). Conjunction errors: Evidence for multiple judgment procedures, including 'signed summation,' *Organizational Behavior and Human Decision Processes,* **37,** 230–253.

Zedeck, S. (1977). An information processing model and approach in the study of motivation. *Organizational Behavior and Human Performance* **18,** 47–77.

Zedeck, S., and Kafry, D. (1977). Capturing rater policies for processing evaluation data. *Organizational Behavior and Human Performance* **18,** 269–294.

INDEX